Methods of Measuring Women's Participation and Production in the Informal Sector

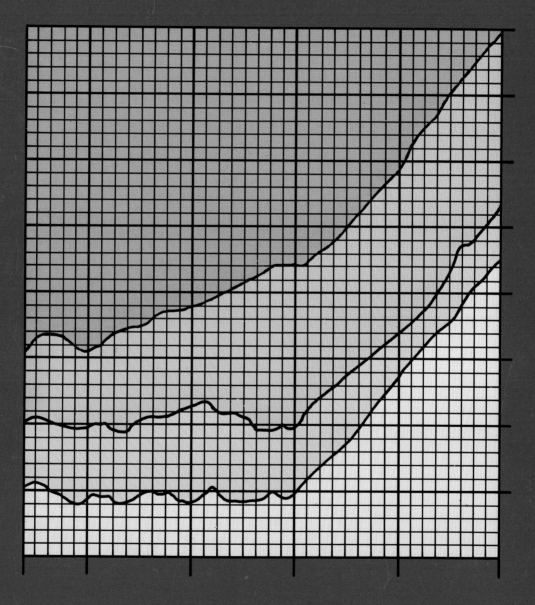

United Nations

ST/ESA/STAT/SER.F/46

DEPARTMENT OF INTERNATIONAL ECONOMIC AND SOCIAL AFFAIRS

STATISTICAL OFFICE
and
INTERNATIONAL RESEARCH AND TRAINING INSTITUTE FOR
THE ADVANCEMENT OF WOMEN

STUDIES IN METHODS   Series F   No. 46

METHODS OF MEASURING WOMEN'S PARTICIPATION AND PRODUCTION IN THE INFORMAL SECTOR

UNITED NATIONS
New York, 1990

NOTE

The designations employed and the presentation of the material in this publication do not imply the expression of any opinion whatsoever on the part of the Secretariat of the United Nations concerning the legal status of any country, territory, city or area or of its authorities, or concerning the delimitation of its frontiers or boundaries.

ST/ESA/STAT/SER.F/46

The present publication is one in a series of reports issued by the United Nations to promote the improvement and use of statistics and indicators on the situation of women. These studies have been concerned with issues such as sex biases in statistics; concepts, methods and training for collecting, compiling and using statistics and indicators on the situation of women; and improving statistics and indicators on women, using household surveys. 1/ These studies have been prepared in response to recommendations of the World Conference of the International Women's Year, the World Conference of the United Nations Decade for Women: Equality, Development and Peace, the World Conference to Review and Appraise the Achievements of the United Nations Decade for Women: Equality, Development and Peace, the Economic and Social Council and its functional commissions concerned with statistics and with the status of women and the Board of Trustees of the International Research and Training Institute for the Advancement of Women (INSTRAW). 2/

The present technical report is concerned with the development of statistical concepts to improve measurement of women's (and men's) participation and production in the informal sector, including both remunerated and unremunerated work, pursuant to implementation of the Nairobi Forward-looking Strategies for the Advancement of Women. In the Nairobi Strategies, adopted in 1985 by the World Conference to Review and Appraise the Achievements of the United Nations Decade for Women: Equality, Development and Peace and endorsed by the General Assembly in its resolution 40/108, the Conference recommended that:

"The remunerated and, in particular, the unremunerated contributions of women to all aspects and sectors of development should be recognized, and appropriate efforts should be made to measure and reflect these contributions in national accounts and economic statistics and in the gross national product." (para. 120)

To follow up this recommendation, INSTRAW organized in October 1986 at Santo Domingo the Expert Group Meeting on Measurement of Women's Income and their Participation and Production in the Informal Sector, in collaboration with the Statistical Office, Department of International Economic and Social Affairs, and the Economic Commission for Latin America and the Caribbean of the United Nations Secretariat. At this meeting, the Expert Group discussed drafts of the reports contained in the present publication on (a) development of appropriate statistical concepts and methods to measure women's participation and production in the informal sector, (b) use of time-use statistics for this purpose, (c) experience in measuring the informal sector in Latin America, and (d) alternative approaches to the measurement of women's economic situation. These reports have been further developed for the present publication to take into account the comments of the Expert Group. 3/

The present publication provides an improved technical basis for development of measurement of the informal sector and women's participation in it, from both the point of view of employment measurement and the point of view of measurement of economic output in national accounts. Thus, for example, work is proceeding at the International Labour Office, INSTRAW, the Statistical Office and the Economic Commission for Latin America and the Caribbean on case studies and statistical research on the informal sector, household economic activities and their relation to national accounts practices that tries to further develop and harmonize these various perspectives in the light of practical experience and current data collection possibilities. 4/

Many of the ideas discussed in the present report can be applied in ongoing national data collection programmes. The most comprehensive and widely used data collection programmes at the national level are population censuses and household surveys. For further discussion of concepts and methods used in these programmes, the reader should consult the relevant United Nations recommendations, handbooks and technical studies, including <u>Principles and Recommendations for Population and Housing Censuses</u> and <u>Handbook of Household Surveys (Revised Edition)</u>. 5/

The <u>Handbook of Household Surveys</u> provides basic guidance on the organization and methodology of household surveys and reviews, at a general level, problems of organization, design, operations and survey content. The <u>Handbook</u> has been followed by a series of technical studies prepared by the National Household Survey Capability Programme (NHSCP), dealing in greater detail with technical issues of survey design and content, and the measurement of household income and expenditure, and by the technical report already noted <u>Improving Statistics and Indicators on Women Using Household Surveys</u>. 6/

The present publication, as well as preceding publications in this series, 1/ has been prepared as part of a joint project of the Statistical Office of the United Nations Secretariat and INSTRAW, located at Santo Domingo, Dominican Republic, to promote the development of statistics and indicators on the situation of women. Further information on the work of the United Nations in this field may be obtained by writing to the Director of the Statistical Office of the United Nations, New York, or the Director of the International Research and Training Institute for the Advancement of Women, Santo Domingo, Dominican Republic.

<u>Notes</u>

1/   The first four publications in this series are <u>Compiling Social Indicators on the Situation of Women</u>, Studies in Methods, Series F, No. 32 (United Nations publication, Sales No. E.84.XVII.2), <u>Improving Concepts and Methods for Statistics and Indicators on the Situation of Women</u>, Series F, No. 33 (United Nations publication, Sales No. E.84.XVII.3), <u>Training Users and Producers in Compiling Statistics and Indicators on Women in Development</u>, Series F, No. 45 (United Nations publication, Sales No. E.87.XVII.6), and <u>Improving Statistics and Indicators on Women Using Household Surveys</u>, Series F, No. 48 (United Nations publication, Sales No. E.88.XVII.11). These reports follow up and elaborate an earlier working paper prepared by the United Nations Secretariat in 1980 entitled "Sex-based stereotypes, sex biases and national data systems" (ST/ESA/STAT/99).

2/   See <u>Report of the World Conference in the International Women's Year, Mexico City, 19 June-2 July 1975</u> (United Nations publication, Sales No. E.76.IV.1), chap. II, sect. A, paras. 161-173; <u>Report of the World Conference of the United Nations Decade for Women: Equality, Development and Peace, Copenhagen, 14-30 July 1980</u> (United Nations publication, Sales No. E.80.IV.3 and Corrigendum), chap. I, sect. A, paras. 257-261; "The Nairobi Forward-looking Strategies for the Advancement of Women", in <u>Report of the World Conference to Review and Appraise the Achievements of the United Nations Decade for Women: Equality, Development and Peace, Nairobi, 15-26 July 1985</u> (United Nations publication, Sales No. E.85.IV.10),

chap. I, sect. A, paras. 58, 64, 120, 122, 130, 282, 312, 317, 333, 351; and
Economic and Social Council resolutions 2061 (LXII) of 12 May 1977, entitled
"Improvement of the data base for measuring the implementation of the World Plan of
Action for the Implementation of the Objectives of the International Women's Year",
and 1981/11 of 6 May 1981, entitled "Social indicators applicable to studies on
women".

3/   The report of the expert group meeting has been issued as document
ESA/STAT/AC.29/8-INSTRAW/AC.3/8.

4/   See International Labour Organisation, Fourteenth International
Conference of Labour Statisticians, Report of the Conference, Geneva,
28 October-6 November 1987 (ICLS/14/D.14), Conference Proceedings, General report,
chap. 2 (Employment in the informal sector), and appendix I, resolution VII;
"Project of the INSTRAW work programme on women and the informal sector of the
economy in collaboration with the United Nations Statistical Office: report and
recommendations for the period 1 April 1987-28 February 1988" (INSTRAW working
paper); and "Development of guidelines on national accounts for women's
contribution to development", report of the Secretary-General to the Statistical
Commission at its twenty-fifth session (E/CN.3/1989/12).

5/   Series M, No. 67 (United Nations publication, Sales No. E.80.XVII.8) and
Series F, No. 31 (United Nations publication, Sales No. E.83.XVII.13).

6/   The NHSCP studies have been issued by the Department of Technical
Co-operation and Development and the Statistical Office of the United Nations
Secretariat. They are: Survey Data Processing: A Review of Issues and Procedures
(DP/UN/INT-81-041/1), Non-Sampling Errors in Household Surveys: Sources,
Assessment and Control (DP/UN/INT-81-041/2), The Role of the NHSCP in Providing
Health Information in Developing Countries (DP/UN/INT-81-041/3), Development and
Design of Survey Questionnaires (INT-84-014), Sampling Frames and Sample Designs
for Integrated Household Survey Programmes (DP/UN/INT-84-014/5E), Measuring
Literacy through Household Surveys: A Technical Study on Literacy Assessment and
Related Education Topics through Household Surveys (DP/UN/INT-88-X01/10E) and
Household Income and Expenditure Surveys: A Technical Study (DP/UN/INT-88-X01/GE).

CONTENTS

CONTENTS (continued)

Part Two

COLLECTION AND COMPILATION OF TIME-USE STATISTICS TO MEASURE THE PARTICIPATION OF WOMEN IN THE INFORMAL SECTOR

CONTENTS (continued)

Part Three

COLLECTING STATISTICS ON THE PARTICIPATION OF WOMEN IN THE
INFORMAL SECTOR: METHODS USED IN LATIN AMERICA

CONTENTS (continued)

Part Four

MEASURING THE ECONOMIC SITUATION OF WOMEN: AN ALTERNATIVE APPROACH

CONTENTS (continued)

Tables

CONTENTS (continued)

Tables (continued)

EXPLANATORY NOTES

Symbols of United Nations documents are composed of capital letters combined with figures.

Reference to "dollars" ($) indicates United States dollars, unless otherwise stated.

Reference to "tons" indicates metric tons, unless otherwise stated.

The term "billion" signifies a thousand million.

Annual rates of growth or change refer to annual compound rates, unless otherwise stated.

A hyphen (-) between years, e.g., 1984-1985, indicates the full period involved, including the beginning and end years; a slash (/) indicates a financial year, school year or crop year, e.g., 1984/85.

A point (.) is used to indicate decimals.

The following symbols have been used in the tables:

Two dots (..) indicate that data are not available or are not separately reported.

A dash (--) indicates that the amount is nil or negligible.

A hyphen (-) indicates that the item is not applicable.

A minus sign (-) before a number indicates a deficit or decrease, except as indicated.

Details and percentages in tables do not necessarily add up to totals because of rounding.

The following abbreviations have been used:

CELADE   Centro Latinoamericano de Demografía (Latin American Demographic Centre)

CIEPLAN   Corporación de investigaciones económicas para Latinoamérica

ECE   Economic Commission for Europe

ECLAC   Economic Commission for Latin America and the Caribbean

ILO   International Labour Organisation

ILPES   Instituto Latinoamericano y del Caribe de Planificación Económica y Social

INSEE   Institut national de statistiques et études économiques

INSTRAW   International Research and Training Institute for the Advancement of Women

ISCO   International Standard Classification of Occupations

ISIC   International Standard Industrial Classification

OECD   Organisation for Economic Co-operation and Development

PNAD   Pesquisa Nacional por Muestra de Domicilio (National Family Budget Survey)

PREALC   Programa Regional del Empleo para América Latina y el Caribe

SNA   System of National Accounts

UNESCO   United Nations Educational, Scientific and Cultural Organization

UNICEF   United Nations Children's Fund

Part One

DEVELOPMENT OF STATISTICAL CONCEPTS AND METHODS ON WOMEN AND THE INFORMAL SECTOR*

---

*   Prepared by Lourdes Urdaneta-Ferrán, consultant to the International Research and Training Institute for the Advancement of Women and the Statistical Office, Department of International Economic and Social Affairs, United Nations Secretariat.

INTRODUCTION

The demand for quantitative information on the participation of women in the economic life of nations and specifically on their contribution to development and economic growth is being voiced with increasing strength and urgency. All too often, however, numerical data used to express that contribution lack the desirable standards of technical quality. This is mostly due to the fact that measurement of economic phenomena presents some intricate problems, the complexity of which is even more pronounced in those areas where economic and social phenomena are closely interrelated. The heart of the problem in such circumstances is to find a statistical unit of measurement and a measuring scale that will simultaneously encompass the appropriate economic and social dimensions. However, it should also be noted that demand for comprehensive statistical data on women's activities is of rather recent date. This may explain why, even in circumstances where none of the difficulties referred to above is present, economic data are not sufficiently disaggregated by sex.

As in all kinds of measurement, measurement of women's contribution to economic growth poses two main questions: first, what should be measured, and second, how to measure it.

Women's activities cover a wide range of categories, possibly wider than those of men, but not all of them are of a kind that could be classified as contributions to economic growth. It is necessary therefore to draw a line between those which are to be considered as pertaining to economic growth and those which are not. Such a delimitation must draw on concepts and definitions already existing in economic literature as well as social statistics and national accounting, 1/ but at the same time whether and how these statistical conventions affect estimates of women's contribution must be examined in detail. It may be necessary to introduce changes in definitions, but these must be harmonized with the rules governing calculations of the main aggregates in national accounting, of which the contribution of women is a part.

Where women's activities are firmly embedded in the market mechanism, there is no doubt about their constituting economic activity and meriting the label of economically "productive", so there can be no argument about their inclusion in women's contribution to economic development.

But doubts have been raised as to whether those pursuits which have no link with the marketplace, or only insubstantial and weak ones, should receive the same treatment. This argument is based on the consideration that such pursuits frequently relate to social functions which by their very nature cannot possibly lead to an exchange between two economic units and consequently fall outside of what would be considered "economic" and "productive" and hence part of economic development and economic growth. This would apply, for example, to tasks and activities destined to satisfy personal needs which could not be performed by a person other than the one whose needs are being satisfied (e.g. taking a bath or having a meal). In such cases, there is clearly no possibility of exchange and such actions are undeniably outside the domain of economic development.

Thus, there are two extremes: on the one hand, activities carried out in a social context, encompassed by exchange and the market; on the other, those activities which by their very nature can not be subject to exchange as they are individualistic and intrinsically not exchangeable. Between these two extremes lies a no man's land where people perform tasks and do work which is not exchanged in the market although possibly it could be, as in the case of household own-account production which is consumed by members of the producing household but conceivably could have been sold in the market. Accordingly, we have to distinguish between production for own consumption where production has a market equivalent and production where such a market equivalent does not exist because consumption and production merge into each other.

The decisive feature, then, is not that there must necessarily be exchange in the market but that such exchange conceivably could occur. This intermediate sphere is in fact one of the areas where national accounting concepts have been shifting, with successive changes widening the perimeters of economic activity. The practical possibility of exchange as development proceeds - that is, amenability to market transactions - can thus be taken in principle as the demarcation line that indicates what to include in measurement; in other words, what to measure in order to establish women's contribution to economic development and growth.

This, however, is still a very general principle and it calls for more detailed examination in order to arrive at practical guidelines for measuring women's contribution to economic growth. This subject will be examined further in the discussion of how to delimit informal economic activity.

A further note on the subject of what should be measured concerning women's participation in economic activities is called for regarding a development which could seem to upset the proposed criterion of "productive activity". Child-bearing has traditionally been considered an example of an activity not amenable to market transactions, but recent technological advances make possible just that. What to do about it? Where such arrangements take place, there is a service performed by one person to the benefit of another against a monetary payment, all of which makes this part of the national product. If women's component in national product is to be considered, such services must be taken into consideration. In other words, in some cases what formerly was classified within the third group (unamenable to market transactions) is passing into the first group (market transactions).

However, it is not proposed at this stage to apply to child-bearing the marketability criterion that has been worked out above. It will be included in the second group, as an activity which is not carried out on an exchange basis but possibly could be. Admittedly, this will be an exception to the general scheme of classification, but it is a justifiable one.

After considering the question of where to draw the limits of women's economic participation something must be said regarding the procedures for its measurement and valuation. Here again, the presence or absence of market transactions will play a dominant role, but this time not as a reference point to establish borderlines but as an indicator of the weight and importance to be assigned to each individual contribution.

Once the dividing line is established and we know what is to be included within measurement and what falls outside it, the question to be answered is how this measurement is to be carried out. Here, two different matters must be considered.

First, concerning the technicalities of measurement proper, the problem is how to add up all the individual activities and what weight to assign to each one. In other words, the activities must ultimately be valued using numerical units in order to measure adequately their overall contribution and permit such comparisons as may be desired. This unavoidably leads to the use of monetary units, such as prices for goods produced or services rendered. However, it might be asked why the measurement of women's contribution has necessarily to be done in monetary terms and not with some other unit of measurement which might be easier to use. 2/ In the case of women's contribution to development and economic growth the question posed is clearly that of measuring one part of a given whole, namely, that part of total economic development and growth that has been created by women. This constitutes one parameter of the projected measurement process and imposes the necessity of using the same statistical units as measurement of total economic development and growth uses, that is, monetary units.

The same conclusion will be reached if the issue is approached from the perspective of comparability. One basic objective of statistical information of an economic and social nature is to facilitate comparisons, but comparisons must refer to the same attributes. For example, one cannot compare weight in one case with volume in another, or the time spent by rural women on household work with the value of total agricultural production. Thus, the attributes, and for that matter the units used to measure these attributes, must be the same. When this conclusion is applied to the subject of measuring women's contribution to economic growth, the same result is obtained: economic aggregates and their components are expressed in monetary units and women's contribution has to be measured in the same way.

Measuring economic aggregates, and especially economic growth, in monetary units is not a procedure without weaknesses, but it is the only effective and feasible one at the present stage of knowledge. Measurement in monetary units means that economic contributions, be they in goods or in services, will be aggregated in terms of prices. 3/ Prices in turn are set in markets, whether big or small. In circumstances where economic output - goods or services - do not go to a market, they do not possess a price. If such contributions are to be accounted for in the total aggregate, prices for them have to be constructed. In some instances, where there exist equal or similar products in the market, constructing adequate prices is relatively easy, but in other circumstances it may present quite serious difficulties.

To state the same idea in a different way: in those cases where women's activities are performed in the way that is usual in modern economic life, that is, as activities which imply an exchange and monetary recompense or, in other words, as activities carried out in the market, the corresponding valuation of each individual activity will not present major difficulties as it can be valued by the price or amount of remuneration paid in the market. However, there also exist extensive areas of women's activities which are contributions to development and economic growth and which fall within the demarcation line mentioned above but which are not market activities. They are performed outside the realm of the market or have only a tenuous connection with it. In such cases, a correct valuation is not easy to determine and different techniques have been developed to assign estimated prices in such circumstances. Some of these techniques will be considered in the chapters that follow.

As to the ever-increasing proportion of women's activities that takes place in modern industrial and commercial enterprises, that is, within the market, there, too, problems exist in measuring women's contribution adequately, but these are of a different kind and will not be treated in the present study. 4/ However, the development of market activities is sometimes construed as a mark of economic development and activities which do not fall within the realm of the market are not only difficult to measure but also are felt to remain outside the dynamics of economic development and growth, something that is supposed to wither away and be replaced progressively by market activities. This leads to underestimation of the importance of such measurements, which in turn affects women more heavily because these conditions prevail more frequently in the case of women's activities than men's. This is why a thorough analysis of activities which take place in these circumstances is essential for the measurement of women's contribution.

The second aspect of the question of how to measure women's contribution is the practical one of sources and types of information required. The paucity of information regarding women's activities is even more pronounced than in other fields of statistics because the subject, at least in its quantitative expression, is of recent origin and there is a lack of sources and procedures whose validity and usefulness have been well established by experience and tradition.

Data collected on women's activities serve many different purposes. Frequently they serve to account for women's contribution to development and growth of the national product, that is, the aggregate of goods and services produced during a certain time period by men and women of a given community. Whatever rules are adopted to define production, they must be valid for both men and women. Moreover, it is not only the definitions that must be equally applicable to men and women. The techniques that serve to fill the empty boxes established by the definitions with concrete information must be such that the necessary data can be obtained for men as well as for women.

Although the last decades have seen considerable progress in the collection of economic data, due mainly to the fact that the development of national accounting methodology and its use has been spreading, such data have been oriented mainly towards the objectives of calculating global aggregates and measuring their interrelationships. In its first stage, the impact of national accounting on practical economic analysis has been based precisely on the fact that it sums up an immense amount of economic statistics which otherwise would be too cumbersome to handle separately. However, in this process individual traits tend to be absorbed into broad general categories and become inaccessible to the analyst.

Once national accounting established itself, however, an increasing number of uses were made of it, and new uses called for new classifications and subdivisions, which in turn often required different techniques of data collection. However, women's contribution to development and growth has been bypassed by most analyses and this fact is reflected in the dearth of data which could throw light on the subject. In some instances, the space given to such data, where they did exist, has been reduced in questionnaires and surveys by stronger demands for other kinds of statistical information which have been considered to pertain more directly to economic analysis and decision-making. But now that the importance of women's contribution is acknowledged and the interplay of market and non-market forces in economic production is increasingly visible, it is evident that the subject belongs not only to the cultural and social spheres but represents a crucial element in economic growth and development.

Data referring to women's activities are increasingly sought, but the supply of such statistics lags markedly behind the demand, even in cases where it is only a question of disaggregation of already existing global data, as in income and expenditure, wages and salaries and agricultural production. More statistics and improvement in their quality of the kind referred to in the present study are indispensable for issues related to women's role, as well as for more reliable global economic analyses and policy decisions. The more important statistical data collection programmes which can be used to focus on the subject are:

(a) Population censuses;

(b) Economic censuses and surveys;

(c) Household surveys and time-use statistics.

These will be taken up in chapter II below and in part two of the present report.

The present study refers to the participation of women in the informal sector of the economy. This sector is without doubt the least documented area of national economies and up to now there has been no consensus as to its precise delimitation. Therefore, before proceeding to explain the techniques that can be used for estimating the contribution of women in this sector, we have to agree on how the boundaries of the informal sector must be considered. This is dealt with in chapter I, which deals with concepts and definitions. Chapter II reviews the statistical sources mentioned above, except for time-use statistics, which are dealt with in more detail in part two. Chapter III reviews some of the techniques that can be used to estimate women's contribution from the scarce data that are usually available at present.

I. CONCEPTS AND DEFINITIONS

A. Scope of informal economic activity and proposals for defining the informal sector

The possibilities and conditions for statistical measurement of women's contribution to development and economic growth were outlined in the Introduction. Now we proceed to consider the statistical concepts and definitions within which such measurement can be carried out with reference to the informal sector. As we are concerned with concrete measurement, these concepts and definitions must comply with two conditions: they must be adequate for the uses to which they will be put and they must be amenable to statistical interpretation.

The concept of the informal sector presents serious difficulties in the way of arriving at a generally acceptable definition and adequate statistical treatment, but the sector is of special relevance as far as women's economic contribution is concerned.

We shall present the subject in the following order. In the first part of the present chapter, we review ideas and definitions for the informal sector that have been proposed in different sources, including the 1968 United Nations System of National Accounts (SNA). 5/ Delimitation of the informal sector in these sources varies depending on specific characteristics which the analyst wishes to bring out. Our particular concern in this review is the suitability of the definition to measure the contribution of one component - the work of women - to a global aggregate measure of economic activity or output. This is followed by a detailed consideration of the informal sector from the perspective of the SNA, that is, informal economic activities which fall within the boundaries of production now set by SNA and consequently at present considered to be a part of gross domestic product. These activities are in turn divided into (a) activities which, although their production is not intended to be sold in the market, are classified by SNA - due to their close comparability to marketed outputs - as within the boundaries of economic production and whose outputs are therefore part of GDP; (b) activities the output of which is destined for the market; and (c) the remaining informal activities whose outputs are considered outside the present boundaries of SNA.

Proposals for defining the informal sector

Many proposals have been made for concepts and definitions to encompass the notion of informality. While abundant, they are often rather loose as to definitions and delimitations. Some of them focus on the characteristics of the activity being performed, as in subsistence production or in the many other types of own-account production that exist. Other proposals centre on the characteristics of the unit performing the activity, such as its size, kinds of power and energy at its disposal, the amount of capital, location, and use of modern or traditional methods of production, the latter with reference to production in the strictly technical sense as well as to its mode of organization and administration.

Proposals to distinguish a special informal sector from other economic activities have been made for many different reasons. Sometimes the intention is to portray the extent of certain social and cultural conditions in a country or a region, especially conditions of marginality or poverty. In other instances, the objective is to measure the possibilities for development of industrial enterprises. Proposals have also been related to the need for information for more flexible fiscal policies, or better financial credit arrangements, or to other circumstances. Sometimes the primary concern is the absolute size of the informal sector and not necessarily its relative size within the national aggregate. Frequently, the attributes which are proposed in order to differentiate this sector or activity from others are features which tend to change in the course of economic and social development and these attributes are intended to serve as indicators of such changes.

In so far as the 1968 SNA deals with the problem, it is concerned to include all activities which should be considered to be part of national production and/or national consumption. The 1968 SNA also presents a number of guidelines for certain supplementary classifications, including a scheme of classification into modern (recent) and traditional modes of production, based on criteria of scale, technology, organization and management. These guidelines are given in chapter IX of the SNA, which deals with the adaptation of the full system to developing countries. The existence of a special sector based on traditional modes of production is considered to be a basic feature of developing countries, "that is the existence side-by-side, of traditional and more recent modes of living, social and economic organization, and carrying on production". 6/

As far as it goes, this provides a quite usable general framework for classification within which women's participation could be evaluated. However, it is a very general framework and more precise indications are needed for proper classification.

The SNA proposes to classify establishments according to mode of production, based on criteria "such as the resources, facilities and technology used in the activities, the manner in which production is organized and managed, and the scale of the operation". 7/ It also mentions that different criteria are appropriate for different activities. Thus, all production carried on within household premises would ipso facto be classified as traditional, while in the case of mining, manufacturing and construction, the dividing line would be the use of power equipment: two horsepower or less would characterize the traditional mode of production. This of course implies low capital intensity and heavy reliance on hand labour. The amount of labour engaged is also considered to be a suitable way of distinguishing between the two modes of production.

In more general terms, it is stated that an important point of reference for distinguishing the modern and the traditional parts of the economy of a developing country is the role and type of market to which they are connected, which could be the export market, the regional market or the local market. Moreover, there could be no market at all, as in the case of subsistence production.

In order to bring these indications one step nearer to the task of collecting statistical data, it should be noted here that in mentioning the different types of markets, the objective is to consider the way in which the producer channels his product to the user. This is only the final stage in the process of production, a process that comprises several stages, such as acquiring inputs, transforming inputs into outputs and disposing of output, all of which should be examined in the search for more precise guidelines of classification.

The first stage in the production process is the preparatory stage in which all the elements - physical and human - which will be used in the successive stages are assembled. In a modern organized enterprise such as a corporation, these activities are usually taken care of by a purchasing department and a department of personnel. In a small-scale enterprise, one person, possibly the owner, will take care of buying the materials necessary and hiring labour. But be it on a large scale or on a small scale, buying goods or non-factor services will take place in what is called the product market and the hiring of personnel in the labour market, so in both cases there exist links to the market. This stage is seldom taken into consideration in definitions of informal activities. However, SNA refers to it when it states that processing of primary products for own consumption should be considered as production if the products which serve as inputs have been produced by the same unit that processes them, but not so if these products have been bought in the market.

The second stage in the production process covers the activity by which the acquired inputs are transformed into the final products of the enterprise. This transformation may take place employing advanced and energy-intensive techniques, an extensive division of labour and huge, highly specialized installations in the case of modern enterprises, while, at the other extreme, the artisan or small family enterprise will transform its inputs working at home, through procedures inherited from the past and without much division of labour or intensive use of external energy sources. Many of the definitions that have been proposed by different authors for the informal sector are based specifically on this stage, such as technology employed in production, volume and types of energy utilized, location of activity, among others.

The third stage refers to the way by which the products created are conveyed to users. In developed market economies and in substantial part also in developing economies, the normal procedure is through sales, that is, through market transactions, and the market in which these transactions take place is, of course, the product market. In areas where there is no market, or sometimes even if there is one, certain producing units do not take part in it; they produce for their own use, that is, the products go from production to use without passing through a market.

The possibility of using the type of market, whether local, national or international, for distinguishing different sectors of a developing economy is based precisely on this last stage in the overall process. When considering the practical feasibility of this approach, it has to be borne in mind that "market" in this context does not mean a certain place where purchases and sales are concluded but the aggregate of transactions arrived at in many different ways - by verbal agreement, mail, telephone or other means of communication. This presents a serious impediment to proper statistical coverage.

While there is a certain correlation between them, each one of the stages outlined has individual characteristics which can be used to establish borderlines separating formal from informal productive units.

Although there is no shortage of criteria that could be used to delineate the informal sector, they are mostly descriptive in a way which does not facilitate quantification. They frequently overlap and sometimes the proposals contradict each other. As to the proposal of SNA for classification by mode of production (modern/traditional), it is general, not specific, and it is stated explicitly that the proposals made on adaptation of the full SNA to the developing countries are experimental. 8/ However, for the purpose of compiling statistics and aggregates - as in the present case of measuring and valuing women's participation in economic activities - a clear-cut definition of the area concerned is indispensable.

The multiplicity of criteria is reflected in the many different terms proposed for this area, such as "informal sector", "subsistence sector", "traditional mode of production", "non-monetary activities", which highlight one or another of the traits that characterize it but do not cover the same ground. For example, non-monetary activities can take place within productive units which are not informal (construction for its own use carried out by an engineering firm), and a traditional mode of production does not exclude monetary transactions (an artisan buying materials in the market).

In the following section we shall consider boundaries for the informal sector in a way that will enable us to measure and assign values to women's participation in it. As we proceed, we will examine the details and borderline cases which present themselves, but, first, it will be useful to sum up the general principles on which the definition considered here is based, which will serve at the same time as a conceptual underpinning to the definition.

B. Informal economic activity within the boundaries of the 1968 United Nations System of National Accounts (SNA)

1. Characteristics of the productive unit versus characteristics of the function performed

As already noted, the definition of informal sector in several different proposals is based either on the characteristics of the productive unit or on the function performed by it.

No problem arises when both the unit and the function show similar characteristics. An example is an engineering firm selling goods to the public. In this case the productive unit - the engineering firm - and the function - selling - are both considered of the modern type. In the case of a family which produces for its own use, here again the productive unit - the family - and the function - producing for its own use - are both considered to be of a traditional type. The characteristics of the unit and the function coincide.

However, this is not necessarily so in other cases. When the characteristics of the productive unit and those of the function which it carries out do not coincide, we have to choose whether classification should be based on one or the other. For some purposes this decision might be of secondary importance, but in order to arrive at a workable definition, it is necessary that the characteristics of the unit should be taken into account to qualify for inclusion in the aggregate we propose to measure. For example, production for own use - which represents a non-monetary activity, at least as far as the disposition of the product is concerned - if carried out by a "formal" unit (as the engineering firm in the example above), should not be included in the "informal" sector as defined here, because the unit manifestly is not an informal unit.

In this context, "unit" means "productive unit". A person could participate in different productive units, as in the case of an employee who after her or his working hours as an employee in a formal enterprise works at home in the family enterprise. A still more complex case is the employee doing household chores at home. These cases will be taken up later in the present report.

2. Role of the market

The other principle of classification is the role of the market. This is an underlying reason for the 1968 SNA proposal to distinguish between traditional and modern modes of production, but, as pointed out above, the role of the market is considered solely in connection with the disposition (sale or own use) of the goods and services produced by the unit. This, on closer examination, appears to be insufficient, as it covers only the last stage of the economic activity of the producing unit.

In the previous section we distinguished between three stages of production: the creation or acquisition of inputs (factor or non-factor inputs), the technical process of transformation (in its broad sense) and the final stage of disposition to the user. Each of these stages has different characteristics in the case of "formal" and "informal" units, but it is especially the first and the last stages where the market enters into the picture. Use of the market typifies the production unit not only in the sense of the destination of its final products but also as the locus of its acquisition of inputs. To be more precise, we have to divide the input market into two classes: the factor market (land, capital and labour) and the market for intermediate goods and services.

The 1968 SNA makes use of this division implicitly in distinguishing between processing of its own (that is not bought on the market) primary products for its own use by the primary products producer, and processing for its own use of primary products bought on the market. This is a useful distinction but it does not take into account the possibility that, while the basic raw material being processed may have been produced by the same person, other inputs, such as auxiliary materials, might have been bought in the market. For example, a farmer using milk from his own cows to produce cheese for his own use might have used chemical inputs bought at a store.

More relevant as far as establishing the scope of informal economic activity is concerned is the relationship of the productive unit to the factor market and specifically the labour market; in other words, whether or not there exists salaried employment. Where there are regularly employed salaried workers, this can be considered a formal production unit. Regularly employed is here taken to mean continuous, constant employment as opposed to occasional employment. Conversely, the absence of regularly employed salaried workers would classify the unit as an informal one. Again, the presence of occasional workers would not alter this classification. However, one important exception, which concerns agricultural production, should be noted. An agricultural production unit can employ regularly a few salaried workers and still be considered an "informal unit". The number will depend on specific conditions in each country.

It must be emphasized that all employeés or workers mentioned in this concept of formal sector are paid. Either they receive a wage or salary or they are paid by the piece or on a commission basis. In all these cases, they are considered salaried employees according to accepted definitions. This distinguishes them from unpaid family workers. A household enterprise could employ unpaid family workers and still continue as an informal unit. Employment of domestic service would not alter this informal status.

Summing up, it can be said that the notion of "formal" or "informal" should be based on the unit performing certain activities and that the unit should be considered of one kind or the other, depending on whether or not it has salaried employees working for it on a regular basis, with the exception of agricultural units.

This way of distinguishing between formal and informal units brings out economic as well as social features, such as the degree of division of labour and the intensity and mode of social exchange relations. As a definition, it is clear-cut and objective. On the practical side, it facilitates the task of collecting statistics inasmuch as situations where there are periodic payments involved, as in the case of wages and salaries, are in a qualitative sense different from those where such regular transactions in terms of money do not occur. This is because, in the first case, even if there is no formal bookkeeping it is more probable that some records exist, albeit in the most elementary form, or are more easily remembered. In addition, regular paid employment brings in a social dimension and concern which tend to be reflected in social security legislation and the existence of labour unions and other such organizations. As far as these institutions possess some kind of records, these can be used as a source of data.

Thus, the difference between units with and without salaried workers, even if only one worker, is deeper and more easily observed from the statistical viewpoint than the difference that might exist between a unit with only one employee and another unit with more than one employee. Furthermore, small establishments with salaried workers can be more easily covered by establishment censuses or sample surveys. They are in many countries an important sector of the economy and in some instances have been taken as part of the informal sector, even when employing only a few employees. Based on the above consideration, that their differences from household enterprises are more pronounced than those from other enterprises, they are considered here as part of the formal sector and outside the scope of the present report. None the less, small establishments with only a few salaried workers may represent an important category for social, economic and financial analysis. In such circumstances, it is desirable to collect data specifically for this group and establishment censuses and sample surveys should be designed in a way that allows data for this group to be obtained so that they can be easily distinguished from the rest of the formal sector.

The differentiating criterion described here departs from some suggestions given in SNA, for example, the suggestion to classify as informal all producing units that carry out production on household premises. Here, it should be remembered that the suggestions presented in SNA with reference to the informal sector are tentative proposals. They are more in the nature of hints as to possible trails which should be explored in what at the time SNA was adopted was mostly unexplored territory. Therefore, more than one definitional possibility is given by SNA even if all of them could not be applied simultaneously or, for that matter, translated into viable guidelines for statistical data collection. In the present situation, in contrast, the task is to arrive at a single definition which encompasses the phenomenon to be measured and, moreover, is amenable to collection of statistical data.

3. The production boundary

The foregoing should allow us to distinguish a formal from an informal unit, but, be it one or the other, it is evident that any unit can carry out quite different kinds of activity and not only productive activities. The question of what is to be considered a productive activity and what not is a difficult one and is at the heart of the issue of adequate measurement of women's activities. It is also a question that is more acute for the informal than for the formal sector, since the latter separates more tangibly productive and non-productive activities, while, in the former, all kinds of activities are clustered together and are nearer to each other in space, in time and even in purpose.

SNA considers as economic production all output produced for the market. Output that is not produced for the market is treated in accordance with some specific characteristics. 9/ Thus, economic production includes on the one hand all output by government and private, non-profit institutions serving households, and on the other, the portion of their output that has been retained by the producers for their own use. However, in the last case, SNA makes an important distinction. In the case of primary producers, all output retained by them plus the processing of these products is considered economic production. But in the case of other producers, as distinct from primary producers, the output retained by them is economic production only when part of it is also sold in the market.

C. Production in the informal sector

Proceeding from this review, we can now examine production in the informal sector. Informal sector production can be classified into two categories: for exchange, and for own use, which correspond broadly to monetary and non-monetary transactions. The significance of this division is twofold. On the one hand, by separating monetary from non-monetary transactions, data are made available which fit much better into monetary analysis. On the other hand, information is provided on the relative importance of the two types of transactions, which is an important feature in as far as one is expected to be increasingly replaced by the other in the process of economic and social development. Let us take up first non-monetary production.

1. Non-monetary production

The concept of non-monetary activity given by SNA includes four main elements: primary production; processing of primary products; fixed capital formation; and valuation.

(a) Primary production

According to SNA, "Some of the goods and services covered in the gross output of industries is not eventually sold in the market, but these items are similar in all essential respects to the goods and services which are marketed. In a number of countries, a significant part of the output of agricultural producers will be consumed in their households." 10/ The term "non-monetary" does not mean that there is no monetary transaction during the production process. The producer can buy fertilizers and seeds, for example, but the output is retained by the producer for his own use.

-13-

SNA states: "Subsistence production of primary products (the characteristic products of agriculture, fishing, forestry and logging, and mining and quarrying) is of considerable importance in the developing countries; and a shift takes place from subsistence to market production as development proceeds." 11/ It has been pointed out in a study carried out by the Organisation for Economic Co-operation and Development (OECD) that non-monetary production forms a substantial part of the total for most developing countries. 12/ In nearly 40 per cent of a sample of countries, non-monetary activities accounted for 20 per cent or more of total gross domestic product (GDP) and for 10 per cent or more in about two-thirds. The main types of activities considered as part of subsistence production in the countries included: production of basic indigenous agricultural foods such as poultry, pigs, goats, bananas and vegetables such as coconuts, maize, sweet potatoes, tapioca; hunting (excluding sport); food gathering (gums and resins, wild rubber, herbs, wild fruits, leaves, roots, and the like); firewood gathering; water-carrying; catching crustacea and molluscs and fishing.

(b) Processing of primary products

Also considered in SNA as non-monetary production is the processing of primary products by the producer for his own consumption, such as production of butter, cheese, wine, oil, cloth or furniture, even if none is produced for the market. Some countries include additional commodities, such as footwear, pottery, small agricultural tools, and food processing in general.

(c) Fixed capital formation

SNA states that all production of fixed assets on own account should, in principle, be included in the gross output of commodities. 13/ This refers to all types of products which have a life expectancy of one year or more and are retained by the producer for his own use irrespective of the final use of the output created by these assets. The items considered include construction works, land improvements, dwellings, copra driers, storage sheds, canoes, nets, traps, water supply.

Thus, total non-monetary production in the informal sector is the sum of primary production, processing of primary products and fixed capital formation carried out by the informal units for their own use.

Barter represents a special case in the sense that it involves exchange which is performed without the use of money. For this reason, it should be included in non-monetary transactions. However, sometimes it is not clear whether the exchange involves money or not, as when real goods are exchanged but one of them has acquired the characteristics of a money surrogate and is being accepted as a means of exchange.

(d) Valuation

Non-monetary production is usually measured in physical units and has to be valued in monetary terms in order to be integrated with the rest of production. This valuation can be attempted through the use of imputed prices. SNA recommends the use of producers' prices of the same or similar products on the market. 14/ Where market prices cannot be satisfactorily determined, labour inputs can be used instead. For both producers' prices and labour inputs it is desirable to take a yearly average. If the estimate is based on labour, all labour inputs, including those of unpaid family workers, should be valued at local wage rates for comparable work.

The market price can be easily used for valuation if at least part of the output produced has been sold in the market, whether or not the producer or the product were the same. If the product is not identical, a similar item can be taken as representative, taking account of differences in quality.

The most problematic area is the processing of primary products for own use when the producer does not usually perform this activity for the market, because the quality differences with similar products sold in the market could be substantial. The type of valuation to be used in such circumstances is a topic of ongoing discussion and the procedures used are compromises between what is ideally desirable and what is practically attainable.

2. Monetary production

Monetary production means that it is directed towards the market. In the case of an informal unit, production will often be in part for the market and in part for own use. The concept of informal marketed production consistent with SNA is "output of household enterprises", where production for the market tends to be more important than for own use. A first definition of household enterprise could be that of a household engaged in an economic activity on its own, which means without outside help. In other words, it is a family business without paid employees. If it is an agricultural activity there could be limited help by paid labourers and it would still be considered a household enterprise. In any other case there could be only casual employees; regular employees - even if only one single employee - would place the production unit in the category of an establishment and therefore outside the informal sector.

The production of the household enterprise can be disaggregated into two types: production and processing of primary products; and production of other types of products and services (manufactures, distributive trade and services, household and other services).

(a) Production and processing of primary products

Primary output as part of monetary production as well as its processing by the producer is similar to non-monetary primary production discussed above but in this case all or part of production is sold in the market. A further difference is that the primary input can be purchased but the output must be, at least partially, sold in the market. In this category are thus included all the agricultural units operating on an own-account basis, while all units with regular salaried help are excluded. The objective and identifying characteristic is that the owner operates his own farm, with or without the help of unpaid family workers. If the proprietor has only managerial functions this unit is probably a formal one.

The informal agricultural household enterprise defined in this way usually carries out production of both types: non-monetary for own use and monetary for the market. The relationship between these two elements, monetary and non-monetary, varies, and as the business progresses, the marketed part grows more than the other. The non-monetary part will be minor when the enterprise becomes formal. Quite often, for example, when a new highway is built through formerly rather isolated regions, an essentially rural environment is opened up to new possibilities and forms of co-operation with the market. Some family members participating in household enterprises withdraw from them and take up paid employment. The formerly prevalent subsistence activities are progressively associated with market activities and often eventually replaced by them. Such market activities might include the sale of fruits, vegetables, flowers or handicrafts to vehicles passing along the highway and the use of the road to take products to more distant market-places and to buy new, productivity-increasing inputs.

Elementary arrangements like the sale of agricultural products on the highway, especially at points where traffic slows down or stops for some reason, might become more complex over time, especially if they tend to be commercially successful. The informal agricultural producer who started selling his product personally or with the help of unpaid family members might engage paid helpers whom he pays by the day or on commission. In both cases, the payee is considered a salaried worker, and if this happens on a regular basis throughout the year the household enterprise belonging initially to the informal sector changes over to the formal sector. However, this mutation will seldom be sudden. It usually comes about gradually and even imperceptibly, as the salaried employment grows from intermittent into steady and regular. For statistical coverage this presents a dilemma, since even the two sides concerned, the employer and the employee, might have different opinions as to whether the job is or is not a steady engagement. In such circumstances, past duration should be the criterion to decide one way or the other.

In this context, another matter has to be mentioned, concerning problems connected with the remuneration of women's employment. The division into formal and informal sectors allows examination of many problems specific to one or the other of these two groups and contributes in this way to better understanding. But neither of these groups is uniform within itself. Within each group there are differences, and at the margin individuals or subgroups in one group may show great affinity to individuals and subgroups in the other group. Where this is the case and where the expected usefulness of the information to be obtained justifies the additional cost, design of statistical inquiries should be directed to obtaining data on marginal cases in the formal as well as informal sectors.

While in the present paper we are interested specifically in the informal sector, we cannot lose sight of the fact that, on the formal side of the borderline, there are cases and subgroups very close to those on the informal side, as for example, those who receive payment by the piece, although they work on materials supplied to them by their employers, work at home and sometimes even with their own tools (production of carpets, clothing, maquila). Their remuneration is usually below minimum standards and more often than not they are not covered by any social legislation. Generally they do not belong to any union and, of special concern here, a majority of them are women who combine this kind of work with caring for children and other housework and therefore are unable to work outside their home. By generally accepted definition such cases are part of the formal sector and beyond the limits of the present paper, but for a comprehensive view of women's contribution and problems related to it, appropriate arrangements should be made for their statistical coverage.

The various activities of production and processing of primary products for the market which are considered here are similar to those examined in the case of subsistence. The main difference is in the scale of operation, especially in the case of products to be marketed. Production for own consumption is quite similar in both cases. This aspect of the productive activity of the household enterprise is usually in the hands of unpaid family workers. The processing of primary products produced by household enterprises is relatively important only if the business is very small, which means the household is close to subsistence level and their processing of primary products is concerned with products directed to the market. Examples are milling of paddy into rice, production of juice or wine, manufacture of syrup or jam or dairy products, processing of fish or meat, as well as manufacturing of agricultural tools, household furniture and domestic utensils.

(b) Other products and services

The foregoing discussion considered household enterprises producing and processing primary products, which implies that most of them are located in rural districts. Now we turn to household enterprises situated in rural or urban areas producing for the market non-primary products, as in the case of manufactures, distributive trade and services, and household and other services.

The typical case is a family business in which members of the family participate but which does not have regular salaried employees. The question might arise whether the definition of household enterprise should also cover those cases where only one person, either living alone or with other members of a family, is active; in other words, what is frequently referred to as "own-account worker". However, this question need only be considered a semantic one, since both multiperson family businesses without salaried help as well as own-account work belong to the informal sector.

Traditional language use distinguishes a single person from a family, but surveys and censuses now speak of one-person households. The decision as to whether they should be covered and presented separately or together with all other households will depend on the relative cost and usefulness.

If an own-account worker accepts a regular salaried job his status changes to salaried employee, even if during off hours he continues to work on own account, provided that his salary represents the major part of his income. A different case is that of an own-account worker who engages another worker and pays him a salary on a regular basis. He too ceases to be an own-account worker and ipso facto passes into the formal sector as an employer. Here, the distinction between informal and formal becomes tenuous. Arguments can be put forward in favour of including an artisan with only one paid regular helper in the informal category. However, this would not solve the problem; it would only shift it on to ground where the distinction is even more difficult.

The condition of selling in the market, in the case of non-primary activities, makes an important difference in some countries as this concept derives from market economies where consumers are at the same time factors of production who receive monetary income and go to the market in order to satisfy their needs. However, the situation in developing countries is that a large part of their population must satisfy their needs producing by and for themselves within the household. Many researchers believe it is advisable that these activities should be treated as productive instead of as general household duties. One implication of not treating such activities as productive is that when a housewife buys material to sew family clothes, her activity is not considered as productive, but if she is a professional dressmaker, the whole of her activity, for the market and for own consumption, is treated as economic.

The main activities carried on by household enterprises are handicrafts, trade, transport and services. The designation handicrafts includes many types of manufacturing, such as making sweets and other food, weaving, sewing, and making jewellery and carpets. The activity may be performed by power-driven machines or by hand and it can be carried out within the household premises or outside. No hired help (unless casual) is required. In the trade and restaurant industries, street vendors frequently constitute the majority of such enterprises, but other trade activities such as intermediaries, guest houses and food establishments, including mobile catering carts, are also common.

Sometimes there are problems in distinguishing an own-account worker from an employee. A person operating a mobile catering cart or a taxi driver could be one or the other. The criterion for deciding is to determine whether he/she is an entrepreneur or not. A person is considered an entrepreneur when he/she owns or leases the capital or the material inputs involved in the business and can dispose of the output. When the capital equipment and/or material inputs are provided to him/her by a proprietor who is another person or firm, then he/she is an employee. Outworkers may be classified, following the rules laid down in the International Classification of Status in Employment, 15/ as employees (where performing work for wage or salary) or own account workers (when operating business without the assistance of paid employees, but possibly with the assistance of unpaid family workers). This is a position that can be seen as intermediate between the status of an employee and that of an entrepreneur; this is the case of a women who assembles products at home using materials or components which have been supplied by the enterprise which will receive the products. The adequate classification of such activity depends on the relationship between the person concerned and the enterprise, the existence of a labour contract and the ownership of the instruments and machinery employed.

Passenger and freight transport on an own-account basis is, in some countries, a very important part of that industry. The vehicle can be owned or leased. The limiting condition is that no regular employee is used. Sometimes transport and trade are performed jointly and hired help is temporary.

Services performed by household enterprises are of many different types: real estate and finance, health and related services, private teaching, street performers and household (domestic) services. In the service sector, the condition of having no hired regular help is still valid in order for a unit to be considered as a household enterprise, but there is something else that has to be considered. Some of the activities mentioned above are carried out by university graduates or similar professionals. Such people, though working on an own-account basis, are frequently, in research done on the subject, not considered as part of the informal sector. Accordingly, they should better be excluded or presented separately. This problem appears only when they work alone. Usually they have regular paid help - receptionists, secretaries, switchboard operators - but even when this is not the case (sometimes they have unpaid family help), it is advisable to leave them out of the informal sector.

With regard to domestic service, it should be borne in mind that this area covers two different situations, both within the informal sector: first, the activities performed by an own-account worker who receives payment for work done, usually per hour; and second, those domestic services which are supplied by persons living in the same household.

Not infrequently, domestic service is performed exclusively for "bed and food". This is, of course, a remuneration in kind, even though a rather sparse one. Sometimes it is argued that such arrangements are justified on the grounds that the person - usually a child or an adolescent - is getting an education or is being employed as an apprentice. The question of how to treat apprentices in household work as well as in any other activity is not easy to answer. Recommendations on population and housing censuses propose creation of a special category of "unpaid apprentices" in countries where it is needed. It is further recommended, however, that this category should not include apprentices who receive pay in kind, or meals and sleeping quarters, who should be classified as employees. This solution is also applicable to our purpose.

Given the definition of the informal sector based on the absence of paid employees, a question might be posed as to the appropriate classification of co-operatives. Co-operatives usually have no salaried employees and the members of a co-operative receive income calculated on the basis of a pre-established agreement. This differentiates them from family enterprises, where such pre-established accords as to the distribution of income do not exist. For that reason, it seems appropriate to include co-operatives in the formal sector and not consider them when dealing with the informal sector.

Activities corresponding to aid given by one household to another for humanitarian or other reasons should be treated in the same way as similar activities for the well-being of the family. In most cases, however, it is impossible to arrive at an acceptable estimate of such activities.

As for illegal activities, these encompass a wide range, from growing and producing narcotics and drugs, peddling, robbing, smuggling, prostitution and illegal gambling to clandestine economic activity, such as evasion of tax or other legal provisions. Some are highly organized and staffed enterprises, others small-scale or even one-person activities corresponding to the informal sector. It has been said that such activities have been growing lately at an accelerated pace. The question that arises here is whether estimates of such activities should be made. The rule followed in national accounts is that illegal activities which are comparable to legal ones, such as smuggling and illegal imports, should be included in the estimates, and this answers the question. Activities which are included in national product, irrespective of whether they are carried out by men or women, have to be included in our estimates of the informal sector if we want to arrive at an acceptable estimate of the role of women in the creation of total national product.

D. Non-monetary production outside SNA

Up to this point we have been examining activities creating a product, either in the form of commodities in the sense of SNA (that is goods and services intended for sale on the market) or what SNA refers to as "other goods and services" (that is, not normally sold in the market). The objective has been to establish a suitable dividing line between two types of sectors, the formal and the informal. Both sectors fall within the limits set by SNA for productive activity and therefore estimates of the value of women's contribution along the lines agreed on up to this point in the discussion will be directly comparable with the total value of the national product as currently defined and of which they are a component. This comparability has to be borne in mind as we proceed to explore the possibility of taking into account women's activities that, by present SNA standards, are not part of national product.

Any change of the production boundary to take account of work activities often carried out primarily by women implies an expansion of what is to be considered as national product. This poses a series of problems, especially if the change is quantitatively substantial and the increase in the national product brought about by this innovation is due to the inclusion of activities without a concomitant monetary flow, as is the case for those which will be considered below. The outstanding problem in this connection is not so much the fact that activities without a monetary counterpart do not have a price (this can be taken care of by imputations) but, far more importantly, the circumstance that national product data are used mostly in the context of other monetary aggregates.

The most important activity from the point of view of women's contribution, given a broader concept of national production which hitherto has not been taken into account, is the work that women do for their families within their homes. This includes activities for children and spouse, cooking, cleaning and generally carrying out a great number of diverse tasks which are indispensable and without which those other activities which are at present included in the national product could not be carried out. Such activities are recorded in the 1968 national accounting framework if they are performed by a hired person because there is a monetary (or in-kind) transaction. They are omitted if they are done by a member of the household, usually a woman, because the monetary transaction is absent. (This is the basis of Pigou's joke about the contraction of the national product due to a man marrying his housekeeper.)

Several questions arise in this connection. Is the inclusion of such activities in national product accounting at all possible? How can they be delineated in a way which would make them accessible to statistical coverage? Where would we look for data that would measure them in a satisfactory way?

The answer to the first question is definitely positive, with the proviso that in order to be useful to different types of analysis the final national accounts aggregate should be presented in two different ways: a comprehensive variant and another exclusively money-related variant. In the latter case, not only will women's unpaid work be omitted from the total, but several other items presently included in the usual presentation of GDP would also not be included. As to the question of how to define woman's work for the upkeep of the family in terms that would clearly isolate what we wish to measure, this is discussed below. The issue of sources of information is the subject of subsequent chapters.

1. Boundaries

It is first necessary to comment on the concepts of the kind of activity and the unit responsible for it. 16/ The activity referred to is the upkeep of the household and it is carried out by a unit without any economic remuneration. In other words, we are not concerned here with paid household work. A unit, as has already been said, means an economic unit, although, in this particular case, the economic unit and the individual person tend to coincide. But, as has been said before, a person can participate in different economic units. The unit can be someone who does not perform any other work besides household chores or somebody who is a student, but it also can be someone working in a factory or an office or in a family enterprise. 17/ In these last instances, the hours spent on household work will be additional to working time in the activities mentioned. If we wish to maintain the same approach used earlier, we would say that such persons participate in two different economic units: on one hand the factory, the office or the family enterprise; and, on the other, the unit in charge of the upkeep of the household.

A factory or office is part of the formal sector of the economy, while the family enterprise and now also the upkeep of the household belong to the informal sector of the economy. The new element of course is the inclusion of household work within the boundaries of economic activity. While such duties are mostly done by women, men also sometimes perform them. For the purpose of measuring women's participation in the national product in this expanded version, these activities should be measured in their entirety, covering women's as well as men's contribution, separating, of course, the corresponding part for each sex.

One of the consequences of including these particular activities in the national product is an increase in what is considered production. This part of production is intended for consumption and, accordingly, consumption also increases. Up to now, such activities have been overlooked. Consumption is counted as the sum of purchases of consumption goods and services (and their equivalents in the case of consumption from own production), while, in the expanded version, consumption would equal the former total plus the value of the new activities. This would bring out more clearly the fact that increasing absorption of housewives by salaried employment and the ensuing increase in formal production is frequently offset by a decrease in the production of the informal sector. Vice versa, a decrease in family upkeep activities by housewives can create a heavier and unforeseen demand for certain services of the formal sector, especially the public sector, as has been observed in some countries where demand for nursery schools and hospitals as well as homes for the elderly has gone up substantially as a consequence of increased salaried employment of women.

The same phenomenon can be viewed in a somewhat different way. Increases in manufacturing of food and textiles by factories are often counterbalanced by a contraction of food processing, weaving and sewing within the household. In all such cases, national accounting figures in their present form tend to distort reality by the impression they give of development. What is presented as an increase is in fact, at least partly, a displacement.

We now return to the problem of how to isolate this household activity from others for the purpose of measurement. As a first step, it has to be seen in more concrete terms. Speaking of it as if it were one single activity implies a high degree of abstraction. In concrete terms, it consists of many different activities, such as tending and teaching children, taking children to school, preparing meals for children, the elderly and spouse, nursing the ill, looking after the house, the garden and possibly animals, carrying on social obligations, and many, many others which it is impossible to list. Most of these activities performed for one's own family have their counterpart in the market - charwomen, cooks, schools, babysitters, transport, medical or paramedical care, restaurants, laundries, commercial house cleaners, intermediaries, errand boys - and even in the much less specialized form of salaried domestic services.

The question gets more involved when instead of, or in addition to, providing services to others, such services are imparted to oneself, as for example cooking for oneself or bathing. In order to fix a limit to such activities which otherwise would stretch out to include all manifestations of human life, we shall remember what has been said at the beginning of the present study about activities amenable or not amenable to exchange. If an activity that gratifies the needs of a person can be performed by another person, there exists the practical possibility of exchange. Where such a possibility exists, the activity should be considered for national accounting purposes as a productive activity and consequently part of GDP in its expanded version. In fact this is being done in the present system in the case of processing of primary products for own use. If an activity cannot be performed by a person other than the one who benefits from it (as in the case of taking a walk) it is not amenable to exchange and thereby removed from a social context and outside the ground covered by national accounting.

This furnishes the boundary we were looking for. Non-marketed activities, with special reference to the chores of housekeeping, should be included in productive activities within the expanded GDP, even if carried out by the same person that enjoys their benefits, whenever there exists the possibility that they could be carried out by others.

Such a solution, however, is open to criticism when it comes to comparing activities to be included with those excluded. For example, it has been pointed out that combing one's hair would be considered productive (because it could be done by a hair dresser) and learning unproductive (because unlike the process of teaching, learning can only be done by the person concerned). This situation resembles somewhat the one that presents itself when the otherwise prosperous banking sector shows, in accordance with general national accounting principles, negative value added. In all such cases, the general principle must be complemented by specific ad hoc decisions in certain singular cases.

Household activity is difficult to measure in terms of its products or outcome. In this, it resembles the public sector, where valuation of output is also beyond our capacity for measurement. For this reason, government services are valued for national accounting purposes at the cost of inputs, which, for the government workforce, is given by the payroll. For household activities, there are no payrolls and their valuation for national accounting purposes has to be based on the time spent on them.

This in turn raises several questions which we will comment on before entering into a description of particular procedures for valuation. First, is household work all toil and exertion or is it also, at least in part, enjoyment by itself? Second, if the output is measured in terms of time spent in producing it, should not productivity be taken into account?

The first question is a reasonable one, inasmuch as activities at home are more independent and unfettered than those in formal production. Where the outputs of these activities are for exchange in the market, they will not be enjoyed directly by their producer, as will be the case for household work, as in all production for own consumption. Thus, there can be an element of enjoyment in the proper execution of the work which is not present, or much less present, in the case of work for the market. This, however, is a difference of degree. Work carried out in a hostile environment, deplorable physical conditions, pressure of time and pecuniary insufficiency is not conducive to enjoyment, while formal production under favourable conditions may produce such satisfaction. Thus, the difference between the two, after all, may not be as pronounced as it might seem.

Another contention related to the same phenomenon refers to productivity of work done at home in comparison with work done under supervision and within the constraints of an organized framework. It asserts that the former is done at a more leisurely pace than the latter. This might be true in some instances but certainly not always. Scarcity of time and the existence of competing needs are constraints in the household as well as elsewhere and pressure by supervisors on the shop floor does not always produce high productivity. In more concrete terms, a housewife does not necessarily produce less per hour than hired domestic help. The issue of productivity has still another side to it: the use of equipment and power supply in the household. Between the mortar and the handmill, the cellar and the icebox, between the open fireplace and the kerosene stove and the kitchen range and the microwave oven, there are differences not only in convenience but also in enhanced productivity, since an hour's work with utensils and equipment may well create more product than the same amount of work without them. It is desirable to take account in our estimates of such differences in productivity. The possibility of doing this depends on the way household activities are valued.

2. Valuation

Several different methods can be used in order to estimate the value of women's (and men's) work in their own households. It should be clear, however, that any practical procedure can only provide an approximation. Activities that lack a monetary counterpart are different in kind - at least as far as their incorporation into national accounts is concerned - from those which take place in the market, as there is no price-tag attached to them. In order to price them, one looks for an equivalent in the market sphere. In this way, we arrive at an imputed price and such a price is of course an approximation. At this point, we have to ask ourselves whether this fact does not detract from the usefulness of our proposition.

The usefulness of national accounting data can be established only by their applications. The use of data on women's activities in their own homes will be more frequently related to analysis and decisions of a longer-term nature than to short-term analysis, let us say in the monetary field, where fine-tuning of policy measures is the most common use, and precision and statistical accuracy are essential. For this reason, such approximations as can be reached in the former case would be unsatisfactory for the last-named example but are quite satisfactory for other purposes. It is for this reason that it is important to insist upon the significance of separating within total national product the part that corresponds to monetary transactions from the non-monetary.

The approaches that are taken to estimate the value of women's activities in their own homes can be divided into two groups. The first is the opportunity cost approach. This term derives from the fact that the price assigned to domestic activity is equal to what the same person would earn in her non-domestic occupation. An hour of domestic activity of a newspaper vendor would be priced at the same amount as she normally would earn in an hour selling newspapers and that of a government employee according to the hourly earnings in her job.

In this approach, the price attached to non-salaried domestic work varies according to the average income of the person who performs it. This approach has its weak as well as strong points. It is weak because the same kind of work is valued differently depending on who does it. This is undesirable from an objective viewpoint. From a subjective point of view, however, this portrays the circumstance where a person with high income will price her time higher than a person with lower average income. Moreover, it contains a large element of abstraction because, in practical terms, it can not be taken for granted that opportunities for additional work always exist, or that additional hours of work would produce the same average income. Furthermore, it can not be applied to those who do not have any other occupation in addition to work in their own home.

The second approach is called "equivalent market function", because it looks for the price of functions or activities in the market that can be considered equivalent to those rendered in one's own home. This can be done in two ways, either by adopting the price paid to domestic servants who discharge all the different duties of this service or by pricing the different activities which the work comprises in accordance with the corresponding market rates. In the first case, women's work at home is priced at a rate equal to domestic servants' wages, possibly adjusted for differences in the number of hours worked. In the second case, one has to determine the time spent on different activities like cooking, cleaning, nursing, teaching and so on, and assign to each one of these pursuits the same prices or fees they get when contracted in the market. It is especially with this procedure that possible differences in quality of service have to be borne in mind. There will usually be not one single price for a certain service (unless regulated by legislation) but a more or less broad band of different prices, possibly expressing differences in quality. This can be taken into consideration when choosing the price level most appropriate for a woman's activities in her own home. Possibilities of refining the estimates will depend mostly on the availability of data. This subject will be considered in later chapters.

While we have centred our attention specifically on activities that can be described as unpaid household services for own consumption, where "own consumption" should be understood as use by the person who provides the service as well as use by her family for consumption, the question remains whether the fact that a certain person performs such activities should or should not affect her status in statistics on the economic activity of the population.

The International Conference of Labour Statisticians established concepts and definitions on the economically active population where reference is made to persons engaged in the production of economic goods and services for own and household consumption. With respect to their statistical classification, such persons are considered as employed if their production constitutes an important contribution to the total consumption of the household. It is also said that the system of statistics on the economic activity of the population should allow for measuring relationships between employment, income and other social and economic characteristics. Therefore, statistics on the economic activity of the population should be developed, to the fullest extent possible, in harmony with other economic and social statistics.

In regard to the subject of household work for own consumption (understanding by "own" the person concerned and her family), this brings out the necessity of imputing a price to it. Otherwise, if this type of activity is included in employment but the corresponding "product" or "income" is not included in the national sectoral aggregate, there is no possibility of measuring the relationship between them, which is one of the objectives of the economic statistics system. In order to reach that objective, both phenomena have to be handled statistically in a parallel way. If this category is to be considered as "employed", it is at the same time "productive" and the product created has to appear in the accounts of the national accounting system.

For the same reason and also for the sake of harmonization in the field of statistical coverage, the concept cited above, which restricts the classification to cases where production constitutes "an important contribution to the total consumption of the household", should be interpreted in a way that makes it consistent with the general definition of the category of employment.

II. SOURCES OF DATA

In this chapter the different sources of statistics that can be used to construct an estimate of women's contribution to economic development will be taken up. It was pointed out earlier that statistical information on women's problems lag far behind the demand that presently exists. Furthermore, in the context of the present study, the search for statistical data centres on the information that is needed to account for women's participation in the informal sector of the economy. Inasmuch as these data usually are not ready-made, compromise with respect to strict observance of definitional rules at the stage of compilation is unavoidable, but it should not go so far as to distort the meaning of the results obtained.

The basic informational building blocks needed refer in part to number of persons, especially women, and in part to the volume and value of goods and services created by them and/or the income perceived. As the present objective is limited to the informal sector, it is necessary to ensure that the women and the values considered are part of that sector.

The task of putting a value on women's participation in the informal sector can be approached either via estimates of the product created by them or via their income, monetary, non-monetary and imputed. In the case of a primitive economy with an observable division of labour by sex, it is also possible to use as a clue to women's activities the disposition of goods and services, that is, mainly consumption.

In the first case, the essential figures refer to quantities produced in different activities and products and their corresponding unit prices. Economic statistics on total production do not usually discriminate between production by men and women. The distinction must be based on other sources, mainly population censuses and/or specialized inquiries. For information on average prices, it is necessary to search in production censuses and surveys, trade bulletins and price lists.

If the income approach is chosen or, more exactly, is chosen for that part of the total estimate for which figures on income are more readily available, the questions to be faced are analogous to those mentioned above and, again, we will have to rely heavily on the population censuses. The fact that we are looking for figures in the informal sector aggravates the difficulties.

The collection of data for national accounting has been likened by one of its outstanding representatives to the work of ants which roam in search of bits and ends that might be used in building their ant-hill. The analogy fits even more the search for data on women's participation in the informal sector. As statistics related directly to women's activities in the informal sector do not generally exist, these statistics have to be compiled and the value of their activities calculated by sifting information and statistical figures prepared for different purposes. Definitional problems apart, the statistical difficulties of this endeavour relate to the fact that the information needed belongs to different statistical areas and the data are not always collected and compiled in a way that allows them to be combined easily.

Statistical information can usually be obtained from information systems specifically designed for statistical purposes or from administrative files where statistical figures are an unintended by-product. But even in the case of specific statistical tools like censuses, if a certain topic has not been taken into account in the design of the questionnaire, the user must try to use whatever data of a general character can serve his purpose and select pieces of information which, although they were not intended for that specific objective, might nevertheless be useful for it. In such circumstances, one has to accept the fact that first estimates will unavoidably be crude. Successive improvements will be the result of better sources, methodology and experience.

Within this situation, which in its general outlines is common to most countries, there still exist substantial differences among countries. We will take up the more important statistical sources usually available in the following order:

(a) Population censuses;

(b) Economic censuses and surveys;

(c) Household sample surveys;

(d) Price statistics, administrative files and other sources.

Given their different aims, each of these makes a different contribution to our research. The population census covers total population and the characteristics of each person. Economic censuses are divided customarily by areas of activity covering the primary, secondary and tertiary sectors. Thus, we consider separately censuses and surveys on agriculture, industry and trade and services. The statistical unit of economic censuses and surveys is the productive unit.

Censuses, demographic as well as economic, are undertaken usually only at relatively long intervals and their results published only after considerable delay. Since, for our purpose, data from censuses are to be combined with other figures, care must be taken to make the necessary adjustments so that both sets of figures correspond to the same year.

After the population and the economic censuses, the third group comprises household sample surveys. The distinguishing feature of national household surveys, which can cover a wide range of different topics, is the fact that the universe on which they are based is the aggregate of households of the country. Because of this, they enable us to discover facts which surveys based on buildings, establishments and enterprises cannot reach.

In addition to these sources, many countries have collected statistics on the use of time, which can shed light on the problems treated here in a way no other type of data can. Chapter III reviews these statistics on the basis of country experiences.

A. Population censuses

The population census is a basic, universal record widely available in most countries. It covers demographic, economic and social data of all persons in a country. The fact that each individual is enumerated and his or her characteristics are recorded separately makes it possible for data on various characteristics to be cross-classified. This constitutes the irreplaceable role of the population census for our purposes.

The census data that have the greatest interest for us are those which relate the population to its economic characteristics. In the United Nations Principles and Recommendations for Population and Housing Censuses, twenty different recommended tabulations are shown dealing with economic characteristics. 18/ There are also other tables pertinent to our endeavour, especially "Households and population in households by size of household and number of economically active members". 19/ These tables as they appear in the United Nations recommendations are not necessarily followed exactly in different countries. However, even if differently combined, the categories and cross-classifications indicated usually appear in country presentations.

The tabulation most appropriate for our purpose is the table "Economically active population by status of employment, industry and sex". 20/ This tabulation is shown for the country as a whole and for major civil divisions, differentiating between rural and urban areas. Status in employment distinguishes among employees, own-account workers, employees, unpaid family workers, members of producers' co-operatives and not classifiable. Industry is classified according to the International Standard Industrial Classification of All Economic Activities (ISIC).

There are also two tables which refer to income. 21/ One presents the economically active population by monthly income, occupation and sex. The other shows households and population in households by annual income and size of household. The recommended geographical division for both is the same as described above for the table on economically active population and occupation is classified according to the International Standard Classification of Occupations (ISCO). Where these tabulations on income are available, they can be of great help in calculating women's income. In many cases, however, they either will not be available or the data collected will be considered of doubtful validity and inferior to those obtained through income and expenditure studies.

One of the characteristics of the informal sector is that its units are small and their economic activities are very much interrelated with other non-economic activities. It is therefore difficult to isolate informal units and even legal and administrative provisions are difficult to enforce in their case.

In countries where laws stipulate a minimum age for primary school leaving and prohibit child labour below a certain age, authorities are reluctant to fix an age limit in population censuses for economic activity below that age. Yet, in spite of such legal and administrative provisions, a great number of children below the minimum age do work, mostly in the informal sector. A similar exclusion occurs in some countries which automatically leave out of the enumeration persons at official retirement age, regardless of whether they are working or not. In developing countries, this category is, however, quantitatively less important than the aforementioned one.

If there is some documentary evidence as to the number of persons thus omitted from the count of the economically active population in the population census, the corresponding correction should be made. Possible sources for such a correction could be household surveys and time-budget studies. Otherwise, the subject should be marked for inclusion in the questionnaire of future surveys.

This under-enumeration of the work-force refers both to women and men. In addition, population censuses show evidence of under-reporting due to sex bias, whereby women who double up as participants in the work force and in household work are reported exclusively in their role of housewives. It is not easy to correct such figures. This type of bias has to be eliminated at the planning stage of censuses. Once the figures have been compiled, only crude corrective adjustments can be made. Some such methods of adjustment are presented in chapter III.

While our main purpose is to point out statistical sources that already exist and can readily be used in estimates of women's social product, some words are called for on action that would add to and improve such sources. Specifically in the case of population censuses, there is much debate going on regarding the question of whether the population census should comprise a very wide range of topics or should be limited to demographic data. Recent trends view the population census as a general frame for specialized sample surveys, micro-data studies and other specific inquiries. Whether this means separate surveys or the addition of specialized questions posed only to a small fraction of the census population depends on local circumstances. The really important issue, however, is the necessity of homogeneous or at least mutually compatible and convertible concepts, definitions and units of measurement.

A category for which the treatment in many population censuses is highly unsatisfactory for our purposes is unpaid family worker. Not only have there been various definitions, but their identification and inclusion in or exclusion from the economically active population has varied from census to census and from country to country. For censuses which followed past guidelines this implies that the corresponding corrections have to be made a posteriori. However, for future censuses, the resolution of the XIII International Conference of Labour Statisticians concerning statistics of the economically active population, unemployment and underemployment creates a new and more favourable situation for future estimates of the role of women. For that reason, it is worthwhile to describe briefly the changes that have been proposed.

The resolution adopts the concept of "economically active population comprising all persons of either sex who furnish the supply of labour for production of goods and services as defined by the United Nations System of National Accounts and Balances". New standards are introduced with respect to the reference period and two concepts are distinguished: "The usually active population", which refers to a long period such as a year, and the "currently active population" or the labour force, which refers to a short period, such as a week or a day.

Those who are employed are comprised of those who are in paid employment during the reference period (performed some work for wage or salary in cash or in kind) and those who are in self-employment (performed some work for profit or family gain in cash or in kind). Persons engaged in the production of goods and services for own and household consumption are to be considered as being employed, with one condition: that their production represents an important contribution to the total consumption of the household.

B. Economic censuses and surveys

1. Agricultural

Agricultural censuses and surveys are the main sources of statistics on agricultural holdings and production of agricultural products. The main classifications used refer to products and regions and the unit of enumeration is the holding, in contrast to population censuses which use the household and the individual within the household.

Prior to 1980, it was recommended that agricultural censuses collect relatively detailed information on all persons living on agricultural holdings. However, following the 1980 World Census of Agriculture, it was recommended to provide information that can be used in conjunction with other statistical sources, such as population and housing censuses or special household surveys. These recommendations now cover specifically: (a) the collection of limited data on demographic characteristics and economic activity of members of the household; (b) the collection of information on the number and sex of hired permanent agricultural workers for each holding; (c) an indication of whether or not occasional agricultural workers are utilized on the holding. This approach implies a greater reliance on combining data from agricultural and population censuses and corresponds to the requirements of measuring women's role in agricultural production, provided that such population and employment data are systematically disaggregated by sex.

There are however two weaknesses in this procedure. The population census normally investigates only the principal economic activity of each person and only during a fixed time-reference period, often one week. Those persons who are connected with agricultural activity only incidentally or during a period which does not coincide with the census reference period are not identified. Where these weaknesses have seriously affected available data from past censuses, additional data on seasonal employment should be obtained through ad hoc inquiries or sample surveys. New United Nations recommendations for population censuses contemplate both a short and a longer time reference period. In addition, the question on main occupation could be supplemented with one regarding secondary occupation.

Agricultural production, as it appears in most agricultural statistics, is divided into crops and livestock and its products. Crops are classified in different groups such as cereals, roots and tubers, pulses, vegetables, fibres, coffee, cocoa and tea, tobacco, sugar cane, natural rubber, grapes and wine, nuts, fruits and berries. Some of these crops are typically destined for extensive processing in specialized agro-industrial production units and rudimentary small-scale processing on small family farms is rather a marginal occurrence. Other crops, such as yam or taro, are typical subsistence foods. Even if ultimately sold on the market, they are usually produced or collected on family farms. Such considerations must be used to identify informal production, at least in the early stage of investigation of women's participation. Caution should be exercised, however, as such characteristics do not remain fixed. An acceptable assumption for one year might not be valid some years thence, especially where economic development proceeds at an accelerated pace. The assertion that a certain procedure was used in a previous investigation on the same subject is not by itself an acceptable argument to use it again.

Some agricultural activities, such as the harvesting and gathering of wild plants, fruits and berries, are carried out almost exclusively by small family farmers and specifically women and children. Data on such activities, however, are scarce. 22/ Not infrequently certain roots and vegetables are explicitly cultivated for animal feed and for this reason they are not included in the production figures that appear in the agricultural census. Frequently women's participation in this type of production outweighs that of men and care must be taken that such production used as inputs in animal husbandry is not left out of the estimates.

With regard to livestock and its products, the situation is similar to that of crops. The decisive and most difficult step is to sort out what part of total production corresponds to the informal sector and within this sector to the work of women. In some instances, statistics for estimates on the first question must be culled from the agricultural census if tabulations exist on production, cross-classified with size of farms. However, the degree of participation of women will usually not be available and will have to be reconstructed from auxiliary sources. The figures on meat production customarily include both commercial and farm slaughter, but frequently data can be separated. The coefficient of women's participation varies considerably in different kinds of meat production, such as beef, mutton, goat, lambs or kids, and it is especially high in the case of poultry meat, where on small farms it usually reaches 100 per cent.

A similar situation exists with respect to milk production, dairy products, cheese, butter and eggs. Unless the farm is of a certain size and/or specialized in a given production, work done by women will be preponderant. The figures and coefficients to be used in the estimate will, again, be a mixture of data from the agricultural census, population census and ad hoc investigations.

Agricultural census data can also be complemented by housing census data. The United Nations recommendations state: "The housing census also provides an opportunity to collect data concerning small-scale agricultural activity carried on where the area in question would not fall within the definition of an agricultural holding. These data sometimes refer to the keeping of poultry, bees and so forth." 23/ Such information is helpful in coming closer to the contribution which the informal sector makes to the economy.

2. Industrial

Industrial censuses provide information on the overall structure and activity of the industrial sector. The industrial sector is conventionally defined to include the following branches of economic activity: mining and quarrying, manufacturing, electricity, gas and water, and construction. A weakness is that industrial censuses are taken at infrequent intervals. However, if supplemented with continuing annual inquiries, they provide indispensable sampling frames and benchmark data. For our purposes, however, these censuses, and often also the annual inquiries, have other shortcomings. These centre on two aspects: limited scope and absence of data on women's activities.

Although the industrial sector is defined to cover all establishments, uncertainties arise concerning the inclusion of small units. International recommendations suggest that units which carry out their productive activities on household premises should be included in industrial statistics only if it is known that they account for a significant portion of total industrial activity. In any case, the recommendations advise that the output of such units should be measured in household or other special surveys and that they could be enumerated in the population census. Whatever the definitional recommendations, in practice, coverage usually falls short of the established limits. Many countries establish a certain cut-off level below which no enumeration is done. In such cases, the non-enumerated units are precisely those which fall within the informal sector. On the other hand, countries where this section of industrial activity is quite important try to include in their industrial censuses all productive units regardless of size.

Before one can decide whether census figures are or are not usable for our purpose, it is therefore necessary to find out what the characteristics, theoretical as well as practical, are with respect to inclusion and exclusion of small-size units. In most cases, however, they cover establishments in which a given minimum number of persons is employed and which thus fall outside the demarcation line we have established for the informal sector. Thus, there exists a real information vacuum regarding small establishments, including one-person establishments, that is, persons working on own account.

In this situation, one has to fall back again on the population census. Recognizing this situation, the United Nations recommendations state that the information needed through the population census on smaller establishments, particularly those operated by self-employed persons, "is the industry and status (as employer, employee, own-account workers, etc.) of economically active persons, the name and address of their establishments (if any) and (for employers) the number of employees. If all of this information appears on the census questionnaire, the data for the small employers and own-account workers can be extracted from the schedule or from the processing documents after the enumeration. If only industry and status appear on the schedule, the remaining information may be obtained from the desired group at the time of the population census enumeration and entered on a separate schedule." 24/

The International Recommendations for Industrial Statistics 1983 recommends a breakdown by sex for "working proprietors", "unpaid family workers" and "employees", assigning this breakdown the same first priority accorded to the respective totals. 25/ However, in respect to "compensation of employees" such a breakdown is given priority 3, a low priority.

Persons engaged in establishment comprise all persons who work in or for the establishment, including working proprietors, active business partners, unpaid family and other unpaid workers. Excluded are home-workers, although it is recommended that they should be enumerated but shown separately as a memorandum item in the published tables. Unpaid family workers are defined as follows: "All persons living in the household of the proprietor of the owning enterprise and working in the establishment without regular pay (that is, without an agreed amount to be paid for work done) for at least one third of the working time normal to the establishment are included in this category. In practice, it may be necessary to broaden this definition to account for non-household members who work without regular pay". As has already been mentioned, the condition that working time of unpaid family workers should represent at least one third of normal working time, as applied in former censuses, has been reduced in recent recommendations to one hour. Mention of non-household members who work without regular pay can be understood to include, inter alia, apprentices.

Wages and salaries comprise payments in cash or in kind made by the employer, including bonuses, cost-of-living allowances as well as vacation and sick leave and such supplements to wages and salaries as are contemplated in the national accounts.

3. Distributive trade and services

These activities, sometimes called the tertiary sector, represent a very considerable part of gross domestic product and total employment in most countries. 26/ Also, to an important extent they are carried out by small units and are widely scattered, apart from the services of government. In developing countries they may represent, along with agriculture, the main activity of the informal sector. Moreover, women's participation in the tertiary sector is substantial.

As to sources of information, this sector is sometimes included in general economic surveys, while, in other instances, data in the field of distributive trade and services, again excluding general government, are collected in separate censuses and surveys. Most of the problems that arise in the use of data for this sector are similar to those presented in reference to data in the industrial sector. In addition to those mentioned there, the following features, characteristic of many of the units, require special attention and correction in the statistics: underenumeration due to the small size of units and the fact that often they operate in homes and do not require special equipment, the existence of itinerant units and the frequency of temporary activity.

In some cases, possible additional sources are administrative records for tax purposes and to meet labour regulations, and the records of social welfare bodies.

C. Household sample surveys

The comments that follow are intended to facilitate the use of data from available household sample surveys and to point out some matters that should be considered in future ones.

Household surveys are surveys which use the household as the sampling unit. Many different types of information can be drawn from household surveys, such as population characteristics, labour force, income and expenditure, household production and others. The United Nations Handbook of Household Surveys (Revised Edition) states: "Household surveys are among the most flexible of all data gathering mechanisms. In principle, almost any subject can be explored, and the concepts and level of detail can be adapted to the requirements of the investigation." 27/

In the past, a major portion of household sample surveys, especially in developing countries, were conducted as household income and expenditure surveys with the principal objective of obtaining weights for the consumer price index. The information obtained from such surveys can be helpful for our purpose, but it is mostly confined to capital cities and important towns or other areas for which it was considered important to have a consumer price index or cost-of-living index.

In the last decade or so, household sample surveys have experienced an extraordinary expansion and today one can say that there is probably no country with a statistical service that does not conduct household surveys of one kind or another. This expansion is due to the fact that demand for socio-economic data has been growing and household surveys are a cost-efficient tool to satisfy that demand. Complete canvasses like censuses are undertaken usually every 10 years, while household surveys can be undertaken with much more frequency and can go into more detail. Household surveys are thus a necessary complement that reflects changes taking place between one census and the next. "Sample household surveys provide a basis for updating census information at least for the nation as a whole or for broad geographical areas. The relationship is essentially a complementary one, between an infrequent but geographically detailed cross-section represented by the census and much more frequent time-series provided by surveys, which reflect continuous changes in society." 28/

Furthermore, household surveys, because they take the household as their unit of enumeration, provide answers to questions which could not be elicited from economic censuses and surveys, which take the establishment as their enumeration unit. An example is the income of persons (commission worker, homeworkers) who work for more than one productive unit.

Household sample surveys can be carried out in many different forms. These include continuing survey programmes and ad hoc surveys, and the surveys can be specialized or cover several subjects. A continuous survey programme has definite advantages over ad hoc surveys, not only because of the experience which is accumulated over time, which produces gains in efficiency and quality, but also because it provides a data base for efficient comparability and permits observation of changes in time (time-series).

The multi-subject survey covers simultaneously several different subjects. All of them could be covered for all households or some questions asked only from a sub-sample of households. One multi-subject survey is usually less costly than several surveys covering the same range of subjects and produces cross-classifications that different small surveys do not allow, or at least, do not allow with the same accuracy. On the other hand, the difficulties in designing and organizing a sample survey covering many topics lead more often than not to a compromise approach.

The data collected can cover a wide range. They are related both to the household and to the individuals living in it. That means that they furnish information on the household as such as well as the demographic and socio-economic characteristics of each household member.

As the household survey is viewed as a complement and extension to a census, the questions have to be designed in a way that makes it possible to disaggregate the broad information given by the census. Where only one question was asked to the individual in the census, several questions can be formulated in a household survey, but the definitions and concepts used in both must be consistent and omissions must be avoided. Thus, what has been said about concepts and definitions in speaking of censuses is also valid in the case of household surveys.

For our immediate purpose, it is important to be aware whether a single survey is part of a wider programme of surveys and whether a given item in the survey can be directly related to some other characteristics within the same survey or if we have to look elsewhere for such additional information.

There is practically no limit to the diversity of subjects that can be covered by household surveys. Those which are more directly related to our purpose are household surveys covering demographic characteristics, income and expenditure, labour force, agriculture and household enterprises, each of which will be considered below.

While all household surveys are sample surveys, not all sample surveys are household surveys. The decisive characteristic is that the sampling unit should be the household. Sometimes it is not easy to distinguish sample surveys based on small-scale production units from a real household survey because a small-scale unit will frequently coincide with a household. The important thing to look for is, again, whether sampling is based on households or some other universe.

1. Demographic characteristics

Whatever the type and specialized coverage of a household survey, it will collect at least some basic information on demographic characteristics, which most certainly will include age and sex. Those surveys which focus on demographic topics will collect demographic information in great detail. The main features investigated comprise general demographic characteristics, fertility, mortality, migration and socio-economic background characteristics.

Among the general demographic characteristics, high priority is assigned to household and family composition. As stated in the Handbook of Household Surveys, these "are not only biological characteristics but also reflect socio-economic, legal, cultural and often religious circumstances. In most developing countries, the household or family is the centre not only of socio-cultural activity, but also of much of economic production and consumption". 29/

A household can be a one-person household or a multi-person household. The latter can in turn be classified as nuclear, extended or composite household. A nuclear household is defined as a household consisting of a single family nucleus. An extended household is a "household consisting of a single family nucleus with other persons related to the nucleus, two or more family nuclei related to each other, with or without additional related persons, or two or more related persons who do not comprise a family nucleus". A composite household is "any household which includes any unrelated person". It is recognized, however, that in this matter conditions can differ considerably from country to country. Thus, "countries may find it appropriate to modify the classification according to national circumstances". 30/

Socio-economic background characteristics collected in household surveys usually cover topics related to education and literacy, some basic economic characteristics like activity status, status in employment, occupation and industry, as well as a classification of urban and rural residence. As has been mentioned already, the latter is of special importance for estimates of women's participation in the informal sector.

2. Income and expenditure

Together with household surveys on household enterprises, whether agricultural or of other types, which will be discussed below, the income and expenditure surveys are among the most useful sources for our purpose. Traditionally, these surveys were used most often for establishing weights for consumer price indices, but this is only one of many possible uses.

From our point of view, the importance of these surveys resides in the fact that they furnish data on the level and the distribution of household income, data which are widely used for compiling household accounts in the systems of national accounts and balances. Moreover, if detailed information is collected not only for the household as a whole but for each individual on each of his or her income items, as is recommended, this puts us in a position to calculate women's income with greater precision than is possible with other sources. It must be borne in mind that answers to questions on income are frequently evasive, especially at the high and low extremes of income distribution, but there can be no doubt that, within the context of a household survey covering income as well as expenditure, such difficulties can be better taken care of than in global canvasses like population censuses. If questions on both income and expenditure are included in the same questionnaire, this provides, up to a point, a check on the figures furnished by the respondent.

When using income and expenditure data from surveys, it is important to determine their geographical scope. While national coverage is usually recommended, sometimes, due to financial considerations, the coverage is more restricted. Another feature that must be examined is the time period. Income patterns of different population groups can show significant seasonal fluctuations and this is especially frequent in the case of women. Several procedures are used in surveys to reduce the impact of seasonal effects. The user of such data should examine these procedures in order to decide whether they take into consideration special problems connected with seasonal fluctuations of incomes of women.

Still another domain where the user of data is advised to examine the underlying methodology used in a survey is the sample design. A sample size which is quite acceptable for the nation taken as a whole can be unsatisfactory for regional analysis or for special population groups. The choice of respondent can also have a substantial influence on the results, as can the choice of statistical units. Some countries exclude one-person households from their surveys, and the treatment of multi-earner households differs from country to country.

More than anything else, however, the definition of income used in the survey must be examined carefully to find out whether it coincides with the definition required for the measurement of women's contribution to national product. United Nations guidelines distinguish between total household income and total available household income. The former comprises the compensation paid to employees in cash and in kind and employers' contribution to social security schemes, the income of members from producers' co-operatives and gross entrepreneurial income of unincorporated enterprises. This last category includes household enterprises. By deducting from this total the amounts paid in direct taxes, social security and pension fund contributions, one obtains the second total, available household income.

3. Labour force

Household surveys focusing on labour force topics can serve a great variety of uses but here we are concerned with their use for the estimate of women's participation in the economy of the country. The information obtained in such surveys covers data on the size and characteristics of the economically active population, but aim also at obtaining information on the potential labour force. Some information on the economically inactive population is also provided.

One characteristic of the labour force is, of course, the amount of income which is received by labour. These data on income, if obtained in sufficient detail and cross-classified by sex, can be of direct use for our purpose, but even where they cannot be obtained in such a direct way, they provide useful information on the distribution of income and on average wages and salaries. Here again, a factor to be examined carefully is to what degree the conceptual approach used in the survey coincides with the definitions and concepts of other sources with which it can be combined, and if it does not, what adjustments could be made to reduce discrepancies.

Where data on the labour force from household surveys are available together with figures obtained in establishment surveys, these should be compared. As the universe on which each is based is different, one cannot expect that the figures will coincide. The basic difference between them is that the former takes into account the activity status of the individual and the latter reflects the situation as observed at the establishment. As expressed in the Handbook of Household Surveys, "Household surveys cover in principle the entire population of interest, including the economically inactive, with establishment surveys generally restricted to employees, who form only a segment of the economically active population. The missing segments include the unemployed, family workers in household enterprises and farms, the self-employed and, in general, all non-wage and salary earners. Moreover, establishments surveys are usually limited to establishments larger than a certain minimum size." 31/

    As can be seen, almost all of the elements missing from establishment surveys are part of the informal sector. These are precisely the segments that can be reached by household surveys, which, due to their flexibility, can also provide the additional information that is essential for cross-classifications. This additional information is mainly demographic characteristics. These are provided in all household surveys on labour force topics and by most household surveys on other subjects as well. The Handbook of Household Surveys specifies: "Demographic and general characteristics of the household and its members are obtained in almost all household surveys or survey rounds and thus are automatically available for analysis in conjunction with details of their labour force characteristics. The items that are of particular relevance in relation to employment characteristics are sex, age, marital status and relationship to the head of household; educational attainment and level of skill and training; size and type of household; urban-rural, locality and geographical area; national or ethnic origin; migration status; and so on". 32/

    There is, however, one subject on which establishment surveys provide more accurate information. Being taken from written documents such as payrolls and accounting records, the figures provided by them will be less affected by measurement and response errors than in the case of household surveys, which are mostly based on oral interviews and figures given from memory.

                            4. Agriculture

    What has been said about surveys based on a production unit compared to surveys based on households takes on a special meaning in the case of agriculture. In cases where a large part of agricultural production originates in small-scale agricultural holdings, these holdings will almost always coincide with household units. However, the concepts of holding and household are liable to different interpretations in different surveys and, reflecting differences in prevailing conditions, the concepts and their use also differ among countries.

    The Programme for the 1980 Census of Agriculture of the Food and Agriculture Organization of the United Nations defines a holding for agricultural census purposes as a "technoeconomic unit of agricultural production comprising all livestock kept and all land used wholly or partly for agricultural purposes and operated under the management of one person or more, without regard to title, legal form, size or location". 33/ This definition includes those engaged in agricultural production, including livestock, with no significant agricultural land or for which land is not an indispensable element of production. This can be interpreted to mean that all livestock kept and all land used wholly or partly for agricultural purposes should be considered a holding. In practice, however, most such units are not enumerated because the authorities set a cut-off point which eliminates from enumeration units below either a minimum number of livestock kept or level of production.

    In the Programme, the definition of household corresponds to that used in the population census; the agricultural households are defined as units where at least one member of the household is operating a holding or where the household head, reference person or main income earner is economically active mainly in agriculture. The topics usually covered in household surveys centred on agriculture basically correspond to the recommendations made by FAO, as they are adapted to the specific requirements of each country. These topics are usually grouped into those on characteristics of individuals, of households and of holdings. With respect to the characteristics of individuals and their economic activity, FAO recommends, among others, the following: activity status; occupation, subdivided into main occupation (in which most of the time is spent), and secondary and subsidiary occupations; industry and status in employment, both divided in the same way as occupation; economic activity on the holding (agricultural work); economic activity off the holding, subdivided by non-agricultural work in the household enterprise, agricultural work on other holdings and non-agricultural work outside the holding; and time worked.

Time worked should be investigated in reference to a short period (hours per week) and a long period (days per years), with the following subdivisions: time worked on the holding, time spent on non-agricultural work in the household enterprise, paid agricultural work on other holdings, paid non-agricultural work outside the household and unpaid work off the holding.

Among the characteristics of the holding are topics referring to the number of permanent workers, distinguishing members of the holder's household and hired workers. This information allows classification of the holding in reference to the informal sector.

5. Household enterprises

As agricultural holdings are usually treated separately in surveys, as discussed in the previous section, the household surveys concerned with enterprises cover the secondary and tertiary sectors, mainly small industries, crafts, petty trade and service industries. These units are all too frequently not covered by other types of inquiries. Many topics in this group are similar or identical to those covered in income and expenditure and labour force surveys, but in addition to these, household enterprise surveys also cover data on production and inputs used in production.

A crucial problem is to separate expenditures on inputs for production from those on consumption, because household enterprise production is closely intertwined with other household activities. Even when the survey establishes time spent on household enterprise activities, the usual situation is such that these activities may be carried out simultaneously with other activities, as in the case of the petty trader who tends his or her store and children at the same time.

Most of the other problems which arise in the use of this type of survey for estimating women's contribution to production have been taken up in the previous section.

D. Price statistics

In so far as some totals and subtotals which comprise women's economic activities will have to be built up from quantity and unit price data, the need arises to find adequate data on prices.

Apart from economic censuses and surveys already mentioned, information on prices can sometimes be gathered from price lists compiled for consumer price indices and special sections of bulletins published by statistical authorities, ministries, marketing boards, financial institutions, and trade associations. Where such information is used it is essential to find the price category that corresponds best to the specific purpose pursued. In the present case, the aim is to arrive at figures which are consistent with those of the national accounts. Therefore, guidance on what prices should be used is the same as that given in the national accounts. These are discussed in detail in A System of National Accounts. 34/

As to data on wages (average wages or minimum wages) for different activities, these can be found in statistical bulletins and publications of the ministries of labour, where they exist. In some cases data can be obtained from trade unions, depending on the specific situation of each country.

E. Administrative records

Administrative records generally vary from country to country more than do censuses and surveys as they conform to special characteristics of national legislation and tax structures. Where there exist provisions concerning women and/or households, there will be some kind of record which can be of use for the purpose at hand. Even in the case where it is considered that the files are incomplete, such figures can serve as appropriate indicators. In using these sources, thought must be given to possible biases they might contain, especially when the purpose for which they were set up is not the same as that for which they are used in estimates on women's work.

A special case is the records of social security institutions. In so far as social provisions are different for men and women, these records contain separate figures by sex or at least data from which the separation can be obtained by reprocessing. The possibility of using records of trade union associations, where they exist, should also be considered.

F. Other sources

Institutes for social studies, departments of universities, religious institutions, women's organizations and other similar bodies sometimes carry out studies and research on subjects which cover ground more or less proximate to our own. A thorough critical analysis of each is a sine qua non for their use. However, they can be very valuable, especially in examining specific problems and to show sources for numerical information that otherwise could have escaped attention.

Whenever figures are presented, their origin has to be examined, whether they were taken from outside sources, in which case these sources have to be analysed, or whether they have been produced by an ad hoc survey, in which case the statistical validity of such figures has to be examined very thoroughly for technical procedures, sampling and non-sampling errors.

For additional information on various statistical sources, their characteristics and treatment of data, the following publications, already cited, can be consulted: <u>A System of National Accounts</u>, <u>Principles and recommendations for Population and Housing Censuses</u>, <u>Programme for the 1980 World Census of Agriculture</u>, <u>International Recommendations on Statistics of the Distributive Trades and Services</u> and <u>Handbook of Household Surveys (Revised Edition)</u>.

G.   Future outlook

As noted, the statistical situation varies greatly from one country to another. Therefore, unavoidably, the sources mentioned in the foregoing paragraphs exist in some countries, are in the process of being created in others, or are in the planning stage in those with a weak statistical structure.

Production of statistics is a costly enterprise and many different groups and topics set claims to priority treatment. Furthermore, the costs involved are mostly monetary, concentrated and highly visible, but the benefits obtained are dispersed and difficult to measure. This makes any cost-benefit analysis almost unmanageable. However, in the case of women's contribution to the social product it is generally accepted that documentation on the subject has not kept up with the realization of its importance.

Two areas present themselves for immediate improvement. One is to add a sub-classification by sex to census and survey questionnaires where it does not exist presently and where it might facilitate estimates of women's economic activity. The other is to produce specific inquiries on the subject designed in such a way as to furnish all the documentation necessary for the purpose and/or to complement other existing sources. This might be most efficiently accomplished through specialized rounds of household sample surveys. The two avenues are interrelated and will have to be pursued simultaneously.

In pursuing them it should be remembered that measuring the role of women in the economy contributes not only to redressing wrongs which concern half of the human population (in fact slightly more than half) but also to creating the tools to plan and achieve higher economic and social attainments for the nations of the world, men as well as women.

III. METHODS OF CALCULATING WOMEN'S CONTRIBUTION TO DEVELOPMENT
     IN THE INFORMAL SECTOR

The methods that can be used to measure women's contribution to development in the informal sector depend in each case on the kind of information available. The methods presented in this chapter rely on statistical sources commonly available in many countries but some reference is also made to procedures requiring data less commonly available, mainly from specialized inquiries. All of the sources considered here were reviewed in chapter II.

The main obstacles to calculating women's contribution arise, as commonly happens, when figures from different sources are to be combined. Data that at first sight appear compatible turn out not to be so after some scrutiny. This scrutiny must be done painstakingly, going into as much detail as possible, because all analysts agree that calculations of women's contribution are highly dependent on the methodologies used in collecting and compiling the underlying data. It will not suffice to take the figures as they are published in summary and detailed tables and to study carefully the footnotes provided in them. In addition, it is necessary to examine the questionnaires that have been used in obtaining the figures and the instructions issued to the enumerators. Wherever possible, personal contacts with the people in charge of the statistical collection programmes should be established. One should also look for any publication that describes or comments on the administration, methodology and results of the inquiry, or which provides any kind of evaluation of it.

Statistics for urban and rural areas often come from different sources and the methodology presented here will likewise incorporate different methods to take these differences into account. Further, the concept of economic activity in the 1968 SNA and concepts corresponding to production boundary discussed above will be treated separately. However, while the totals arrived at by estimates should correspond to the concepts they purport to measure, the separate steps which lead to the estimates do not necessarily follow the main lines of the production flows as delineated in SNA.

Another overall consideration is that although we are concerned with production carried out by women and concentrate therefore on sectors of particular interest to them, the methods presented here can be applied equally to measure men's as well as women's contributions to the economy. This has the advantage that women's contributions can be compared to those of men, not only at the national level but also as far as certain specific sectors are concerned.

As the outlook here is restricted to the informal sector, which is characterized by small units, it should be kept in mind when dealing with methods and sources for determining this sector's output that these are considerably less precise than those used for larger and more accounting-conscious units. This, however, should not stand in the way of employing such methods and sources. In spite of any weakness in the resulting estimates, they not only shed light on phenomena and situations where, as far as their quantitative characteristics are concerned, we presently grope in the dark, but they also contribute to improving the accuracy of the global estimates. In considering precision and accuracy, one has to accept the fact that first estimates will unavoidably be crude. Improvement will come from development of better sources, improved methodology and experience.

It bears emphasizing that the methods used have to be adapted to existing sources, which vary considerably from country to country. For this reason, suggestions as to how to proceed necessarily have to be general and more in the nature of examples that could be helpful in finding the approach best suited to particular local circumstances.

The production to be considered can be summarized in the following production flows:

1. Rural areas:

    (a) According to 1968 SNA concepts:

    (i) Primary production for own consumption;

    (ii) Processing of primary products by producer for own consumption;

    (iii) Households' agricultural and non agricultural production for the market;

    (iv) Own-account fixed capital formation by households:

        1. Construction of own dwellings;

        2. For agricultural and non-agricultural enterprises;

    (b) Outside 1968 SNA concepts but within extended version:

    (i) Production for own use of non-primary products, when selling none on the market;

    (ii) Other household activities;

2. Urban areas:

    (a) According to 1968 SNA concepts:

    (i) Production of non-primary products for own consumption when selling part on the market;

    (ii) Sales by household enterprises;

    (iii) Own-account fixed capital formation by households:

        1. Construction of own dwellings;

        2. For household enterprises;

    (b) Outside 1968 SNA concepts, but within extended version:

    (i) Production of non-primary products when selling none to the market;

    (ii) Other household activities.

The definition of the informal sector in terms of small units must be kept in mind here, and all the flows shown in this scheme should refer only to such units. For example, some doubts might arise in connection with flow 1(a)(ii), processing of primary products by producer for own consumption, where the type of producer is not clearly specified. Although the bulk of such consumption will be in informal units, that is, on small farms, it will occur also in bigger units. What to do with milk or cheese produced on a large farm classified as a formal unit that is being consumed by the family who owns it? If we had adopted "type of flow" (that is, produced for own consumption) instead of "type of unit" to identify what we understand by informal sector, production consumed by the producer would be taken into consideration. According to the definition used here, however, the example falls outside the output of the informal sector.

This is true also for flows 2(a)(i) and (iii), which should comprise only informal units, thus excluding production for own use of units classified as formal, be it the own-account construction of an additional wing in a factory or sweets consumed by owners of a pastry shop which has grown beyond the size of a family enterprise without regular paid employees.

In order to undertake the estimation of production in the informal sector, it is necessary to clearly distinguish informal units from formal ones. Once the informal sector has been identified, the following steps are needed to determine the value of production for each of the flows mentioned above, and to measure what part of this output is contributed by women.

At present, there are not many statistical sources that permit application of the definition of informal adopted in the present study. This situation might suggest abandoning the terms of the proposed definition for others easier to follow. However, this definition is not necessarily so complex to implement. The main reason for linking the characteristic of formal or informal to the producer unit is that a product in itself cannot be considered informal or formal. It is the unit producing it which is classified as formal or informal, and a unit can change from being part of one sector to being part of the other. The cut-off point for the boundary between them is in a way arbitrary but this is not the first time statisticians would resort to use of an arbitrary convention to make an important distinction. The criterion of not having employees is a useful one. It is based on the notion that, once a producer unit has employees, it has to comply with certain requirements that eventually will characterize it as a formal unit. Nevertheless, to set the limit in terms of one, two or any other number of employees instead of no employees is a matter where, in the final analysis, national circumstances must be taken into account.

The following sections contain suggestions on how to proceed with statistics that might be available. Since the available statistics and other circumstances of each country differ widely, it is only possible to present elements of a methodology, to draw on and adopt in each case.

A. Rural areas

Methodologies used to estimate production in rural areas usually focus on flows based on type of industry and/or type of product. They are not related to production flows by specific types of use or disposition (for example market or non-market), with the possible exception of production for own consumption. In the

-44-

present case, however, where the specific purpose is to determine that part of production which is due to women's efforts, the analysis of production flows according to their destination plays an essential role.

Items 1(a)(i)-(iii) in the list above belong to the category of primary activities, which comprise mainly agriculture, hunting, forestry and fishing. In these industries, the methodology used to estimate production differs according to the type of producing unit. Estimates of production for large and average size farms are based on one kind of statistics and those for small farms on another. As we are concerned here with the informal rural sector, which has been defined to include only small farms, we will deal only with those sources and methods that are relevant to them. From the point of view mentioned above referring to the characterization of production flows according to their destination, these farms are engaged in the following types of activities: they produce for sale in the market and also for their own use, and usually they produce more than one product, especially when it is for own consumption.

1. Production for own consumption

When consumption is from own production we can expect that it will comprise products typically included in the usual subsistence level diet. We can take advantage of this fact to undertake estimates of production where other sources of information are lacking. The methodology for these estimates must be based on the specific nature of each product. For countries where exhaustive estimates of production for own consumption are already available, the task is how to go about estimating that part of total production which has been produced by women. Where separate estimates of production for own consumption are not available, or such figures as have been given are considered grossly underestimated, it is necessary to calculate this production first. In doing so, it should be borne in mind that one of the purposes of the estimation is to determine women's participation in the production process. This is the idea underlying the following propositions.

Women in rural areas almost always take part in production and on small farms their participation may be considerable. However, their participation is not always reflected in statistics, especially in the case of housewives, because they tend to consider themselves exclusively as housewives and the enumerators count them in that category, losing sight of the fact that, even if they are not paid, they are farmworkers as well as housewives. This malpractice often reflects the way the questions are formulated in censuses and surveys. Frequently, there is only one generic question as to work done and the resulting reply classifies the woman as "housewife". Additional questions usually produce quite different results but they have to be formulated in very concrete terms, citing examples such as, Do you keep fowls, goats or pigs? Do you mend fishing nets? Do you gather berries or mushrooms? Do you pound your own corn? Do you sell part of the food made by you? Do you help in the field? In addition, the language used has to be familiar to the respondent.

Underreporting has been verified not only in individual cases but also by statistical analysis of census figures and, for this reason, estimates of women's participation in production based on these biased figures are far off the mark. While cases of housewives on small farms who do not participate in production are not out of the question (a case in point might be on account of serious disability), the frequency of such cases overall is such that they can be considered as negligible. This leads us to include all women on small farms whom the census classifies as "homemaker" in the category of unpaid family workers.

Usually, the procedure followed to estimate production in rural areas either of crops or livestock is based on the type of product. To relate the production flows mentioned above to specific products, many assumptions have to be made. It can be assumed that production of primary products exclusively for own consumption is limited to certain products only, depending on the country and the area or region. It can also be assumed that some of these products are exclusively of concern to women. Again, this will differ by country and region. Therefore, this procedure requires a detailed study of local circumstances and can only be applied based on such a study.

2. Other flows

The production of primary products (a) for both own consumption and the market, and (b) only for the market, (c) for own consumption after processing and (d) for own-account fixed capital formation, cannot be assigned so easily to women. They participate in the process of production but their share is more variable.

In the initial phases of study on the subject, rather crude assumptions, based on limited observations, must be made. At this stage, they are unavoidable but will pave the way to more dependable calculations in the future. At a later stage, it will be necessary to look for more advanced sources of information and, where possible, to contribute to their development, taking care that they correspond to the requirements for measuring women's contribution to development and economic growth. The most adequate type of sources are surveys on the economic production households and on time use, especially in the much-neglected setting of rural areas.

A crude approximation of women's participation can be attempted using national accounts and population figures. For studies of this nature, it is first of all essential to determine whether or not the value of the work women are engaged in is significant relative to the whole or is minimal. To reach a conclusion on this point, the first step is to find production estimates by kind of product in agriculture and determine which product estimates include, or should include, production for own consumption. This information provides a basis for deciding whether production for own consumption should be studied in more depth. Usually, in every country and region, each agricultural product has its own characteristics: it may be for export or for internal consumption; it may require investment which cannot be supported by small farms; or it may be of a kind only produced by very small agricultural units. These product characteristics can also be related to sex or age. Some tasks specifically related to each type of production are usually done by women, others by children.

Second, because we are measuring women's participation in terms of their labour input, it is necessary to determine the cost structure of each product. For each one, the labour must be ascertained, paid as well as unpaid and including work done by own-account workers. In other words, labour as a factor of production must be measured, not only the remuneration of employees.

Third, there are certain products and services for which it is feasible to make assumptions as to whether the type of unit concerned is formal or informal.

Examples are products produced mainly for subsistence, such as yams, firewood collection and water carrying. At the other extreme are cash crops for export or industrial use such as coffee, cocoa and tea. Between these extremes are products for which such _a priori_ classification is not feasible, so that indicators of the relative role of informal and formal units in their total production are needed. For this purpose, agricultural census or survey results could be used, if they contained data on the number of employees and the value of the production by farm and by product.

Fourth, data on economically active population in rural areas by sex are needed. If there are no data on labour inputs by sex, which could be known through specialized _ad hoc_ studies or household surveys, then one of the following two courses of action can be adopted:

(a) Assume that the labour inputs for selected products correspond to male and female labour force according to their relative numbers;

(b) Attribute to women's work on certain specific types of products.

These results will give a general idea of the importance of women's participation in the production process in agricultural activity. Their participation in other occupations is estimated separately.

Flow 1(a)(iv) in the scheme for rural areas refers to own-account capital formation on small farms. A considerable amount of capital formation created by the farmer himself takes place on small units, such as preparing land, planting long-lived trees, all kinds of construction for people, animals or tools, knitting of fishing nets, digging of wells and many more. These activities do not receive much attention in statistical work and women's participation in them varies considerably by region. Efforts to quantify them should be made step by step, without assigning high priority at the outset, until it is established that women do participate in these activities to a considerable extent.

Even though agriculture is usually by far the most important activity in rural areas, one should not lose sight of those cases where non-agricultural activities are important. Such activities may consist of manufacturing and trading on own account and own initiative or on the basis of contracts offered by industrial or trading enterprises to rural households. This kind of work is done mostly by women

B. Urban areas

The urban sector is essentially a sector based on exchange. Therefore, in the sense defined here, there is no significant production for own consumption within the production boundary of the 1968 SNA.

The participation of women in production in the urban sector extends to almost all activities, although with profound regional differences. Their work in the informal sector, as defined here, can be characterized in terms of status in employment either as working on own-account or as unpaid family worker. (In certain cases a family enterprise might employ salaried as well as unpaid family workers but by the definition used here such family enterprises would belong to the formal sector. In such cases, placing the contribution of these unpaid family workers in the informal sector is an imperfection that will disappear after the statistical sources for these calculations have improved.) This establishes the units we are concerned with. The total numbers of own-account and unpaid family workers, classified by sex, are obtained from census data.

The next step is to determine the time spent on specific economic activities. In this case, time spent on economic activities is a decisive variable which should be investigated separately from time spent on other activities. If the census or survey records only the main activity of a person, time spent on other activities will be lost altogether. This requires some kind of correction. Whether this is done using results from an ad hoc inquiry or from time budget studies will depend on availability of data and the possibility of organizing this kind of investigation, as well as the amplitude and depth of the procedures used.

Once the time spent on an activity has been determined and the number of persons involved cross-classified according to time spent, one has to establish appropriate valuation. The customary procedure is to multiply the person-hours spent in an activity by the current average wage in the same or a similar type of industry or craft. Instead of an average wage, the minimum local wage rate is sometimes used. A more sophisticated procedure consists of determining the value of the product originating in an activity and imputing relative labour cost. Imputed labour cost is based in this instance on the relative cost of labour in similar activities in the market sphere, usually understood as $L/P \times 100$, where L is income accruing to labour and P is value of product. Income to labour from the activity includes wages and salaries as well as other enterprise expenditures for labour in cash and kind as detailed in SNA.

Based on such data, one obtains total labour cost in the activity in the informal sector. From this, the part corresponding to women can be derived simply as a proportion of female to male unpaid family workers or, if information is available, as a proportion of hours worked by female unpaid family members to total hours worked.

In the case of own-account workers, the value of their contribution is equal to the value of their output, marketed or used by themselves, either for consumption or for capital formation, minus the cost of inputs bought. Where possible and appropriate, depreciation of capital goods such as sewing machines, looms, tools, as well as financial charges including interest and the like should be deducted.

In both cases, unpaid family worker as well as own-account worker, the information obtained relates to income generated in production in the informal sector. However, persons working in the informal sector could also receive income from other sources - as part-time employees or as property income or transfer incomes. This raises a question that is connected with the uses that will be made of these figures. If the main interest is in identifying the amount which represents the purchasing capacity of women, something that market researchers would be interested in, a strong argument can be made for including such additional sources of personal income. However, as the present report is concerned with women's participation in informal sector production, these other incomes should not be included unless their part-time salaries were paid by an informal unit. However, this would involve information on sources of income which is usually hard to obtain.

Data on average number of hours in employment during a week by sex, urban or rural residence, type of industry or activity performed and status in employment are furnished by censuses and household surveys. Many censuses and household surveys also provide tabulations based on data on income earned, classified by sex, industry, occupation and status in employment. These data usually relate only to urban population, but some also include rural population. They are used in estimating personal and family income distribution according to income classes. This information in most cases is limited to cash income from labour.

Income distribution tabulations from censuses and household surveys of various types (surveys of income and expenditure, household activities or focused on labour force characteristics) require additional adjustments because usually they are not totally consistent with production estimates from national accounts. Their coverage in terms of the population they represent can be adjusted with the help of data on economically active population classified by sex, residence, industry and occupation and status in employment, but in the last case only the own-account and unpaid family workers are considered. For each income interval, the average earnings of women in each industry and occupation can be estimated. This allows comparisons to be made with the average earnings of their male counterparts.

It also has to be taken into account that income is often under-reported. In order to arrive at income totals from labour data which are compatible with SNA, adjustments to the average in each interval should be made. Often tabulations on income distribution present an open-ended interval. It is then necessary to estimate an average income for this interval.

The information on income distribution necessary to follow these procedures has to be obtained in very detailed form - by industry and occupation, status in employment rural and urban - because, for each one of these groups, the adjustment is different.

Once a distribution of women's income from labour in the informal sector has been calculated, one can estimate women's participation in the production process in the informal sector. This procedure is also valid for income from paid employment and for women as well as men.

The data on income distribution, combined with those referred to above on number of hours worked by type of industry and occupation, provide an hourly average income, which is useful for comparisons.

As for the totals, they should include imputations for the income of unpaid family workers. The assumption to use in their case is either (a) to consider the minimum salary in each industry or occupation, or (b) to distribute unpaid family workers in the same way as paid employees in the same industry or occupation, eliminating the upper ranges of income.

If no income data are available, it is necessary to turn to labour inputs expressed in hours, that is, time spent in the production process. In order to transform these figures into indicators of women's participation, it is also necessary to estimate total labour inputs.

The use of income distribution data instead of figures published by trade associations or ministries of labour on average wage rates in different industries might appear as an unnecessary detour. However, this is necessary because average wage rates usually are not subdivided by sex. To use such overall wage rates for estimates of women's income would introduce a serious distortion.

C. Outside 1968 SNA concepts but within the extended version

Censuses and household surveys provide data on the number of women over a certain age who are counted as homemakers. This information is insufficient for estimating the value of household work done by women. For this purpose, we need the number of all women who do household work: those who work exclusively in domestic tasks at home and those who also work in economic activity and therefore are included in the labour force.

Population censuses and household surveys usually obtain information, by sex, on status in employment, urban or rural residence and type of industry or occupation. In addition, time-use surveys provide details on how the economically active population and those outside the labour force use their time, but not every country where such studies have been done publishes cross-tabulations using all these classifications. Even those who can produce such tabulations on request do not have data on women that allow classifying them in subgroups distinguishing housewives from other women, both for "economically active" women and for those outside the labour force.

A housewife is a woman who besides household economic activities has the responsibility of running the household. The assumption is that in each household there is one housewife. The term housewife is misleading because she could be unmarried. Homemaker is better but it is used already only for those outside of the labour force, thus excluding women who combine household economic and non-economic activities. Information on "housewives" should be requested in time-use questionnaires. The special importance of time-use studies lies in the fact that they are the only source for breakdowns which distinguish between housewives and non-housewives and, within each of these two groups, between those in the labour force and those outside it.

The next stage is to find the value of women's household work. For this, we need the estimates of production for the market discussed previously. However, in trying to combine these data with those from time-use studies, an additional problem arises. Time-use statistics are concerned with time; they do not attempt to measure value. The connection between time spent on some kind of production and the value of that production is often called productivity. This, however, has a special connotation in this instance, because the amount of time spent on producing some good or service will vary, depending not only on skill and tools employed but also on the fact that time is more scarce in one case than in another. Housewives without any other occupation have more hours at their disposal than those who perform these same activities in addition to work outside the home. Should hours of work at home be valued uniformly in both cases? Different studies have given different answers to this question.

To sum up: if there are data on women concerning residence, status in employment, type of industry or occupation, hours worked per week (or on any other time period) and income distribution by class intervals, and if they can be cross-tabulated, it is possible to estimate women's contribution in the production process as delineated by the 1968 SNA. To go beyond the 1968 SNA boundaries and take into account household work, time-use studies are indispensable. With improved computing capabilities, special tabulations and cross-classifications, in this case as in many other aspects discussed above, are more easily done. Thus, the main concern presently is the availability of field data.

Notes

1/   The concept of the production boundary and various criteria for defining it are examined in detail in T. P. Hill, "On goods and services", Review of Income and Wealth, Series 23, No. 4 (December 1977).

2/   For example, the introduction of population figures into SNA would create an additional dimension for measurement of the informal sector and women's contribution.

3/   It is here that weaknesses may show up. This procedure makes certain assumptions about the behaviour of the market mechanism. Where these assumptions fail, the integration of the aggregates may be affected, as, for example, in a case where there is unequal pay for equal work.

4/   If, for example, women are discriminated against in salaries, that means the same work is paid a lower amount if done by women and this creates a discrepancy between aggregate values in real and in monetary terms. Attempts have been made to overcome such contradictions in a similar way as price differences in time for the same good or service are treated in statistical time series at constant prices.

5/   A System of National Accounts, Studies in Methods, Series F, No. 2, Rev. 3 (United Nations publication, Sales No. E.69.XVII.3).

6/   Ibid., para. 9.5.

7/   Ibid., para. 9.17.

8/   Ibid., para. 9.2.

9/   Ibid., paras. 6.18-6.25.

10/   Ibid., para. 6.18.

11/   Ibid., para. 6.19.

12/   D. W. Blades, Non-Monetary (Subsistence) Activities in the National Accounts of Developing Countries (Paris, Development Centre, OECD, 1975).

13/   A System of National Accounts ..., para. 6.23.

14/   Ibid., para. 6.19.

15/   Principles and Recommendations for Population and Housing Censuses, Statistical Papers, Series M. No. 67 (United Nations publication, Sales No. E.80.XVII.8), para. 2.206.

16/ The words "activity" and "unit" instead of "transaction" and "transactor" as they appear in SNA are used here in order to avoid the impression that more than one person is necessarily involved. Another possibility is "actor" and "action".

17/ The activity that is being discussed here is of course distinct from other work in a family enterprise, although the two could be quite similar, as in the case of a household member weaving a basket for the family enterprise and watching over a child.

18/ Principles and Recommendations ..., illustrations P37-P56.

19/ Ibid., illustration P17.

20/ Ibid., illustration P41.

21/ Ibid, illustrations P55 and P56.

22/ The FAO Production Yearbook, 1983, vol. 37 (Rome, Food and Agriculture Organization of the United Nations) states: "Statistics on fruit, especially tropical fruit, are unavailable in many countries, and the coverage of the reporting countries suffers from lack of uniformity. Generally, production data relate to plantation crops or orchard crops grown mainly for sale. Data on production from scattered trees used mainly for home consumption are not usually collected. Production from wild plants, particularly berries, which is of some importance in certain countries, is generally disregarded by national statistical services."

23/ Principles and Recommendations ..., para. 1.33.

24/ Ibid., paras. 1.35-1.36.

25/ International Recommendations for Industrial Statistics, 1983, Statistical Papers, Series M, No. 48, Rev.1 (United Nations publication, Sales No. E.83.XVII.8).

26/ This sector is conventionally defined to include wholesale and retail trade and restaurants and hotels, transport, storage and communication, financing, insurance, real estate and business services and community, social and personal services.

27/ Handbook of Household Survey, Revised Edition, Studies in Methods, Series F, No. 31 (United Nations publication, Sales No. E.83.XVII.13), para. 1.12.

28/ Ibid., para. 1.7.

29/ Ibid., para. 9.6.

30/ Ibid., para. 9.26.

31/ Ibid., para. 11.10.

32/ Ibid., para. 11.61.

Notes (continued)

33/ FAO Production Yearbook (Rome, 1976), p. 16.

34/ A System of National Accounts ..., chap. IV.

Part Two

COLLECTION AND COMPILATION OF TIME-USE STATISTICS TO MEASURE
THE PARTICIPATION OF WOMEN IN THE INFORMAL SECTOR*

_____

    *   Prepared by the Statistical Office, Department of International Economic and Social Affairs, United Nations Secretariat.

-55-

INTRODUCTION

Time budgets or time-use studies provide a unique source of information on the participation of women in the informal sector. They cover productive activities both outside and inside the household and they can capture activities of short duration which are characteristic of women's various activities in the informal and domestic sectors. With a time budget study, whether one is performing productive activities is not decided on the basis of one or two questions about primary or secondary activity but emerges from a detailed activity listing. This method overcomes any cultural preconception that women are engaged only in housework and that all other tasks are of marginal or minimal importance.

I. NATIONAL STUDIES IN DEVELOPING COUNTRIES

A. Issues in conducting and using time-use studies in developing countries

Since the mid-1970s, many time-use studies focusing on women's productive activities have been undertaken in developing countries. Two main, interrelated sets of concerns have been investigated in these studies. One concerns the utilization of human resources in the household, particularly women and children, and the second, improvement in the measurement of employment, unemployment and underemployment.

The first approach concerns studies in which the household and the allocation of time by its members provide the basic framework of analysis. Time-use studies within this perspective were stimulated by the development of an economic model, the so-called "new home economics," which focuses on the ways households allocate human resources to market and nonmarket work, reproduction and leisure. Using this perspective, economists as well as nutritionists, anthropologists and demographers have been interested in time-use statistics to address a variety of concerns which relate to women's participation in the informal sector. These include the division of labour in households, nutrition and subsistence production and the value of children. 1/

In the second approach, time-use statistics are used to derive more meaningful and accurate measures of economic activity. A recent discussion of the underenumeration of women's work in India illustrates the importance of time-use statistics. It points out that, even if definitions of work include the unpaid but productive activities that women perform in the home, "they may still miss enumeration because they are treated as part and parcel of housework by the members of the household themselves ... . As a result, while reporting as respondents, household members, whether males or females, normally merge these work items with 'housework' and only 'housework' gets recorded in the census or the NSS (National Sample Survey) field records." 2/

A related problem, also discussed in the analysis of the Indian data, is that the value of women's productive tasks in the informal sector, such as "attending to domestic cattle producing a small quantity of milk and manufacturing butter, ghee, lassi, curd, buttermilk only for household consumption, feeding a couple of poultry birds which produce eggs which are consumed by household members or even participation in minor construction or repairs of residential house, cow sheds, etc.", is regarded as small, at least in comparison to the overall time spent in housework. 3/ The detailed accounting of activities provided by time-use statistics is therefore important in identifying the many productive tasks women perform and also in indicating the relative time or value of productive tasks in the home.

Another analysis, also based on data for India, sheds light on the extent of underenumeration of women's work using conventional measures. 4/ It compares the estimates of the economically active population based on the National Sample Survey with those of small village studies using time allocation methods. The time allocation studies were conducted by the Institute for Social Studies Trust in six villages. The time spent in a broad range of 42 activities was recorded for all household members. Annex 1 presents a brief description of the studies (items 7 (a) and (b)). The village studies show, for example, that, among poor and destitute families, women were engaged in providing domestic service to other households in the village and in begging and prostitution. All are income-producing activities but begging and prostitution were not coded as occupations and domestic service was poorly enumerated in the National Sample Survey. Moreover, women who in the time allocation study were shown to spend time in agriculture and/or animal husbandry were not enumerated as workers in the studies using conventional methods.

The time allocation studies conducted in India by the Institute of Social Studies Trust have yielded important insights into women's work, particularly in the informal sector, and have contributed to a recommendation by the National Committee on Women's Work and Employment for a time-use survey based on a larger, more representative sample. The study, based on a subsample of the India National Sample Survey, was undertaken in 1983 by the National Council of Applied Economic Research (see annex I, item 7 (e)). One objective of the survey was to compare the estimates of economic activity gained from intensive time-use methods with those of the National Sample Survey using conventional methods. Additional methodological issues investigated were the use of female and male interviewers and the use of participant observation and interview methods to collect information on time use. Results of this study are not yet available.

Time-use surveys, while having numerous advantages for studying issues of women and work in developing countries, also present great difficulties. In developing countries, people do not think of their activities in terms of clock time, nor can they be expected to keep diaries listing their daily activities. Instead, in one method, a detailed account of activities is maintained by observers who live in a village for a period of time, often spending up to a week with a single family and returning several times during a year to capture the seasonal variation in activities. Another method used successfully in developing countries is an interview where each member of a household reconstructs the sequence of activities, usually for the day before the interview. Intensive observation and interview methods require well-trained and well-supervised interviewers and a great amount of interview time. 5/ The analysis of time-budget data can also present great problems, given the numerous records maintained for a single person and/or for a single household.

The complexity of the data and the cost of time-budget surveys per person or household surveyed limit the possibility of using the method with large population samples in developing countries. However, small, in-depth, time-use studies can play an important role in national data programmes. As exploratory studies, they generate information on the daily lives of specific populations which in turn can be used to design a framework for questioning in a larger survey. For example, in studying women's activities in the informal sector, a small, in-depth, time-use study reveals the various kinds of tasks performed and their importance. Based on these findings, questions can be asked about the specific activities in a subsequent national sample survey.

Time allocation studies have also been recommended by ILO as a validity check in post-enumeration surveys. 6/ Time-use surveys might also be undertaken in developing countries as a component of a larger survey investigating seasonal or cyclical variations in household characteristics and activities, such as the 1974/75 Rural Income Distribution Survey in Botswana (see annex I, item 1).

An alternative to the detailed time budget study, in which the sequence and duration of activities are listed for a specific period, is a simplified activity time schedule in which information including time allocation is asked about a limited number of activities. 7/ This approach was tested by ILO in a 1981 rural survey in Kerala, India, and in a 1983/84 survey in Costa Rica. In the study in India, 716 currently married women aged 25-50 years were interviewed. Twelve major economic activities were specified, all of which are included in standard definitions of labour force activities. For each activity performed, information was collected on the nature of the activity, the amount of time spent on it per day/season, whether performed for family or others, whether performed at home or inside or outside the village, and whether income was received or product sold. However, the results of this work study are not yet available.

B. Measures of work-hours in the informal sector

Time allocation studies undertaken in developing countries show that women engage in a wide range of productive activities in the household that are included within the economic activity boundary set by national accounts as well as in domestic activities that are outside the accounts framework, and that the total burden of work for women is greater than for men. Examples are provided by the following three studies: the 1974/75 Botswana Rural Income Distribution Survey, the 1978 Status of Women Project in Nepal and the 1979 Côte d'Ivoire National Household Food Consumption and Budgetary Survey. (See annex I for methods of data collection and other general information on these studies.) These studies are useful as illustrations because they are relatively current, they provide information on a wide range of activities, that is, the activities performed in a 12 to 24-hour period, they use a relatively large sample size, given the in-depth methods utilized, and they have as a primary objective the investigation of women's activities in the informal sector.

Each of these studies uses a very detailed listing of economic activities. The list developed for the survey in Nepal (see annex II) contains 97 activities, of which 47 are classified as productive. These are divided among animal husbandry, agriculture, hunting and gathering, manufacturing, food processing, participation in the local economy and home construction. Eight categories are provided for domestic activities and six categories for child rearing and child care. Somewhat similar classifications were used in the Botswana and Côte d'Ivoire studies.

Tables 1, 2 and 3 present general statistics on the various productive activities of men and women. Table 1 reports data for Botswana on the percentage distribution of time between activities rather than mean amounts of time spent on activities. 8/ The data indicate that women's contribution to the income of the family is significant in that women's activities account for 40 per cent of the total time spent in all of the so-called income-earning activities. Within the sub-categories of income-earning activities, about two thirds of the time spent in crop husbandry, trading, vending, processing and hunting and gathering is women's. Moreover, women account for more than 80 per cent of time allocated to housework and men only 18 per cent.

Table 1. Distribution of time spent on selected activities,
by sex, Botswana, 1974/75 a/

(Percentage)

Activities	Men	Women
Crop husbandry	36.9	63.1
Animal husbandry	88.5	11.5
Wage labour	65.9	34.1
Trading, vending, processing	32.3	67.7
Hunting or gathering	38.2	61.7
All income-earning activities	60.3	39.7
Repairing, new building	34.2	65.8
Fetching water	18.5	81.5
Child care	16.2	83.8
Housework	15.4	84.6
All housekeeping activities	18.3	81.7

Source: E. Mueller, "Time use and household characteristics in rural Botswana - some preliminary findings" (Ann Arbor, Population Studies Center, University of Michigan, 1978).

a/   Individuals over age 6.

Actual time allocation figures are shown in table 2 for farmers in the Côte d'Ivoire and in table 3 for males and females in six villages in Nepal. The three major categories are: "conventional economic activities" in the Côte d'Ivoire study and "labour force participation" in the Nepal study; "subsistence economic activities"; and "domestic work". They summarize roughly comparable activities across the two studies. The total work day for farm women in the Côte d'Ivoire and for rural women in Nepal is considerably longer than that for men, roughly two hours more per day in the Côte d'Ivoire and three hours more in Nepal. By the same token, the work day for both men and women in Nepal - 10.86 hours per day and 7.51 respectively - is higher than that for either women or men in the Côte d'Ivoire, where it is 6.9 hours for women and 4.7 for men.

Table 2. Time allocation of farmers aged 15 years and over,
by sex, Côte d'Ivoire, 1979 a/

(Hours per day)

Activities	Women	Men
Conventional economic activities b/	2.3	3.9
Subsistence economic activities c/	1.2	0.3
Domestic work d/	3.4	0.5
Total work	6.9	4.7

Source: Côte d'Ivoire, Direction de la statistique, Household Food Consumption and Budgetary Survey, 1979.

a/ Estimates based on a one-week survey of households conducted four times during the year.

b/ Includes animal husbandry, agriculture, trade and manufacturing.

c/ Includes wood and water collection, gathering, fishing and hunting, gardening, food processing, home construction and repair.

d/ Includes cooking, laundry, cleaning, shopping and child care.

Table 3. Comparative time-use pattern for men and women
aged 15 years and over, six villages in
Nepal, 1979

(Hours per day)

Activities	Men	Women
Labour force participation	5.81	4.62
Animal husbandry	1.43	0.97
Agriculture	2.73	2.74
Manufacturing	0.42	0.45
Market activities (in-village)	1.24	0.46
Subsistence economic activities	0.91	2.16
Hunting and gathering	0.17	0.05
Fuel collection	0.24	0.38
Fetching water	0.07	0.67
House construction	0.25	0.08
Food processing	0.18	0.97
Domestic work	0.79	4.03
Cooking/serving	0.27	2.05
Cleaning dishes and pots	0.03	0.39
Cleaning house/mud plastering	0.04	0.46
Laundry	0.02	0.15
Shopping	0.24	0.17
Other domestic	0.04	0.13
Child care and rearing	0.16	0.69
Total work	7.51	10.81

Source: M. Acharya, Time Use Data and Living Standards Measurement Study,
LSMS Working Paper No. 18 (Washington, D.C., World Bank, 1982), p. 41.

There are several difficulties in the analysis of these data for issues
concerning women's participation in the informal sector. First, a fundamental
distinction in the framework proposed in this report is that drawn between monetary
and non-monetary production within the production boundary set by the United
Nations System of National Accounts; in other words, between market and subsistence
production. However, in time-use surveys, certainly in those reviewed here but
also in others, the two sets of activities are not entirely distinct. For example,
in the Nepal study, the activities in the broad categories - animal husbandry,
agriculture, hunting and gathering, manufacturing and food processing - are all
classified as "conventional economic" although goods produced may be used for
family consumption rather than sold (see annex II). Similarly, the subsistence

category, which encompasses hunting and gathering, fuel collection, fetching water, house construction and food processing, may include activities which produce goods for sale on the market. A broadly similar classification of activities is found in the Côte d'Ivoire and Botswana studies.

It should be noted that, although activities producing for the market and for subsistence are separate categories in the United Nations System of National Accounts, countries do not always make separate estimates in their calculations of national production. Data on which to base such estimates are not readily available. Although time budget studies provide highly detailed information on activities, they cannot discriminate fully between market and subsistence production, since what determines whether an activity is one or the other is not the nature of the activity but the destination of the product produced. Time-use statistics could, however, be used in conjunction with supplementary questions concerning what goods are produced and what proportion are produced for sale and for subsistence. These percentages, applied to the time-use data, could then yield estimates of the time spent in monetary and non-monetary production.

Secondly, the statistics presented in tables 1-3 refer to averages for total populations, not just to persons who actually performed the activities. For developed countries, time-use statistics on the work of women and men are classified by employment status. However, for developing countries, they usually are not presented with any classification that would relate the data to those who are likely to perform the activity. In the small localized populations studied in developing countries, there may be little variation across women in what tasks are performed, but the degree to which this is true is not known. Time budget data would be more meaningful if the proportion of each age and sex category participating in the activity were indicated and if the average time spent was reported only for those who did such work. 9/ The classification of respondents by ownership of productive assets would also be desirable, 10/ as for example in the tabulations for the Côte d'Ivoire, (table 2), which, however, relate to farmers only.

In developing countries, time-use surveys have been undertaken mainly in rural areas because of the difficulty of collecting information on women's productive activities using other methods. There have been only a few time-use studies in urban areas. These include the 1979 Côte d'Ivoire study, which, in addition to the rural sample discussed above, had two urban samples, one for Abidjan and the other for other urban areas; a 1965 survey in Lima-Callao, Peru, a site in the international comparative time-budget project (see table 7); and more recently a 1982 national urban survey in Venezuela (see table 6).

In urban areas in developing countries, employment in the informal sector is mainly as own-account worker or unpaid family labour. The extent to which these kinds of work would be shown in the results of a time budget study would depend on a number of factors, including the particular sample, the detail of the categories and the development of the formal sector in the area studied. Productive activities in the informal sector are said to be important activities in the urban samples of the Côte d'Ivoire study. However, they are not reflected in statistics from the Venezuela and Peru time-use studies. The last two studies do not distinguish unpaid family labour or own-account work from other kinds of employment.

II. NATIONAL STUDIES IN DEVELOPED COUNTRIES

In developed countries, a substantial amount of time budget research has been carried out by commercial enterprises interested in programme planning and marketing of advertising media, and more generally. Time allocation studies have also been conducted by national statistical offices and research institutions in many European countries and in Japan to provide information on activities not covered by other official statistics programmes, for example, leisure, household work and family care. These time allocation statistics have been used to measure unpaid activities performed in the home, to analyse the relationships between market and domestic labour and to serve as a basis for quantifying domestic work in monetary terms comparable to production included in national accounts.

In internationally comparative time-budget research, a most ambitious effort began in 1964 under the sponsorship of UNESCO and the International Social Science Council. Research institutions in the following 12 countries participated in the study: Belgium, Bulgaria, Czechoslovakia, Federal Republic of Germany, German Democratic Republic, Hungary, Peru, Poland, United States of American, Union of Soviet Socialist Republics and Yugoslavia. In these countries, time-budget information was collected on a probability sample of the urban population, using standardized methods of interviewing and coding.

Following the 1964-1966 multinational research, several additional studies were conducted in the United States at the Institute for Social Research. In a 1975 study, households were interviewed four times during a year and a subsample of these respondents and their children were again interviewed four times during 1981. These data constitute a rich source of information for the study of factors that affect the allocation of time in paid and unpaid work among family members and in households. 11/

In reports prepared for the European Meetings on Statistics and Indicators on Women, held in 1985 and 1987, several national statistical offices discussed their on-going experiences with time-use surveys for policy-relevant statistics on women. 12/ These included Canada, Czechoslovakia, Finland, France, Hungary, the Netherlands, Norway and Sweden. These countries, with the exception of Sweden, periodically collect time-use statistics as part of their national statistical programmes. In Sweden, a pilot time-budget study was conducted in 1984-85. A recent European time-use survey of particular interest to the study of women's unpaid work is a 1980/81 study conducted in Norway by the Central Bureau of Statistics which has as a special focus the care of dependent persons (children and the elderly). 13/ Annex I presents a brief description of some of the most recent time budget studies in these and other developed countries.

The usefulness of time budget surveys as a tool to evaluate women's work and production in the informal sector in developed countries is examined in the two sections that follow. Section A considers measures of work hours in informal economic activity inside the production boundary of the United Nations System of National Accounts; section B considers measures of hours of work in activities outside SNA.

These analyses suggest that, in the European region, participation in informal activities within the SNA production boundary is of marginal importance except in agriculture. Even in agriculture, however, in the circumstances of these countries, it may not be appropriate to consider this work as in the informal sector. In these countries, small farms are operated by the households which own them. There are no regular employees and the farms are socially and economically well-organized and established and account for a substantial portion of national agricultural output. For purposes of the following analyses, farming on own land is not considered in the informal sector. With this exclusion, work in the informal sector is mainly in the category of non-monetary production outside SNA, specifically household work and family care.

A. Informal economic activity inside the production boundary
    of the United Nations System of National Accounts (SNA)

Within SNA, the informal sector may include (a) any activity in primary production and processing undertaken on other than own land and as a secondary activity; such work could be undertaken by agricultural employees, members of agricultural producers' co-operatives and nonagricultural workers (all working without employees), and (b) own-account work in trade, industry and services.

The first category refers to activities mainly in agricultural production and also, although probably to a more limited degree, in processing of primary products. The critical factors in determining whether an activity is classified in the informal sector here are (a) the ownership of land on which the production takes place and (b) the primary occupation of the person performing the work. Hence, the work of family members on a farm they own would not be in the informal sector, nor would the cultivation of fruit or vegetable gardens by families on their own farms. However, the cultivation by members of an agricultural co-operative of plots of land provided to them by the co-operative would be classified as work in the informal sector, as would gardening undertaken by non-farm families and all own-account retail marketing of primary products.

The second category would include various kinds of secondary and tertiary sector activities, the criterion for their classification as informal being work on own-account. What is included under this category as informal is critically dependent on the status in employment of the worker, that is, whether he is working on own-account and not as an employer or employee. "Grey" or "black market" work as an employee would not be included, but "unregistered" own-account work would be. Most production for own consumption in home and car maintenance, sewing, and the like would not be included here as it is not within the SNA production boundary.

The time-use data show that agricultural work in the informal sector is important in Hungary and Czechoslovakia. In both countries, agriculture is collectivized and members of co-operatives receive small plots of land which they cultivate individually. In Hungary, there are both so-called household plots provided by co-operatives to members and auxiliary plots, or gardens, which are cultivated by people whose main occupation is not necessarily in agriculture. Work on these small plots reflects the secondary labours of persons employed in an enterprise or co-operative as well as work by pensioners and homemakers. In so far as the estimates represent work undertaken on own-account and as a secondary activity, that is, normally by persons who are otherwise employed, this production would fall within the boundary of primary production in the informal sector.

The 1976-77 study in Hungary shows that supplementary agricultural work on small plots accounts for 52 minutes per day for female, economically active earners and 61 minutes in the daily schedule of male active earners and, among not economically active, 46 minutes for women and 105 minutes for men, per day. These figures reflect the time spent in activities such as raising vegetables, cultivating vegetable gardens, orchards and vineyards as well as related tasks as, for example, the repair of machines, purchase of materials, sale of products, and transportation, which are connected with agricultural production on small plots. It has been estimated that informal production in small plots provided 13 per cent of the total disposable income of the Hungarian population in 1977. 14/

In Czechoslovakia, the daily time spent working on own farms by homeworkers who are not employed and by co-operative farmers is significant. Homemakers spend about 45 minutes on weekdays in this labour and female co-operative farmers spend 58 minutes, while male co-operative farmers spend an hour. The time spent by other categories of economically active workers is much less; for example, it is only 63 minutes a day for female employees and 13 minutes for male employees; 28 minutes for male manual workers and 16 minutes for females. 15/

The data for Hungary may be compared with those for Poland and Finland through an analysis of national time budget surveys of the three countries conducted during the latter half of the 1970s. 16/ Because the methods and the samples of the three surveys are somewhat different, the Polish and the Finnish data can be compared only through cross-reference with the Hungarian data. Specifically, the Hungary/Poland tabulations reflect age categories 18-69 of a sample over an entire year and the Hungary/Finland estimates are based on age categories 15-65 over the autumn months only. Table 4 presents data for Hungary and Poland and table 5 for Hungary and Finland.

Table 4. Time budget of men and women aged 15-69 years
Hungary and Poland

(Hours per day)

Activities	Men		Women	
	Hungary	Poland	Hungary	Poland
Gainful work	5.56	6.10	3.51	3.38
Primary employment	4.46	3.54	2.55	2.20
Income-supplementing non-agricultural work	0.05	0.13	0.02	0.04
Agricultural work on own plot	1.05	1.43	0.54	1.04
Other work	-	-	-	-

Source: R. Andorka and I. Harcsa, "Economic development and the use of time in Hungary, Poland and Finland", in D. As, A. Harvey, E. Wnuk-Lipinski and I. Niemi, Time Use Studies: Dimensions and Applications (Helsinki, Central Statistical Office, 1986), p. 29.

Table 5.   Time budget of men and women aged 15-65 years,
            Hungary and Finland

(Hours per day)

Activities	Men		Women	
	Hungary	Finland	Hungary	Finland
Gainful work	<u>6.01</u>	<u>4.25</u>	<u>3.57</u>	<u>3.11</u>
Primary employment	4.59	3.43	3.05	2.50
Income-supplementing non-agricultural work	0.03	0.03	0.01	0.02
Agricultural work on own plot	0.59	0.39	0.51	0.19

<u>Source</u>: R. Andorka and I. Harcsa, "Economic development and the use of time in Hungary, Poland and Finland", in D. As, A. Harvey, E. Wnuk-Lipinski and I. Niemi, <u>Time Use Studies: Dimensions and Applications</u> (Helsinki, Central Statistical Office, 1986), p. 30.

In tables 4 and 5, the category "agricultural work on own plot" (the original reads "farms") appears to reflect work in the informal sector since primary employment is tabulated as a separate category. As indicated in table 4, the time expenditure in agricultural work as a secondary activity is slightly greater for Polish men than for Hungarian men (one hour and 43 minutes as compared with one hour and 5 minutes); it is also slightly greater for Polish women than for Hungarian women (one hour and 4 minutes as compared with 54 minutes). The time estimates in table 5 show that Hungarians spend more time in agricultural work as a secondary activity than the Finns. Specifically, Hungarian men spend 59 minutes a day in comparison to 39 minutes for Finnish men and Hungarian women spend 51 minutes while Finnish women spend only 19 minutes a day.

Differences in the agrarian structures of the three countries are consistent with the variation observed in agricultural labour in the so-called informal sector. In Poland, agriculture is not collectivized as in Hungary, so that in 1982, 76 per cent of land in Poland was in small private farms. Farm work and employment outside of agriculture are often combined by Polish farmers, with both the heads of farm households and other members working for cash in activities outside agriculture. In Finland, family-operated small holdings no longer exist. Farms are operated by the owners with no assistance from other family members or wage labour. The time figures for agriculture as a secondary activity in Finland are lower than in Hungary and Finland and would appear to reflect mainly farming as a hobby.

Income supplementing non-agricultural work in the three countries accounts for very small amounts of time. Polish men spend 13 minutes a day but women in Poland and men and women in Finland and Hungary spend 5 minutes or less a day in these activities.

B. Non-monetary production outside SNA

In the developed countries, women's production in the informal sector is mainly in housework and family care and time-use statistics are the key source of data on this area of activities. The Multinational Comparative Time-Budget Research Project undertaken in the 1960s by 12 countries is a useful beginning point in considering international guidelines on the classification of these activities. 17/

About 30 of the approximately 100 categories in the project's classification were devoted to the diverse set of activities involved in family and household care. The specific activities and the three broad groups under which they were usually tabulated are as follows:

Housework	Child care	Shopping and services
Prepare food	Baby care (under age 5)	Marketing (everyday needs)
Meal clean up	Child care (age 5 and over)	Shopping (durable goods)
Clean home	Help on homework	Personal care
Outdoor chores	Talk to children	Medical care
Laundry, ironing	Indoor playing	Administrative/or public
Clothes upkeep	Outdoor playing	services
Other upkeep	Child health	Repair service
Gardening, animal care	Other babysitting	Waiting in line
Heat, water supply	Travel with child	Other services
Other duties		Travel services

Within the general scheme, certain countries participating in the project specified a few additional activities. For example, in the United States survey, "sewing, canning" and "helping adults" were added.

It appears from the available information that participating countries still largely follow the classification of household work and family care specified in the Multinational Project. For example, although the classification scheme for the 1974/75 study in France had a total of 200 specific categories in contrast to the 100 for the Multinational Project, the categories of household work and family care used in tabulations appear to be consistent. However, car repair and maintenance and nursing at home are treated as specific categories in the French scheme. Published tabulations of the French data group the various household work/family care activities so that activities and their market substitutes can be matched as shown in the following list:

Household activities	Market alternative
1. Cooking, washing up, shopping including transport, queueing up and putting purchases away	Meals in restaurants, snacks in cafés
2. Cleaning, indoors and outdoors; washing and ironing house linen; gardening; heating; purchasing household durables; home repairs and maintenance; tidying up	Hotel room

3.	Sewing and mending garments	Services of a dressmaker
4.	Washing and ironing small items	Services of a home helper
5.	Car repair and maintenance	Services of a garage mechanic
6.	Care of infants	Services of a day-care centre; nurse for infants
7.	Care of children aged 1 to 14; medical care outside the home; other maternal care; indoor and outdoor games; outings; transport of children; care of animals	Services of a child nurse or assistant nurse
8.	Nursing at home; nursing adults	Services of a trained nurse or assistant nurse
9.	Supervision of lessons and homework; reading aloud from books other than school books	Services of a private tutor
10.	Miscellaneous: accounts, filing, letter writing, dealing with administrative questions (including time spent waiting)	Services of a private secretary

The 1980/81 Norwegian time-use survey uses about the same number of specific activities as the Multinational Project and groups them within the categories (a) housework, (b) maintenance, (c) purchase of goods and services, (d) other household work and family care and (e) travel in connection with household work and family care (see annex II).

Concerning specific activity categories, the Norwegian study adds "private production of food" and, under the category maintenance, specifies in detail such tasks as construction and larger remodelling, painting and smaller remodelling, maintenance and repair of car/motorcycle and maintenance and repair of other equipment. Another difference is that all travel is treated together while, in the Multinational Project, travel associated with family care is separated from travel related to shopping and services.

In the Norwegian study, as in a number of other studies in the ECE region, adult care is a specific category. Interest in the private care given to persons who are dependent due to long term illness, disability or old age is growing, owing to the aging of the population and governmental concerns over the growth of public services. A special focus of the Norwegian study was the care given to dependants. Since the time-use diaries were relevant for only the population engaged in care-giving at the point of the survey, a questionnaire asking retrospective information on care-giving activities was also administered.

Table 6. Division of labour in households, by sex, Venezuela, 1982

(Hours per day)

	Unemployed women	Employed women	Employed men
Employment a/	- -	5.3	6.6
Housekeeping b/	5.7	3.1	0.5
Total work	5.7	8.4	7.1

Source: "Division of labour, time diary and economic values of work performed in households in Venezuela, 1982", Anuario Estadistico (Caracas, Central Bank of Venezuela, 1983), table 2-1.

a/ Includes primary employment, secondary employment, other employment and commuting.

b/ Includes cooking, housecleaning, laundry, shopping, gardening, pet care, other housework, child care and activities with children.

Table 6 presents tabulations from the Venezuela study on the work activities of men and women, the results of which are similar to those for developed countries shown in table 7. In interpreting these data, it must be recognized that the tabulations are based on a seven-day week and thus include time-use during the weekend as well as weekdays. This is one factor explaining why the daily averages for hours of work are less than the standard eight-hour day.

In developed countries, women's participation in the informal sector is mainly in the category of non-monetary production outside the SNA, that is, in housework and family care. Tables 7 and 8 present time-use statistics for housework, family care, and market work, based on the Multinational Comparative Time-Budget Research Project and the 1981 Basic Survey of Social Life in Japan. For many of the 12 countries included in the comparative project (table 7), more recent national budget data are available. However the data contained in table 7 are a unique source of internationally comparable, time-use statistics and a rich source of information for the study of factors that affect the allocation of time in paid and unpaid work among family members and in households. The data are presented in four broad categories: housework, which includes cooking, home chores, laundry and marketing; household obligations, which includes garden and animal care, errands and purchasing durable goods, home repairs and other household duties such as carrying water and gathering wood; child care; and market work. In the category of household obligations, such activities as home repairs and gathering wood are within the SNA framework. However, the data for these activities are not reported separately and, in any case, the activities would be significant in only a few settings.

The data from the Japanese study are also of special interest in that the large sample size (209,000 persons) provides for the systematic analysis of the relation of different phases of the family life cycle and household composition on the time spent in housework and child care.

Table 7. Time spent in household and market work, selected studies in 12 countries

(Hours per week) a/

	Housework b/			Household obligations c/			Child care d/			Total housework			Market work e/			Total work		
	House-wives	Em-ployed women	Em-ployed men	House-wives	Em-ployed women	Em-ployed men	House-wives	Em-ployed women	Em-ployed men	House-wives	Em-ployed women	Em-ployed men	House-wives	Em-ployed women	Em-ployed men	House-wives	Em-ployed women	Em-ployed men
Belgium	41.28	18.95	1.93	3.13	2.47	3.67	4.65	1.77	0.83	49.07	23.18	6.43	1.68	39.47	49.58	50.75	62.65	56.02
Bulgaria, Kazanlik	39.23	20.75	6.10	12.28	3.07	6.27	5.17	2.62	1.48	56.68	26.43	13.85	0.08	44.90	49.37	56.77	71.33	63.22
Czechoslovakia, Olomouc	43.35	29.40	6.50	5.78	3.75	5.43	9.82	4.03	2.20	58.95	37.18	14.13	2.40	38.27	47.80	61.35	75.45	61.93
France (six cities)	40.18	21.10	3.77	3.65	2.32	5.47	11.73	3.07	1.30	55.57	26.48	10.53	0.33	41.80	50.18	55.90	68.28	60.72
Germany, F. R. (100 districts)	40.88	24.93	1.82	5.63	4.00	6.77	6.47	3.00	1.03	52.98	31.93	9.62	1.20	35.68	51.50	54.18	67.62	61.12
Germany, F. R., Osnabruck	39.02	22.07	2.28	4.43	2.70	6.20	6.50	2.32	0.92	49.95	27.08	9.40	0.90	36.35	47.80	50.85	63.43	57.20
German Dem. Rep., Hoyerswer	45.90	28.93	7.23	3.35	2.03	5.20	12.13	4.98	2.55	61.38	35.95	14.98	0.58	42.82	53.07	61.97	78.77	68.05
Hungary, Cyor	45.17	28.07	3.45	12.85	2.68	7.85	5.10	4.03	2.32	63.12	34.78	13.62	5.68	44.35	52.03	68.80	79.13	65.65
Peru, Lima-Callao	43.65	17.10	2.12	2.02	1.60	2.12	5.63	2.27	0.77	51.30	20.97	5.00	0.42	38.20	48.53	51.72	59.17	53.53
Poland, Torun	43.22	23.00	4.88	5.45	2.27	4.22	7.77	4.02	2.87	56.43	29.28	11.97	0.25	42.03	48.33	56.68	71.32	60.35
USA (44 cities)	32.83	17.78	3.33	6.30	4.72	4.78	8.65	2.47	1.30	47.78	24.97	9.42	0.50	40.37	47.93	48.28	65.33	57.40
USA, Jackson	34.50	17.58	3.68	5.27	4.78	5.02	8.83	2.10	1.20	48.60	24.47	9.90	0.67	40.37	48.63	49.27	64.83	58.50
USSR, Pskov	39.68	23.23	4.03	10.02	4.12	6.18	6.78	4.83	3.57	56.48	32.18	13.78	0.33	40.40	42.63	56.82	72.58	56.42
Yugoslavia, Kragujevac	42.57	25.82	3.10	4.80	2.58	4.95	3.70	3.33	1.38	51.07	31.73	9.43	1.20	36.05	45.57	52.27	67.78	55.00
Yugoslavia, Maribor	48.23	29.77	3.85	17.18	4.33	10.50	5.82	3.63	2.17	71.23	37.73	16.52	1.55	42.67	48.23	72.78	80.40	64.75

Source: The Use of Time: Daily Activities of Urban and Suburban Population in Twelve Countries, A. Szalai, ed. (The Hague, Mouton, 1972).

a/ For housewives the weekly averages are based on the figures for weekdays and Sundays, with the Sunday averages taken also for Saturday; for employed men and women, the weekly averages are based on workdays and days off.

b/ Includes cooking, home chores, laundry and marketing.

c/ Includes garden and animal care, errands and purchasing durable goods, home repairs and other household duties including carrying water and gathering wood.

d/ Refers to time actually spent caring for the child, playing with him or her and helping with homework.

e/ Includes time spent on main job, secondary job, commuting and other job related activities except eating at the work place.

Table 8. Basic survey on social life, Japan, 1981

(Hours per week)

Activities	Housewives a/ (15,677)	Women employed part time b/ (9,640)	Women employed full time c/ (13,787)	Employed men d/ (34,397)
Total housework	45.5	31.5	15.4	..
Housekeeping and child care	39.2	27.3	12.6	..
Shopping	6.3	4.2	2.8	..
Market work e/	2.1	35.0	51.8	44.1
Total work	47.6	66.5	67.2	44.1

Source: The Survey on Time Use and Leisure Activities - Major Results and Analyses (Tokyo, Statistics Bureau, 1983).

Note: Numbers in parenthesis refer to number of persons in the sample.

a/   Refers to women who indicate "keeping home" as "main daily activity".

b/   Refers to women who indicate "engaged in work while keeping house" as "main daily activity".

c/   Refers to women who indicate "engaged mainly in work" as "main daily activity".

d/   Refers to men who indicate "engaged mainly in work" as "main daily activity". The numbers of men who indicated "keeping house" as "main daily activity" and "engaged in work while keeping house" were negligible, that is 217 and 419 respectively.

e/   Includes commuting and farm work.

Notes

1/   See, for example, the following volumes containing proceedings and studies from three workshops on this subject: Household Studies Workshop, (Singapore, 1976), H. P. Binswanger and others, eds., <u>Rural Household Studies in Asia</u> (Singapore, Singapore University Press, 1980); "Symposium on households economics" (Manila, 1977), <u>The Philippine Economic Journal</u>, vol. XVII, Nos. 1 and 2 (1978); Seminar convened by the Asian Development Seminar Program, <u>Time-Use Data</u>, (New York, Asia Society, 1978). See also V. A. Miralao, "Methodological issues in the collection and analyses of women's time-use data", Occasional Paper No. 3, Integration of Women in Development Programme, Asian and Pacific Development Centre (Kuala Lumpur, Malaysia).

2/   S. Bhattacharya, "On the issue of underenumeration of women's work in the Indian data collection system", in D. Jain and N. Banerjee, eds., <u>Tyranny of the Household</u> (New Delhi, Vikas Publishing, 1985), p. 209.

3/   <u>Ibid</u>.

4/   D. Jain, "The household trap: Report on a field survey of family activity patterns", in D. Jain and N. Banerjee, <u>op. cit</u>., pp. 215-248.

5/   For a detailed discussion of the advantages and disadvantages of different methods of collecting time-use data, see M. Cain, "Household time budgets", Bangladesh Institute of Development Studies, VFS Methodology Report No. 1 (1977), and R. Dixon-Mueller, "Women's Work in Third World Agriculture", <u>Women, Work and Development</u>, No. 9 (Geneva, International Labour Organisation, 1985), pp. 36-42.

6/   Eighth International Conference of Labour Statisticians, resolution concerning statistics of the labour force, employment and unemployment (Geneva, International Labour Organisation, 1954).

7/   R. Anker, "Female labour force participation in developing countries: a critique of current definitions and data collection methods", <u>International Labour Review</u> (1983), and R. Anker, "Research on women's role and demographic change: Survey questionnaires for households, women, men and communities, with background explanations" (Geneva, International Labour Organisation, 1980).

8/   The distribution of time among activities was considered more reliable than the absolute amounts of time spent on activities: "Undoubtedly people in rural Botswana do not keep precise track of time during their daily activities; they merely know that they devoted half of the day to one activity and half to another. In cases where the respondent reported time use in terms of fractions of the day the interviewers were instructed to assume a day of 12 hours (roughly the time from sunrise to sunset)." D. Chernichovsky and E. Mueller, "The household economy of rural Botswana: An African case", World Bank Staff Working Paper No. 715 (Washington, D.C., World Bank 1985).

9/   M. Cain, "The economic activities of children in a village in Bangladesh", in H. Binswanger and others, eds., <u>Rural Household Studies in Asia</u> (Singapore, Singapore University Press, 1980).

10/   R. Dixon-Mueller, loc. cit., p. 43.

11/   T. Juster and F. Stafford, eds., Time, Goods and Well Being (Ann Arbor, Michigan, Institute for Social Research, 1985).

12/   Joint ECE/INSTRAW Meeting on Statistics and Indicators on the Role and Situation of Women, Geneva, 11-14 March 1985, and the European Informal Meeting on Statistics and Indicators on Women, Geneva, 15-19 June 1989. The summary of the main conclusions reached at the 1985 meeting is contained in document CES/AC.60/24 and the 1987 meeting in document CES/599.

13/   S. Lingson, "Time use survey in Norway", paper prepared for the International Time-Use Workshop held at the Institute for Social Research, Ann Arbor, Michigan, 20-21 May 1982.

14/   R. Andorka and I. Harcsa, "Economic development and the use of time in Hungary, Poland and Finland", in D. As, A. Harvey, E. Wnuk-Lipinski and I. Niemi, Time Use Studies: Dimensions and Applications (Helsinki, Central Statistical Office, 1986).

15/   Ibid.

16/   Ibid.

17/   The Use of Time: Daily Activities of Urban and Suburban Populations in Twelve Countries, Alexander Szalai, ed. (The Hague, Mouton, 1972).

TIME-USE SURVEYS IN 13 COUNTRIES

Country and agency or principal investigator	Survey title and date	Population sampled	Sample
1. Botswana			
Central Statistical Office, Gaborone	Rural income distribution survey 1974/75	Rural households*	All members aged 6+ in 1,074 households

Method of data collection	Survey instrument	Time sample	Activity category	Reports issued
Interview - recall	Lined form for listing activities chronologically for previous day, noting duration	Each household visited monthly for 12 months; day of the week recorded but not systematically rotated	41 activities classified into 19 categories	Sherrie Kussondji and Eva Mueller, "The economic and demographic status of female-headed households in rural Botswana", 1981 Population Studies Center, University of Michigan, "Time use in rural Botswana"

* Households with income tax records in government files (5 per cent of total) were not covered in the field survey, and 12 per cent of the population in areas of low population density were covered only by a very small sample.

Time-use surveys in 13 countries (continued)

Country and agency or principal investigator	Survey title and date	Population sampled	Sample	Reports issued
2. Côte d'Ivoire				
Direction de la Statistique	Household food consumption and budgetary survey, 1979	National urban and rural samples	Household members aged 10 and over in 720 households in Abidjan, 720 households in other urban areas, 720 households in rural areas	A. J. Berio, "The analysis of time allocation and activity patterns in nutrition and rural development planning", Food and Nutrition Bulletin vol. 6, No. 1; A. J. Berio, "The use of time allocation data in developing countries in influencing development policies for estimating energy requirements"; (paper presented at International Research Group on Time Budget and Social Activities, Helsinki, August 1984)

Method of data collection	Survey instrument	Time sample	Activity category
Continuous observation (recall for activities performed in absence of observer)	Blank sheet with 15-minute intervals in 24-hr. period	One week for households in urban areas and one week 4 times a year	Coded, using detailed categories for food-related activities and more general categories for other activities

Time-use surveys in 13 countries (continued)

Country and agency or principal investigator	Survey title and date	Population sampled	Sample
3. Czechoslovakia			
Federal Statistical Office	Survey on the use of time, June 1979-May 1980	National sample	34,871 persons 15-69 years of age in 16,583 households

Method of data collection	Survey instrument	Time sample	Activity category	Reports issued
Self-administered diary	Form for recording activities in 10 minute intervals for 24 hour period.	Random sample of days covering the entire year with each individual providing a diary for one day	92 activities classified with 10 major categories	Federal Statistical Office, Czechoslovak Statistics No. 71, October 1981 (vol. 1); No. 53, July 1982 (vol. 2)

Time-use surveys in 13 countries (continued)

Country and agency or principal investigator	Survey title and date	Population sampled	Sample
4. Finland			
Central Bureau of Statistics	Time use study Sept-Nov 1979 (collected in connection with manpower survey)	National sample	7,355 persons aged 10-64 years from National Register of persons not living in institutions

Method of data collection	Survey instrument	Time sample	Activity category	Reports issued
Self-administered diary	Lined form for listing activities at one-half hour intervals between midnight and 5 a.m. and at 10-minute intervals between 5 a.m. and midnight	Two successive days	95 categories	R. Andorka, I. Harcsa and I. Niemi, "Use of time in Hungary and in Finland," Central Statistical Office of Finland, Studies No. 101 (1983); I. Niemi, "The 1979 time-use study methods", Central Statistical Office of Finland, Studies No. 91; I. Niemi, S. Klinski, and M. M. Liikkanen, "Use of time in Finland", Central Statistical Office of Finland, Studies No. 65 (1981)

Time-use surveys in 13 countries (continued)

Country and agency or principal investigator	Survey title and date	Population sampled	Sample
5. France			
National Institute of Statistics and Economic Studies (INSEE)	(a) 1974-1975 Time-Use Survey	Urban	6,640 persons aged 18 years and over in 10,000 households
	(b) 1985-1986 Time-Use Survey	National	24,000 persons aged 15 years and over in 16,000 households

Method of data collection	Survey instrument	Time sample	Activity category	Reports issued
(a) Self-administered diary distributed by interviewer the day before and on day after diary day; interviewer and respondent check diary and list others present and location of activities	(a) Diary for listing primary and secondary activities chronologically showing duration	(a) One day for each respondent apportioned over days of the week	(a) 200 for coding and 73 for tabulations	(a) M. T. Huet, Y. Lemel et C. Roy, "Les emplois du temps des citadins", Documents rectangles (December 1978), reédité en Archives et documents, no. 59; A. Fouquet et A. Chadeau, "Le travail domestique: essai de quantification", Archives et documents, no. 32 (1981); A. Chadeau et A. Fouquet, "Peut-on mesurer le travail domestique", Economie et Statisque", no. 136 (September 1981); (b) G. Grimler, C. Roy, "Les Emplois du temps en France" Premiers Resultats, no. 100 (Paris, INSEE, juin 1987);
(b) Same as above except that the survey concerns two respondents if the household has more than one person	(b) Same as above	(b) Same as above	(b) Same as above	

Time-use surveys in 13 countries (continued)

Method of data collection	Survey instrument	Time sample	Activity category	Reports issued
5. France (continued)				C. Roy "92 minutes de vaisselle ...", Informations socialise, no. 5 (1987); D. Bessy, "Des femmes plus tournées vers l'exterieur", Regard sur l'Ile de France (Paris, INSEE); "Les emplois du temps", Données générales (Paris, INSEE)

Time-use surveys in 13 countries (continued)

Country and agency or principal investigator	Survey title and date	Population sampled	Sample
6. Hungary			
Central Statistical Office	(a) Time budget, 1976/77	National	7,000 persons aged 15-69 sampled from census line 0.1 per cent sample population
	(b) Time budget, 1986/87	National	10,500 persons aged 15-79

Method of data collection	Survey instrument	Time sample	Activity category	Reports issued
(a) and (b) Interview - recall	Interviewer recorded activities in designated preceding day with time activity began and ended as well as any supplementary activity and the place and with whom the activities were performed	Four interviews per person representing four seasons of the year	Type of activities: 100; location of activities: 37; participants: 1,010	R. Andorka and I. Harcsa and I. Niemi, "Use of time in Hungary and in Finland", Central Statistical Office of Finland, Studies No. 101 (Helsinki, 1983), R. Andorka and B. Falussy, "The way of the Hungarian society as reflected by the time budget survey of 1976-1977", Acta Oeconomica, vol. 26, Nos. 3-4 (1981); Social Indicators Research No. 11 (1982)

Time-use surveys in 13 countries (continued)

Country and agency or principal investigator	Survey title and date	Population sampled	Sample	Methods of data collection
7. India				
(a) Institute of Social Studies Trust (New Delhi)	Muluk village study, 1976	One village Pre-test	Adult female members of 5 households	Observation*
(b) Institute of Social Studies Trust (New Delhi)	Time allocation study, 1976/77	6 rural villages	All members aged 5+ in 127 households	Observation*
(c) Institute of Social Studies Trust (New Delhi)	Milk maids of Kaira survey	10 villages	Adult female 124 households	Interview – activity-oriented; Recall for previous day

Survey instrument	Time unit	Activity categories	Reports issued
(a) Form with half hour intervals and spaces for recording primary and secondary activities and tools used for each	5 visits per household over 8 weeks, each visit for 2 consecutive days with recording from 5 a.m. to 5 p.m.	42 categories	D. Jain and M. Chand, "Report on a time allocation study; its methodological implication" (1982)
(b) For rounds 1–4 form with half hour intervals and spaces for recording primary and secondary activities and tools used for each; for rounds 5–6 activities listed and space for recording time	6 visits per household over year, usually between 11 a.m. and 1 p.m. lasting until 8 p.m.	42 categories	Ibid.

* Information on time spent away from home based on recall for hours when observer is not in the home.

-81-

Time-use surveys in 13 countries (continued)

Survey instrument	Time unit	Activity categories	Reports issued
7. India (continued)			
(c) Form with half hour interval for non-sleeping hours, approximately 14-16 hours	1 visit	4 categories: 1. Dairying activities 2. Agricultural activities 3. Domestic work 4. Total house worked	D. Jain assisted by M. Singh and M. Chand, Women's Quest for Power (New Delhi, Vikas Publishing, 1980)

Country and agency or principal investigator	Survey title and date	Population sampled	Sample	Methods of data collection
(d) National Council of Applied Economic Research	Integrating women's interest in development planning, 1983	22 villages	Adult females 1,000 households	Interview - recall for previous day
(e) National Council of Applied Economic Research	Time allocation survey, 1983	-	All household members aged 5 and over	Interview - recall for previous day, and observation period spot check and observation with recall

Time-use surveys in 13 countries (continued)

Survey instrument	Time sample	Activity category	Reports issued
7. India (continued)			
(d) Form with half intervals for non-sleeping hours approximately 14-16 hours	1. Visit 2. Time spent on fetching fuel 3. Child care 4. Economic activity	4 categories: 1. Time spent on fetching water 2. Time spent on fetching fuel 3. Child care 4. Economic activity	"Integrating women into the State five-year plan", (Ministry of Social Welfare, Government of India, in preparation)
(e) Recall for previous day and observation with recall - lined form with half hour intervals 4 a.m. to 11 p.m. Observation - lined form with 3 hour intervals - 6 a.m. to 9 p.m.	Multiple visits, 5 day period	21 activities	-

Time-use surveys in 13 countries (continued)

Country and agency or principal investigator	Survey title and date	Population sampled	Sample
8. Japan			
Statistics Bureau	Survey on time-use and leisure activities, 1981	National	209,000 persons 15 years old and over living in 83,000 households

Method of data collection	Survey instrument	Time sample	Activity category	Reports issued
Self-administered diary with visits by the enumerator before and after completion of diary	Abbreviated form with space to record activities performed in half hour intervals for 24-hour period; respondent classified activities into 18 predefined categories	Designated day	18 categories	"The survey of time-use and leisure activities 1981 - major results and analyses" (Statistics Bureau, Prime Minister's Office, Tokyo)

Time-use surveys in 13 countries (continued)

Country and agency or principal investigator	Survey title and date	Population sampled	Sample
9. Nepal			
Tribhuvan University	Status of women project, 1978	8 villages as a country cross-section	192 households (24 households in each village representing its caste composition)

Method of data collection	Survey instrument	Time sample	Activity category	Reports issued
Observation – periodic visits	Forms with a precoded and predefined activity list on the vertical column and a person code of household members on the household line	Each household visited every other day at random designated times for 26 weeks in 4 villages, for 52 weeks in other 4 villages	97 activities classified in 12 major categories	The Status of Women in Nepal, vol. I, Background Reports (issued in five parts); vol. II (issued in nine parts: eight village studies and one monograph summarizing the major findings of village studies, 1981)

Time-use surveys in 13 countries (continued)

Country and agency or principal investigator	Survey title and date	Population sampled	Sample
10. Netherlands			
(a) Netherlands Central Bureau of Statistics with several other institutions	Time-use survey, 1985	National	4,125 persons 12 years and over
(b) Netherlands Central Bureau of Statistics	Time-use survey, 1987	National	All members aged 12 years or over in 9,000 households

Method of data collection	Survey instrument	Time sample	Activity categories	Reports issued
(a) Self-administered diary with interviews before and after completion of the diary	Diary for recording activities in 15-minute intervals according to a defined set of activities	Designated week	225 activities classified in 10 major categories	In preparation
(b) Self-administered diary plus an interview (including an instructive interview for a part of the previous day) with head of household or partner plus one self-administered questionnaire per person	Diary for recording activities in 15-minute intervals according to a defined set of activities	Two days	107 activities classified in 9 major categories	-

Time-use surveys in 13 countries (continued)

Country and agency or principal investigator	Survey title and date	Population sampled	Sample
11. Norway			
Central Bureau of Statistics	Time Use Survey, October 1980 – September 1981	National	5,205 persons, 16-74 years of age*

Method of data collection	Survey instrument	Time sample	Activity category	Reports issued
Self-administered diary and questionnaire	Lined form for listing activities in 15-minute intervals and for recording with whom activities performed	2 designated days	90	"The time budget survey, 1980/81" (NOS B378, Central Bureau of Statistics, 1983); Susan Lingsom and Anne Lise Ellingsaeter, "Work, leisure and time spent with others, changes in time use in the 70s" (SA No. 49, Central Bureau of Statistics); Susan Lingsom, "Informal care of sick and elderly" (SOS No. 57, Central Bureau of Statistics, 1985); Sigmund Gronmo and Susan Lingsom, "Increasing equality in household work; patterns of time use change in Norway", European Sociological Review

* The non-response rate was 42 per cent.

Time-use surveys in 13 countries (continued)

Country and agency or principal investigator	Survey title and date	Population sampled	Sample
12. Poland			
Central Statistical Office	1984 time-budget survey in Poland	National sample of households, excluding those in which a member engages in own-account work outside agriculture or is a professional	45,087 persons aged 18 and over in 21,600 households

Method of data collection	Survey instrument	Time sample	Activity categories	Reports issued
Self-administered diary	Lined form for listing activities in 15-minute intervals	Random sample of households	53	"Dobowy budzet ozasu mieszkancow Plski w 1984 r." (24-hour time-budget of the population in Poland, 1984) (GUS, 1985);

"Analiza budzetu ozasu mieszkanców Polski w latach 1976 i 1974" (An analysis of time budget of the population in Poland in the years 1976 and 1984) (Studia i Prace Statystyczne", GUS, 1987) |

Time-use surveys in 13 countries (continued)

Country and agency or principal investigator	Survey title and date	Population sampled	Sample
13. Venezuela Ministry for the Participation of Women in Development	Division of labour, time diary and economic value of work performed in households in Venezuela, 1982	National urban sample	2,657 persons, 18 years and older in 998 households in 10 largest cities

Method of data collection	Survey instrument	Time sample	Activity category	Reports issued
Interview-recall for previous day	Lined form for listing activities for previous day 24-hour period; respondent classified activities into 37 predefined categories	..	37	Ministry for the Participation of Women in Development, "Division of labour, time diary and economic value of work performed in households in Venezuela", vol. I, and Statistical Annex, vol. II (Caracas, Central Bank of Venezuela, November 1983)

Source: Information compiled by the Statistical Office, United Nations Secretariat.

ILLUSTRATIVE CLASSIFICATIONS OF ACTIVITIES

A. NEPAL

PRODUCTIVE ACTIVITIES

A. Animal husbandry

01010   Herding
01020   Care and feeding of animals
         within compound (Medical treatment,
         shoeing, grooming)
01030   Fodder collection
01040   Castration/Breeding
01050   Shearing
01060   Milking
01070   Butchering
01080   Other

B. Agriculture

02010   Land preparation (ploughing, use of
         kodale, harrowing, beating clods,
         slash and burn)
02020   Terrace upkeep and routine repair of
         irrigation channels
02030   Collecting and preparing organic
         fertilizer
02040   Carrying and spreading organic
         chemical fertilizer
02050   Planting operations (seed bed
         preparation, sowing, transplanting)
02060   Weeding
02070   Irrigation
02080   Harvesting (bundling, drying crop
         residue, storing or bagging grain)
02090   Threshing and cleaning grain
02100   Horticulture
02110   Kitchen Gardening
02120   Seed selection and storage
02130   Guarding/protection of crops
         (in field and harvest)
         Other

C. Hunting and gathering

03010   Hunting wild animals, birds, etc.
03020   Fishing
03030   Gathering of materials for craft
         production (hemp, hotels, bamboo,
         leaves, etc.)
03050   Collecting of medical herbs
         (juniper, jaributi)
03060   Other

D. Manufacturing

04011   Textile (includes entire process from
         cleaning wool, through spinning,
         setting up loom, dyeing, weaving)
04012   Rope/basketry (grass mats, ropes
         fishnets, baskets, etc.)
04013   Making and repairing of tools
04014   Leather work
04015   Sewing (in own home)
04016   Other

E. Food processing

04021   Husking/drying grains, post husking
04022   Roasting, grinding, chiura making, oil
04023   Liquor making
04024   Food preservation (drying of meat and
         vegetables, pickle making)
04025   Preparation of dairy products
         (ghee, curds)
04026   Other

F. Participation in local economy

10010   Government service
10020   Wage labour (agriculture, construction,
         animal husbandry, portering, fuel
         gathering, etc. when done for wages in
         cash or kind)
10030   Trade (sale of food grains, dairy
         products and other food stuffs,
         livestock, manufacturing goods)
10040   Hotel, tea-shop, beer house, store
10050   Lending/borrowing
10060   Medical and religious service
         (for wages)

G. Home construction

07010 Building and repairing own house
07020 Construction and repair of own
       compound or field walls, animal
       sheds and out-building
07030 Well digging

DOMESTIC ACTIVITIES

H. Domestic activities

05010 Cooking/serving
05020 Cleaning dishes and pots
05030 Cleaning house/mud plastering
05040 Washing clothes and bedding
05050 Fetching and preparing fuel -
       (this was subsequently moved
       to "Hunting and gathering")
05060 Fetching water
05070 Shopping
05080 Other

I. Child rearing and child care

06010 Child birth/recovery period
06020 Tending
06030 Feeding
06040 Bathing/cleaning
06050 Oiling and massaging
06060 Other

J. Education

09010 Academic (in-village)
09020 Non-formal
09030 Other

K. Other activities

11010 Grooming and personal hygiene
11030 Sickness/treatment
11040 Eating

SOCIAL ACTIVITIES/OBLIGATIONS AND LEISURE

L. Social activities/obligations

08010 Voluntary labour
08020 Political service (Panchayat, etc.)
08030 Voluntary community service (school,
       committee, youth organization, women's
       organization, etc.

M. Leisure

11020 Ritual (for self or neighbour)
11050 Drinking of alcoholic beverages
11060 Gambling/card playing
11070 In-village visiting
11080 Inter-village visiting
11090 Sleeping
11100 Other

EXTENDED ABSENCE FROM VILLAGE

N. Out of village for employment/production

12010 Army service
12020 Government service
12030 Wage labour
12040 Trading
12050 Herding
12060 Miscellaneous services/employment

O. Out of village for social/education

12050 Attending school or training
12080 Other
12090 Visiting relatives

Source: M. Acharya and L. Bennet, The Rural Women of Nepal: An Aggregate Analysis and Summary of Eight Village Studies (Kathmandu, Tribhuvan University Centre for Economic Development and Administration, 1981), pp. 340-344.

B. NORWAY

Housework

Food preparation, setting of table, serving
Baking bread
Dish washing
Cleaning table
House cleaning
Washing and ironing
Mending of clothes
Heating, wood chopping, drawing water
Private production of food

Family Care

Child care
Escorting children
Help with school-work
Play with children
Conversations with children
Reading for children
Other child care
Care to adults
Help to other households

Maintenance

Care of garden/property
Care of animals
Construction, larger remodelling
Painting, smaller remodelling
Maintenance and repair and car/motorcycle
Maintenance and repair of other equipment

Purchase of goods and services

Purchase of grocery goods
Other and unspecified purchase
Medical treatment
Visit to public offices and institutions
Other errands

Other household work and family care

Other household work and family care

Travel in connection with household work and family care

Travel in connection with household work and family care

Source: Norwegian time-budget survey 1980/81.

Part Three

COLLECTING STATISTICS ON THE PARTICIPATION OF WOMEN IN THE
INFORMAL SECTOR: METHODS USED IN LATIN AMERICA*

_____

     *   Prepared by the Economic Commission for Latin America and the Caribbean
of the United Nations Secretariat, with the assistance of Arturo León, a consultant
to the Secretariat, and with financial support from the International Research and
Training Institute for the Advancement of Women.

INTRODUCTION AND PRINCIPAL CONCLUSIONS

The momentum of activities which developed with the inception of the International Women's Year and during the United Nations Decade for Women: Equality, Development and Peace resulted in considerable advancement of studies carried out on women in Latin America. Before then, however, starting in 1970, the International Labour Organisation's Regional Employment Programme for Latin America and the Caribbean (PREALC) developed a pioneering programme of studies on segmentation of labour markets and on the informal sector in the region. However, until relatively recently there were few if any studies relating these two issues, that is, on women in the informal sector, and none which dealt with this subject from a methodological perspective. The present study is a review of recent experience in the region regarding these topics. It is based on the experience gained by researchers in ECLAC on the topic of women's work.

The study adopts the perspective of users dissatisfied with the statistical information available to measure women's activities in the informal sector - and not the perspective of statisticians. It systematically brings together the latest available data on women in the informal sector in Latin America and, from a methodological viewpoint, provides some suggestions on how to treat this information for both statistical and analytical purposes.

This part of the report comprises the following: Chapter I outlines aspects of women's work which cause it to be considered as non-work or hard-to-measure work, and highlights the greater invisibility of women's informal work. This chapter also shows the importance of adequate measurement of this sector for design of social and economic policies.

Chapter II analyses the invisibility of women's work in the informal sector. It describes the principal ways in which the informal sector has been defined and points out the difficulties of measuring it. It also provides a typology of the women's work in the informal sector covering the visible and invisible sub-sectors.

Chapter III explores the potential usefulness of population censuses and household surveys to measure the informal sector and finds that a more exhaustive utilization of such information allows for a relatively adequate description and analysis of the women's work in the visible informal sector. Special emphasis is given to the analytical usefulness of appropriate design of household records in censuses and household surveys and to ways of exploiting these sources of information more effectively.

Chapter IV provides suggestions based on the experiences reviewed in Latin America for measuring women's work in the informal sector through household surveys. Specific suggestions are made to improve measurement of the participation and income of women in the informal sector, following the typology described in chapter II. This chapter also draws on experience in analysing household surveys in ECLAC's data bank and indicates some of the principal limitations of this type of information.

The main conclusions of the study are as follows:

(a)   Given the great heterogeneity of the informal sector and especially of women's work in it, analytical characterization of sub-sectors must necessarily precede adequate measurement. The study therefore suggests a typology of women's work in the informal sector based on the following dimensions: place of work, degree to which the activity resembles domestic chores, destination of goods and services produced, legality and degree of social acceptance of the activities, degree of involvement with the formal sector, degree of technical and social complexity, the activity itself and its stability over time. These dimensions basically permit distinguishing the following types of activities:

(i)   Visible informal sector;

(ii)   Petty trade;

(iii)   Invisible informal sector;

(iv)   Domestic service;

(b)   The manner in which censuses and household surveys measure the various sub-sectors within the informal sector is evaluated using this typology. It is found that both censuses and household surveys permit relatively precise measurement of women's participation in the visible informal sector, though the latter have some advantages as opposed to censuses. Household surveys are most useful when carried out at least once a year by well-trained interviewers and when designed specifically to include complete investigation of the relevant employment variables;

(c)   A substantial improvement in the measurement of women's participation in the informal sector using household surveys is possible by investigating some additional variables, such as size of economic units and place of work. Surveys can contribute to measurement of women's participation in the informal sector with much more precision through the design of household records which permit analysis of the family unit and women's work in it;

(d)   The invisible informal sector poses greater problems for measurement through household surveys. The main problems stem from failure to ascertain the economic activities actually performed by women as well as failure to appraise the contribution they make to gross domestic product and the income they produce for the household. Even greater difficulties arise in trying to measure women's participation in the informal invisible sector in agriculture, where the absence of any clear distinction between economic and non-economic domestic activities makes the task of counting the economically active population and the product generated by women more difficult.

Taking these findings into account, the following specific suggestions are made for further study:

(a)   Inclusion in household surveys of a special module containing questions geared towards the population which considers itself not economically active. It is very important that this module include a detailed breakdown of the various activities that women perform. This facilitates the identification and recognition of economic activities which are most frequently considered as being non-economic domestic work. In surveys in rural areas, the module should include a special listing of agricultural activities. It should also include own-account as well as petty trade activities performed by women;

(b) Identification of informal visible activities may be substantially improved by incorporating into household surveys some questions directed to ascertaining the work performed in small family enterprises established within or outside the household. The two basic variables are size of the establishment and place where the job is performed;

(c) Improvement of information collected for other variables which are already incorporated in the majority of household surveys of the region. This should include detailed recording of generational relationships of household members, excluding live-in domestic service. It is also necessary to investigate all the work activities performed by unpaid family members, recording the number of hours dedicated to each type of activity;

(d) In the process of coding, recording of activities in the greatest possible detail so that the occupations of women can be more clearly identified.

Specific recommendations are also made to improve the measurement of income through household surveys, especially income obtained by the self-employed. The problems noted in this regard include high margins of understatement of profits and benefits; difficulties in ascertaining the average income of family enterprises; failure to record the value of production for own consumption in the household; and difficulties in estimating net earnings, that is, after subtracting the value of inputs. Other important sources of problems in measuring income generated by women concern the accurate evaluation of the economic contribution made by unpaid family workers to household economic activity and in some surveys, failure to separate incomes derived from principal and secondary occupations, making it difficult to determine and analyse income for each activity.

In the light of these problems, the following suggestions are made:

(a) Investigate the income derived from own-account activities over a longer reference period. For certain activities, twelve months is appropriate;

(b) Register the value of goods produced and sold separately from the cost of inputs used in their production;

(c) Record the quantity and the value of goods and services produced and consumed within the household;

(d) Separate the income from the principal occupation from income from secondary activities, especially intermittent ones.

This study has found that measurement of income is one of the areas which presents the greatest difficulty, especially as it concerns self-employment and unpaid economic activities. Undoubtedly, more precise knowledge of women's activity in the informal sector will result in better assessment of their contribution to household production and income.

I. SPECIAL CHARACTERISTICS OF WOMEN'S WORK

A. Division of labour by gender

The work performed by women is essential for the maintenance and survival of societies. In the present study, it is assumed that women perform principally two types of work. The more important is reproductive activity and domestic work performed in the household which is essential to the reproduction of the population, the socialization of future generations and the replenishment of the labour force. The second type of work, which may be called social or societal work, is carried out in the extra-domestic sphere and in the labour market. In this work, women generate incomes and become part of the so-called economically active population. These types of work, domestic and social, are found in all societies. The definition of tasks as being domestic or social varies from one society to another and with levels of social and economic development, but women are widely expected to be responsible for domestic work as a primary obligation.

In the Latin American and Caribbean region, family care and reproduction of the population are carried out by women in domestic units. Women and their domestic units are generally responsible for family maintenance and for reproduction, though this responsibility does not imply direct execution of all of the related tasks on the part of all women.

In general, the tasks accomplished through domestic work may be grouped as follows:

   (a) Management and distribution of the family budget and own-account production;

   (b) Buying or producing goods and services for processing and consumption;

   (c) Transforming purchased goods for consumption and direct production of services for consumption;

   (d) Upbringing and socialization of children.

As penetration by the market economy advances, these tasks are increasingly fulfilled by services which are bought in the market or which are provided through public and private organizations. In subsistence economies, where the level of technology is very low, the domestic unit combines both productive and reproductive tasks and the distinction between women's and men's work is clear, with men mainly assuming productive tasks, while women perform both productive and reproductive tasks. 1/ As access to higher incomes develops, the distinction between domestic work and social work becomes sharper: the quantity of goods and services bought in the market grows, thereby reducing the proportion of goods and services produced by domestic work.

Economic and social development has promoted the general, global trend towards transferring production of goods and services to the market and reducing the activity of transforming inputs inside households for private household consumption. An example is pre-school education. Formerly, early socialization, up to six or seven years of age, took place in the household. Presently, in the urban areas of the relatively more developed countries and especially for the middle and upper classes, these tasks are mainly performed by social institutions. In other words, there are great differences in the amounts of domestic work performed in households as a function of the degree of development of the country and of the social class in question.

However, despite the fact that the long-term trend is the growth of goods and services in the market and consequent drop in activities which are carried out within the household, in periods of economic crisis, this trend may be reversed and family units may cover a broader spectrum of activities. In the case of women, this may mean that they must increase their social and domestic work. For women in the more deprived groups, the trend will be to maximize the replacement of purchased goods with those which can be produced in the household and to develop various strategies to increase family income, that is, to undertake paid activities in the labour market. This is particularly difficult in a context of economic crisis, which tends to push women not only into informal activities paid in cash but also into those paid in kind. Thus, women undertake activities such as taking in laundry, child care, cooking, and the like, activities which, when done for households of other social classes are paid, whereas when performed for relatives within their own environment are considered as exchanges of services and which may not even be considered by women themselves as work. This is an important source of understatement of women's participation in the labour force in censuses and surveys.

Nevertheless, the primary responsibility of women in the area of reproduction makes them secondary workers in the area of social production. In consequence, women constitute a labour force with its own characteristics. The division of labour by gender not only results in the subordination of women in the domestic sphere - where their work is underestimated because it does not produce any exchange value - but also reinforces their subordination in the labour market.

However, the line which separates domestic from social activities is not clear-cut, since it refers to ideological appraisals which differ according to the country and levels of development, and which, therefore, show a number of ambiguities. These arise from lack of clarity in defining work and respond to various ideological perspectives. They become more evident when the topic of the informal sector is discussed. This is so because in referring to the informal sector, in most cases, the reference is to activities which are rooted in the diffuse separation of the domestic and social spheres.

B. Women in the labour force

1. Concepts and definitions

The concept of the labour force that emerged with the changes introduced by the United States census of 1940, which included the unemployed for the first time, confirmed a new way of assessing the labour force, which is defined as the population working or looking for work. This definition, which was elaborated by and is suited for a developed market economy, was transferred to countries which do not have totally integrated markets and where different modes of production are co-existent. The concept of a population of workers which is different from the general population implies a production system in which work is differentiated from other activities that satisfy life itself. This differentiation is not so clear-cut in less developed modes of production.

In fact, what defines the concept of the labour force, as Felicia Reicher Madeira states 2/, is the advancement of capitalism, that is, how many individuals have been incorporated into its growing trend of commercialization and monetization of social relations whose prototype is the sale of labour transformed into merchandise. In the mean time, market and money preoccupations transform individuals employed in activities which involve commercialization of products and remuneration into an entrepreneurial class responsible for social production, on whom most others are dependent, including most women.

The definition of economically active population used in surveys and censuses makes it difficult to adequately measure women's economic activity because of its special nature. Some of the difficulties are discussed below.

The first difficulty is definition of the boundary of what is considered production of goods and services. In general, work which produces goods and services is culturally defined as that which corresponds to social activities which are paid, continuous and full time. In this way, most of women's work is not adequately recorded to the extent that its basic characteristics are those of discontinuity linked to family life cycles, seasonality, especially in rural areas, and part-time in the traditional sectors of the economy, in family enterprises or through self-employment. 3/ Thus, the characteristics of women's work are closely linked to the informal sector of the economy.

Second, application of the definition does not take into account domestic work carried out within the household as work. This entails not recording an important number of activities which serve to reproduce the labour force and society as a whole. An ILO study indicates that, for eight countries in Latin America, more work is undertaken within the household than outside it. 4/ In terms of value, measurements suggest that domestic work may provide between one third and one half of families' monetary income. The figure is even greater in the case of poorer families.

Third, the definition of economic activity used thus far provides a poor measure of work which produces goods and services for own consumption. In general, activities which do not produce for the market may be one of three types: (a) direct production for own consumption, (b) processing of products for own consumption (grain grinding, preparation and preservation of food, processing of cheese, butter, and the like), and (c) activities for own use such as capital investment, especially in the area of construction and additions to own housing. According to international recommendations, all people involved in production for own consumption should be considered active "if such production comprises an important contribution to the total consumption of the family". 5/

In most of the economies of the region, production for own consumption is very high. Nor is production for own consumption only a rural phenomenon. It acquires important dimensions in urban areas. In Latin America, urban-rural differentials in the extent of monetization are extreme, and the variety of subsistence activities which can be performed in cities is even more considerable than in rural areas. Undoubtedly, undertaking numerous tasks in productive domestic activities is a mechanism of adaptation of low-income families in urban areas to a low daily minimum wage received by the family members with remunerated jobs. Depending on the level of income, cleaning house, minding children and preparing food are not the only domestic tasks that urban women perform. They may also devote themselves to mending clothes, tending animals and cultivating vegetables, gathering firewood and fetching water, and so on. The scope of these activities of the urban housewife is possibly narrower than that of the farm housewife but if their value is measured in comparison to the monetary value of these same services acquired in the market, the importance of domestic production in urban areas becomes unmistakeable. 6/

In Latin American economies, where the productive contribution of women is very large because the market has not yet had a strong impact, neither the destination of the product (consumption/sale) nor the separation between productive and domestic work is absolutely clear-cut. This fact prevents censuses and surveys from adequately measuring women's economic contribution since production for own consumption performed by women is not distinguishable by women themselves nor by interviewers from domestic activities which have been defined as non-economic.

2. Issues in implementation

Census information is processed according to individual variables and not household variables. This means that basic dimensions which affect the participation of women's labour such as the life cycle are not considered. The stage of the life cycle in which the family finds itself determines, for women, the maximum and minimum amount of work to be carried out and, from the point of view of the labour force concept, their greater or lesser "availability" for the labour market. In summary, it may be pointed out that, in the region, women's "availability" for participating in the formal labour market is typically highest when they are under 35 years old, single or separated, divorced or widowed, or highly educated (more than 10 years of study), and when they have no children. All of these variables of an individual nature can be related to the family life cycle, which is defined in terms of turning points in the development of the family unit.

These turning points may be grouped into three broad periods: (a) formation of couples and birth of first children; (b) period of couples with school-aged children; and (c) period of couples living alone when the children have married, have established other family units or have become financially independent by entering the labour market. These three stages (which can, in turn, be sub-divided into others) are not necessarily fulfilled in each family unit, as some families divorce (creating women heads of household) or do not have children or the children do not become independent even after becoming of age. This diversity of situations implies that, in each stage of the household life cycle, the amount of domestic and social work required will be different and will determine, to a large degree, the possibility of women becoming incorporated into the formal labour market. Consideration of the life cycle stage of the family is very important in the search for meaningful relationships accounting for the participation of women in the labour market.

However, censuses and surveys in the region consider that 10-15 years is the minimum age limit to be considered economically active. This means that important groups of children and young people who work in subsistence economies in both rural and urban areas remain uncounted. Likewise, the period of reference in which economic activity is investigated in censuses and surveys - generally the week prior to the interview - fails to include many activities performed by women which are of a seasonal or sporadic nature.

Moreover, the minimum amount of work-time required for a person to be considered economically active - and which, in the region, varies from country to country - leaves out many unpaid family members, especially women and children, in those countries where the limit is high (15 hours or more per week). This omission was revealed by the methodological survey conducted by the International Labour Organisation in Costa Rica in 1983. This survey included in the questionnaire a special module designed to investigate "marginal activities" performed by women. The data showed that these women work an average of less than 15 hours a week. The number of women in the group was four times the number of those who declared themselves as being own-account workers and who had been identified in the main part of the questionnaire. 7/ This means that an important group of women is not included in the economically active population and their economic contribution to the household or to the social product is unrecorded, also disturbing measurement of the magnitude of the underemployed population.

Analysis of the activities declared by this group of women in the Costa Rican survey showed that most of them could be classified within the informal sector, which points to the fact that, in household surveys and censuses, there is significant undercounting of women in informal activities. This confirms the view of PREALC and that of other research institutions that the characteristics of labour employed in the informal sector are opposite to those found in the formal sector. The majority of the workers in the informal sector are women (even when the measurement excludes domestic employees), the very young or old of both sexes, heads of households (especially women), the less-educated and migrants. 8/ In summary, what the studies show regarding the composition of the informal sector is that this sector complements the formal sector in the sense that the former overcomes the difficulties of incorporating labour into the latter.

Women's obligations in reproduction and family care strongly limit their participation in the labour market, especially in the case of poorer women. It is difficult for them to fill occupations requiring them to keep a set schedule, to leave the household and not to consider domestic work as their principal task. For this reason, women have a more important role in the informal labour market. A study conducted in the region by PREALC based on census samples (see A.4 of the annex) demonstrates that around 1980, excluding domestic service from the informal sector, the proportion of women employed in the urban informal sector fluctuated between 6 per cent (Panama) and 26 per cent (Paraguay). These magnitudes are considerably higher if we consider the participation of women in the invisible informal sector, in other words, that part of the informal sector which is not measured in censuses and surveys. 9/ This underreporting is due both to the form in which the labour force has been defined and to problems involved in the measurement of the economically active population.

In comparing the two main sources of information used to categorize the labour force, censuses and household surveys, one has to conclude that although the census allows for universality and simultaneity of the information which is much greater than that provided by household surveys, the latter lend greater depth and precision to the measurement.

For the study of the informal sector, household surveys are more useful instruments than censuses. This is because they scrutinize more carefully the characteristics of the activity and of employment and unemployment, interviewers are trained, the study of the secondary activities (which the censuses do not consider) is included, they provide greater possibilities to use the household as a unit of analysis and importantly, in most countries they are conducted at least once a year, permitting better follow-up of the condition of activity of the population over various periods. However, the special characteristics of women's work discussed in this section show that household surveys also have important limitations for adequate enumeration of the female population employed in the informal sector. This is a result of the invisibility of women's work and, especially, of much of women's work in the informal sector of the economy.

C.   Women in the informal sector of the economy and their importance in policy planning

One of the central objectives of adequate conceptualization and measurement of the informal sector, including both the population's participation in the sector and the product and income generated, is to support the design of policies which will effectively reach social and economic target groups.

The "welfarist" approach to planning in which important sectors of the population appear only as recipients of goods and services granted by the Government 10/ fails to consider, to the extent to which it follows the labour force approach, that large sectors of the population usually considered as not economically active produce an important proportion of household goods and services and also of social product.

For this reason, measurement of women's contribution within the informal sector will make it possible, from the perspective of social and economic planning, to overcome a series of deficiencies which have not allowed women to benefit from social and economic policies. In particular, the following aspects require recognition:

(a) Women's economic contribution through productive work and household work;

(b) The need to acquire a more thorough knowledge of the existing division of labour within the household, determining economic as well as extra-economic contributions of each member. Policies designed for household heads do not necessarily mean an improvement for all the members of the household;

(c) The fact that urban informal sectors tend to concentrate spatially, in "pockets of informality". Planning efforts and social services should therefore focus on such areas.

An adequate knowledge of women in the visible informal sector would permit specific policies geared towards the following:

(a) Generating technical assistance and financing for women employed in the informal sector. When credit is granted, it is generally assigned to the owner of the land in the case of small agricultural producers, or to the owners of family enterprises where other members of the household work. If recognition were given to the fact that groups of women who work in the informal sector are also household heads, it would be possible to design policies which would allow them access to credit lines to improve equipment and purchase raw materials;

(b) Training women employed in this sector to augment their productivity and efficiency and thereby increase their incomes;

(c) Implementing policies related to commercialization, purchase of production inputs, sub-contracting and the like. These policies are of special importance for women who work in activities such as food processing and sales, especially those without a fixed working location;

(d) Developing policies and programmes related to technological improvement to improve the organization of production and production techniques, and to provide technical assistance. Such policies are very important for artisan women;

(e) Implementing legal policies concerning salary standards, social security and working standards. Here, emphasis should be placed on putting out systems and contract and commission arrangements.

Workers in domestic service form another special group for which specific policies need to be designed. The extent of exploitation of these workers stems from the type of labour relationship, especially in the case of workers living in the household. 11/ This is because, despite the relatively high degree of formalization within the sector, since it is governed in most cases by a working contract, a minimum salary and social security, the salaries are the lowest in the registered labour sector. 12/

In view of the magnitude of the invisible informal sector, improved measurement of the sector could make a significant contribution to the design of adequate policies to permit women to work less strenuously and more efficiently in their productive chores, as for example:

(a) Policies to alleviate domestic chores, thus allowing women more time to carry out paid activities in the informal sector. Making day-care centres and schools available is essential to this objective;

(b) Occupational policies geared towards women who appear not to be economically active (housewives) but who are employed in the informal sector. Traditional employment and salary policies do not reach these women to the extent that they earn their income as own-account workers. Knowledge and measurement of the invisible informal sector is of utmost importance in the design of income and employment-generating policies to reach these women.

However, the design of policies designed to influence production in households is difficult. This poses the need to plan from the viewpoint of the household members themselves. In this sense, it is important to bear in mind the need to increase their potential as a group, by increasing their training and skills as well as their organization. But policies aimed at their potential for action as a group are difficult to implement, given the highly competitive nature of their activities. However, it is possible to identify areas in which adequate organization could enable households to negotiate with government agencies to obtain credits, inputs, training, and the like, which they are unable to achieve on an individual basis.

II. INVISIBILITY OF WORK PERFORMED BY WOMEN IN THE INFORMAL SECTOR

A. Concepts and definitions of the informal sector

The magnitudes of the informal sector and of the different segments of the labour market in general depend on the definitions adopted and the measurement possibilities provided by censuses and surveys. There are three main perspectives or approaches to measurement to be distinguished since they pose different measurement problems. 13/ The first emphasizes the heterogeneity of the economic system, including the production units, the type of activities which they perform and their growth potential. From this point of view, identification of the informal sector focuses on the differences between the enterprises or economic units of this sector compared to those of the formal sector. Characteristics highlighted in this perspective are the size, organization, type of technology and human resources predominant in each sector. In this approach, the main characteristics of the productive units in the informal sector are: small size (usually not more than four persons), intensive utilization of labour with minimal capital, use of simple technologies, ease of access to such units by workers and of the units to the market) predominance of the family-owned property system, use of unskilled labour, lack of organization and of formal contracts, and frequent use of payments in kind.

In general, measurement of the informal sector using the concepts based on productive units cannot be done with information on household characteristics; in fact, it can only be done on the basis of economic censuses and surveys. Nevertheless, some variables covered by household surveys allow identification of at least part of the labour force of this sector. For instance, regarding the size of the economic units, data can be used on the number of workers employed in the establishments where the respondents work. Depending on the definition adopted, it may be considered that employees working in economic units with less than five workers belong to the informal sector.

Another example is the use of data collected in some household surveys with regard to social security. Among paid workers, lack of contributions to the social security system may be used as an indicator of the informality of contractual relationships.

The second perspective is based on the labour market approach and focuses on "the employment issue, absorption of labour force, distribution of occupational opportunities and education, together with the factors determining the supply and demand of labour". 14/ In this case, segmentation of the labour market can be analysed by means of the individual characteristics which define the incorporation of the economically active population into production: employment status, industry and occupation. The criterion used to separate the formal sector from the informal one is the existence or not of salaried workers. In this perspective, the formal or modern sector comprises workers employed in productive units where the salary relationship to work is predominant. Residually, the informal sector is that in which individuals have no such relationship. In a formal sense, this distinction applies to all members of the labour force, regardless of the size of the productive unit or the industrial activity in which they work.

In this second approach, the key variables to define the informal sector are the activity status, which allows identification of the population employed, and employment status or occupational category, which establishes the type of work relationship, paid or unpaid.

The third perspective attempts to determine the differences in the levels of the population's income and welfare. The informal sector in this case is comprised of those individuals or families whose income is lower than a certain predetermined level "considered indispensable with regards to social welfare". 15/ In this approach, the unit of analysis is the household or family and not individuals considered separately. The emphasis is placed on survival strategies adopted by lower-income households as to the distribution of the family labour force and, in general, as to the distribution of different roles among household members. Studies on poverty which have quantified the number of such households and characteristics of different roles in them can be considered as typical of this perspective. While their purpose is not to identify the informal sector, most of these studies have shown that the majority of the people living in poor households work in this sector.

B.   Assessment of women's participation in the informal sector

All the available evidence from household surveys as to the magnitude of women's participation rates indicates, (a) that the definition of the informal sector currently used - the view of the labour market which mainly considers the occupational category and the condition of activity - underestimates the size of this sector, and (b) that this sector is a heterogeneous one as to qualification and income levels. It is thus appropriate to ask which type of activities in the informal sector can be better identified with household surveys. In other words, which are the most "visible" own-account and unpaid occupations in surveys, which sectors of economic activity have the highest concentrations of women registered as being in the informal sector and what are the main problems of the measurement procedures which are based on household surveys? 16/

It can be said that the economic activities of the informal sector registered in surveys correspond basically to the small production units and established commerce which could be called the "visible informal sector". Why are these activities "visible" in the statistical sense? In other words, why are these activities the ones better enumerated by the household surveys conducted in most Latin American countries?

Obviously the answer to this question cannot be found in the surveys themselves, but some hypotheses can be made using some indirect, empirical support provided by such surveys. The first consideration is that the informal sector detected is determined by the manner in which the condition of the activity is investigated. This is the key variable which defines who belongs to the economically active population and, within it, who are the employed persons. From this classification, one goes on to define the informal sector with the data obtained on the category of employment, occupation and other variables such as industry, size of the establishment, income, education, etc., according to the operational criterion adopted to define it. The hypothesis is that the method used to assess the condition of activity in household surveys, based on the labour force framework, underenumerates in a higher proportion women who carry out activities typical of the informal sector as compared with those working in the formal sector of the economy.

As stated in the preceding section, a limitation in assessing the activity status of women is the use of a short reference period, such as a week. If one of the characteristics of informal occupations is instability, with frequent turnover, surveys will tend to register the most stable activities of the informal sector such as small commercial establishments, and work done in small enterprises and artisan workshops, whose production and demand are not subject to seasonal fluctuations.

There are other difficulties associated with the manner in which activity status is investigated, which account for the understatement of women's work and have a bearing on measurement of the informal sector. One concerns the wording of questions or items used in questionnaires to classify the population as being economically active or not economically active. The cultural pattern which identifies work with paid activities performed outside the household, in institutions or firms, is evident in the answers given by women and results in underenumeration of the female economically active population. To the extent that women performing economic activities within the household - activities which are often difficult to separate from domestic work - declare that their main activity in the reference week is "domestic chores", they are classified as not economically active and, consequently, excluded from the sector. The same is true for women and for young and aged persons who declare themselves as being students, retired or in other categories of not economically active. There is, therefore, a hazy area comprising economic activities which should lead to the classification of women who carry out such activities in the informal sector. These are unpaid jobs carried out by own-account workers or family members who collaborate in small family enterprises.

Other difficulties in measuring the informal sector concern the nature of activities in the sector. Regardless of how the activity status is studied, jobs which are legally banned or those which are not socially accepted are generally not declared in censuses and household surveys and the persons who perform them appear as not economically active or as performing some other activity. This is the case for work performed on the streets by unlicensed peddlers, trash scavengers, prostitutes and other activities which may be considered illegal. However, according to the United Nations System of National Accounts, these are economic activities which, if enumerated, would be included in the informal sector.

Other activities in the informal sector are often not declared because they do not meet various legal requirements or pay municipal taxes, or are carried out in small enterprises and workshops established within households. This is another example of economic activities of small-scale production and trade termed "invisible".

Moreover, international occupational classifications pose limitations when used to describe a great number of activities carried out in the informal sector and not considered in the classifications. For instance, greater Santiago (Chile) has experienced the appearance of so-called "frequency controllers" (commonly referred to as "mutes"), generally young men, who inform bus drivers of the distance and the approximate time lag between their vehicle and the preceding one on the same route. This information is used in deciding to increase or slow down in order to get a larger number of passengers, and is provided for a fixed tariff.

It is a paid service and those who provide it are informal workers. Classifications in use do not consider this activity and, if it were declared in a survey, it would be very difficult to classify it in one of ISCO categories. It would possibly be considered an unidentified occupation or not classifiable. Based on this example, the inclusion of these residual groups in the informal sector does not seem inappropriate.

C. Typology of women's participation in the informal sector - visibility and invisibility

If the conceptual framework of the System of National Accounts, which gives a definition of economic and non-economic activities, is adopted, various criteria can be established to determine which of these activities constitute part of the informal sector. In preceding chapters, emphasis was placed on the definition of the informal sector based on the category of employment and on the limitation of this definition.

It is, therefore, necessary to make a prior typology of the informal sector, indicating the activities and individuals included in each category, to detect the main difficulties of measurement in each case, in view of the fact that they do not all pose the same problems. On this basis, it is possible to indicate how attempts can be made to overcome them.

The typology suggested in the present study assumes that the economic activities of the informal sector can be characterized according to various dimensions. The characteristics of each sub-sector (or type) are considered relative to the polar or extreme situations within each dimension, as they are combined in different ways in each individual activity. We are, therefore, dealing with a complex of analytical distinction to ascertain the different forms in which the activities of the informal sector take place in reality.

The following dimensions are considered:

(a) Physical location of work: the distance between the dwelling or household and the place where the activity is normally performed. On the one hand are the activities carried out inside the household (for example, the work of own-account tailors, done at home) and, on the other hand, small enterprises and services located outside the dwelling or household (for example, a fruit-stand at the market). This dimension is particularly important for the analysis of women's work in general and the participation of women in the informal sector;

(b) The extent to which the activity resembles domestic chores, that is, chores associated with family and household responsibilities. Polar situations are activities which are indistinguishable from domestic chores (taking care of children, food preparation, washing and ironing, etc.) and (at the other extreme) those which are typically deemed "work" - the production and sale of goods and services for the market, or paid work done outside the household. This dimension stresses the degree of statistical invisibility of work which women do in their own households or outside these and which, according to SNA, should be considered economic activity when done in exchange for compensation whether in cash or kind;

(c)   The destination of the goods and services produced.   The extreme situations are processing of primary goods and the production for own consumption, on the one hand, and market production, on the other.   SNA considers both under the concept of economic activity, whether or not an exchange of goods or services takes place in the market.   This dimension is important since the production of goods in the household, when carried out by women, tends not to be recorded in surveys or censuses, even in the most obvious cases where part of the production is sold in the market (for example, fabric for children's wear, part of which is sold);

(d)   The legality and degree of social acceptance of activities: This dimension not only emphasizes whether activities are illicit or not, a distinction made by SNA and for the treatment of which specific recommendations are made, but also the difficulty confronted by household surveys to record certain activities which, because they are illegal or deemed undignified or degrading, are normally not declared;

(e)   The strength of links with formal sector activities.   This dimension refers to the extent to which activities constitute part of the production network of economic units in the formal sector of the economy.   In the extreme case of maximum linkage are activities such as "maquila" and, in general, the prevailing practice of some enterprises of carrying out their production process outside factories and in households on the basis of the putting out system.   At the other extreme are those activities which have no economic links with the formal sector and for which estimation of their contribution to gross domestic product poses problems.   Examples are care of minors by women who do not reside in the same household and the processing of primary goods for own-consumption in the household;

(f)   The degree of technical and social complexity of the activity.   This dimension includes the degree of complexity of the chores performed and the extent to which these presuppose the participation of individuals in structured activities in which there is a technical and social division of labour.   At one extreme there is, for example, trading done on the streets by self-employed peddlers, those who manage their own resources and labour force without being subject to strict labour norms and standards such as working schedule, quality control and the like.   At the other extreme is work done in small workshops and micro-enterprises where activities are carried out within the framework of organized labour relationships;

(g)   The stability of activities over time.   This dimension considers whether the activity performed is subject to variations over time as a result of market conditions or because of the nature of the activity itself.   Its purpose is to distinguish those types of activities whose instability over time makes it more probable for a person to be classified as not economically active as a result of short reference periods, the month of the year in which the survey is taken, or the manner in which questions are asked.   An example is the sale of products in fairs or markets only on weekends.   If during five of the seven days of the week the person performs "domestic chores", it is highly probable that this person will declare himself or herself as not economically active, implicitly adopting a criterion of principal activity performed.   If the questionnaire does not consider all the activities performed during the reference week, the work done on the remaining two days will be overlooked, as will the contribution this person makes to the national product and to household income.

On the basis of these dimensions the following typology of women's participation in the informal sector can be elaborated:

(a) Visible informal sector;

(i) Private employers and employees in small industrial enterprises, commercial establishments and repair workshops;

(ii) Own-account workers and all family members involved in industrial, commercial and service activities for the market, working outside the home at fixed premises;

(iii) Own-account workers and unpaid family workers producing and selling goods for the market and working at home;

(iv) Economic activities carried out on behalf of firms in the formal sector and performed at home without salaried workers being hired formally. This subsector includes "maquila" and putting out jobs carried out by household members, working as own-account workers or unpaid family helpers;

(b) Own-account street workers without fixed premises, including petty trade and both legal and illegal economic activities:

(i) Street vendors of food and other manufactured goods purchased for resale or sold on behalf of firms;

(ii) Personal services offered by own-account workers. This includes shoe-shine boys, unlicensed parking attendants and night watchmen hired by private individuals;

(iii) Activities involving the salvaging of goods for resale: collection of newspapers, bottles and other similar "door to door" activities, and searching for items on the streets in order to sell them;

(iv) Prostitution, begging and illegal acquisition of goods by theft or robbery for subsequent sale;

(c) Invisible informal sector: this subsector includes economic activities which are normally performed by women and which do not appear in the statistics produced by surveys and censuses for three main reasons:

(i) Failure to declare economic activities which resemble domestic tasks, due to the cultural tendency of interviewers and respondents to associate work with full-time paid activities outside the home;

(ii) Failure to record economic activities as a result of incorrect application of the precedence rule according to which activity status has priority over inactive status. This rule establishes that, whatever the duration of the work carried out during the reference period, the individual must be counted as part of the labour force; thus, if the survey does not investigate activities performed by individuals declaring themselves to be inactive, they will not be recorded;

(iii) Failure to record economic activities performed outside the reference period;

(d) Domestic service:

(i) Resident domestic employees, i.e., those performing domestic tasks in exchange for a wage and usually living in the household they serve;

(ii) Non-resident domestic employees, i.e., those women who provide paid services on an own-account basis in one or more households and do not live in them.

III. MEASUREMENT OF THE INFORMAL SECTOR USING CENSUSES AND SURVEYS

The two preceding chapters discuss the main constraints found in population censuses and household surveys in measuring the participation of women in economic activity and the even greater difficulties which arise in measuring their participation, income and contribution to production in the informal sector. With these limitations in mind, the present chapter points out ways of using these two basic sources of information to study the participation of women in the informal sector. Some suggestions are also made to improve measurement and analysis of the informal sector using data from household surveys and censuses by better identification of target groups, for the design and implementation of economic and social policies geared towards improving conditions of life and work in the sector.

A. Population censuses

1. Measurement of the informal sector with census-based data

Latin American population censuses, especially those taken in the 1970s and 1980s, have served as a basic source of information for a great many studies on demographic and economic phenomena. Using various analytical and methodological approaches and with various objectives in mind, research has been conducted on fertility, mortality, migration, participation in economic activity, social structure, educational level, quantification and description of poverty, among others. This profusion of studies based on censuses has been closely linked to increases in the capacity for processing the information from censuses or census samples in countries throughout the region. This greater capacity has been augmented by the introduction of computerized systems for the exploitation of data bases in statistical offices and institutes, a circumstance which has given researchers more access to the data collected in censuses and expedited publication of preliminary data based on census samples.

The Latin American Demographic Centre (CELADE) has played a very important role in this field since the early 1970s with the creation of a data bank of files containing census samples and, in some cases, complete censuses of the majority of the countries in Latin America and the Caribbean. These data are available to users on magnetic tapes or from special tabulations which can be obtained on request from CELADE. 17/

However, in spite of the existence of these data bases and rapid access to census information at relatively low cost, these sources have not been extensively used to measure and analyse the informal sector. It was only starting in 1986 that the ILO Regional Employment Programme for Latin America and the Caribbean (PREALC), availing itself of census-based microdata for a significant number of countries in the region, requested special tabulations for the purpose of analysing the evolution of different segments of the labour market over the 1960-1980 period and exploring the relationships between the informal sector of the economy and a series of variables at the individual level which characterize labour market segmentation as a function of labour supply. It could be said that this represents the first detailed analysis of the informal sector with disaggregated census data in the perspective of an international comparison of the changes which have taken place over the last two decades in various Latin American countries.

Although it is not within the scope of the present report to give a detailed description of the main conclusions of this research, it is mentioned here because it constitutes a good example of the uses which can be made of census microdata and also because it serves as a reference framework for highlighting the usefulness of census data available in the region and to show the possibilities of measuring the informal sector with census-based data.

Table A.4 (a) of the annex indicates how the segments of the labour market can be delineated according to the definition of the economically active population used in the censuses. The same table shows that access to microdata and the possibility of making special cross-tabulations allow several distinctions to be made within the economically active population, which are not possible when working with published census data. Economic variables in the censuses of the six countries considered allows the use of a common definition for the informal sector. The definition is the one used in many studies when there is no information available on the characteristics of the economic units or on income levels of the population. Moreover, it is thus possible to classify the population employed in the formal and informal sectors by industry and to separate domestic service from the remaining activities. The population employed in agriculture is divided into two subsectors, traditional and modern, and the classification of the economically active population is completed with the inclusion of unemployed persons.

Table A.4 (b) of the annex shows the relative magnitude of each of the segments defined and its composition by sex. Data are expanded sample figures from censuses of six Latin American countries taken in the 1970s and the 1980s.

It must be pointed out that, regardless of the measurement problems of the activity status which population censuses pose - more serious in the case of women, for informal activities and in the agricultural sector - such an information source continues to be irreplaceable for making international comparisons and examining long-term trends.

The PREALC study illustrates the potential usefulness of census data when there is access to microdata and three or more variables can be studied according to specific research or policy design purposes. In general, these tabulations are not available in the census publications provided by statistical offices. In the PREALC study, a uniform set of tabulations permits a very detailed analysis of the different sectors of the labour market. Variables considered are: residence of the population (metropolitan areas, capital cities, urban and rural areas); age (various age groups are distinguished, allowing identification of the youngest and oldest population in the informal sector); sex; relation to the head of household (it is possible to determine economic participation of head of household, spouse, children and other relatives and non-relatives of the head of household in the different sectors and to show the participation of the secondary labour force in the informal sector); education (various educational levels are established on the basis of the number of years of attendance at the primary, secondary and university levels, to analyse the relative educational attainment of the labour force in the formal and informal sectors).

Some of the cross-tabulations include four variables: residence, sex, age, and relation to head of household. Thus, it is possible to analyse, for instance, how the informal sector changed over the last decade in the metropolitan areas of the six countries under consideration, with an indication of women's participation in a secondary labour force in specific age groups. This type of information is particularly important in assessing the characteristics of this sector and its significance as a target group of economic and social policies.

In the following paragraphs, other ways of using the census which are of particular interest for the study of women's participation in the informal sector are described.

2. Relationship between individual characteristics and household characteristics and construction of household records

Most of the research based on census data, including that utilizing data bases, has analysed the personal characteristics of the population under study without establishing relations between such individual characteristics and their households' characteristics. Very few attempts have been made to link information on members of the same household. To some extent, this is because conceptual frameworks have mainly been concerned with analysis of individual behaviour in the labour market. However, it has been increasingly recognized that the household is the relevant unit of analysis for the study of the female labour force and for the design of employment policies.

The decision of whether or not to participate in the labour market and the possibilities of satisfying the needs of its different members depend on the decisions adopted in the household as a function of its resources, including number of persons of working age, education levels and skills, capital resources and the expectations of its members. Decisions with regard to which members of the family participate in the labour market and how and when they do so have come to be considered part of household survival strategies, particularly in lower-income strata.

Regarding participation of women in the informal sector, the need to establish relationships between their individual characteristics and those of other household members is even clearer. Numerous studies have demonstrated that, from the labour force point of view or supply, women's participation in economic activity is strongly conditioned by their obligation to perform domestic chores. 18/ In addition, studies have emphasized that the participation of women in the informal sector is closely linked to the characteristics of participation of household heads or of the main economic provider, which may facilitate participation of spouses and daughters as own-account workers or as unpaid family members if the head of the household is already in the informal sector, or promote the participation of women in this sector if the main household provider is unemployed. The latter situation characterizes the behaviour of the secondary labour force in periods of crisis during which there is an increase in unemployment in the formal sector.

Census data bases permit the creation of computational records of households which can link the characteristics of individuals with their household and housing characteristics. In this way, it is possible to cross-tabulate both types of variables, thereby significantly enriching the analysis.

Two examples illustrate this point. First, participation of women in the urban informal sector is closely linked to the presence of other household members in that sector. There is evidence that when the head of household carries out activity in the informal sector, the women of the household tend to participate in the same sector. In this case, the household records make it possible to analyse the relationship between the economic activities of heads of household and of spouses. A possible conclusion is that any design of policies geared towards improving the situation of women participating in the informal sector must take into account intra-family situations, and the contribution made by women to total household income.

Second, it has been pointed out that assessment of economic activity in rural areas through censuses does not adequately detect the economic participation of women in activities related to the production of goods and the processing of primary products for own-consumption. This is reflected in the low female participation rates reported by censuses and in the small number of rural women classified as unpaid family workers. The construction of a household record permits estimating the number of women of working age residing in households where the head and other active members are rural workers in the traditional agricultural sector. Based on this information, estimates can be made of women who declare themselves not economically active but who participate in the production of goods for own-consumption.

It should be noted that one of the reasons that this type of analysis of census data was not previously made was the difficulty of access to the appropriate data bases for computerized processing. At present, the existence of data banks such as that of CELADE and the availability of statistical computing packages suited to the construction of household records permits making this type of analysis at relatively low cost. Widely available statistical programmes include among their routines the linking of data on individuals in the same household. This permits users to create files suited to their own analyses. The experience accumulated by CELADE and by the ECLAC Statistical Division in processing census and household surveys in the region indicates that when microdata are available, complex tabulations may be made which include four or more simultaneous variables, combining the individual characteristics of those interviewed with aggregate household variables. Limitations of this type of analysis basically result from the size of the samples and the restrictions imposed by a small number of cases when making generalizations for the entire population.

3. Using census data for small geographical areas

Recently the Latin American Demographic Centre initiated a project designed to make it easier to obtain census tabulations for small, previously delimited geographic areas within each country. This project is based on a study carried out in 1983 with the support of Canada's International Development Research Center. This study demonstrated that many national statistical agencies in Latin America and the Caribbean confronted great difficulties in supplying governmental and private organizations with the geographically disaggregated population data required for infrastructure planning for the provision of social services. [19/] To facilitate users' access to disaggregated census data, CELADE implemented a microcomputer-based approach for producing small area tabulations from census microdata, rapidly, at low cost and without programmer assistance. [20/]

The system, called REDATAM, offers many advantages and opens new possibilities for the exploitation of population censuses. The processing of complete census information for predetermined areas or census zones, according to users' needs, is envisaged. Given the purpose of the analysis, a selection can be made of the

geographical units of interest and the tabulations prepared on this basis. Besides
the reduction in costs and processing time, REDATAM provides a further advantage.
It permits studies based on complete enumeration, avoiding the limitations of
census samples, which generally pose serious problems because of the small number
of cases for analysis. At the same time, it permits studies based on those
demographic and economic characteristics of the population in which the user is
interested, without need of processing the complete census.

The REDATAM system is designed so as to permit the user to define the context
of studies based on census cartography and on the definition of census areas used
in the census. In this manner, special tabulations of individual, household or
housing characteristics can be made for a set of census areas which offer certain
common traits and which define, for instance, a neighbourhood within a specific
area or district of the country. To the degree that areas of interest do not
normally correspond to administrative or political limits, the system allows users
to construct their real zone of interest by disaggregating the census information
corresponding to small areas, such as the segments of census enumeration. 21/

The study of the participation of women in the informal sector can be
substantially improved with microcomputer access to the data base of the REDATAM
system. For instance, it is possible to think of in-depth studies of households
located in rural and urban areas in which agricultural activity is linked to
different types of crops or in which specific types of land-holding structures
exist. In defining these specific areas, agricultural and livestock censuses or
surveys can be used to provide data on the characteristics of agricultural
holding. In this manner, census data can be related to data from other sources of
information. The comparative study of women's labour force participation as a
function of the characteristics of the households where they reside, together with
the particularities of agricultural and livestock related activities (for instance,
whether salaried labour or the presence of temporary workers is predominant or
not), can shed some light on the ways women participate in agricultural activity.
Likewise, it is possible to establish relationships between women's participation
in production for own-consumption and estimates of the value of agricultural
production reported in agricultural surveys or censuses. This type of study may
serve to improve the evaluation of the quality of census data when these are
compared with data from other sources.

In urban or metropolitan areas, access to disaggregated data and the
definition of ad hoc geographical areas permit focusing on the use of census data
corresponding to neighbourhoods or city districts in which the lower-income
population is concentrated and on those where it is more likely that women are
participating in the informal sector of the economy. The enormous spatial
segregation of the population in Latin American metropolises facilitates the
identification of those city zones where the population resides in poverty
conditions and thus of the target groups of social policies.

These focused studies can also serve to design experimental surveys and to
apply special questionnaires geared towards ascertaining information on women in
the informal sector, avoiding costly sample designs which are frequently
insufficient to study the characteristics of the population which live in specific
geographical areas.

4. Use of the census programme for data collection experiments

The carrying out of censuses and all the related activities that a census operation entails provide a good opportunity for statistical offices to plan and execute experimental censuses and surveys to collect information about certain topics in some specific geographical areas or to test new questions or items designed to collect information already contemplated in census questionnaires in a different manner. Resources invested in the census operation, preparation of interviewers, the massive campaigns which are generally carried out in order to obtain the collaboration of the population, as well as the compulsory nature of the operation, are all conditions which make the census a favourable occasion to perform experimental censuses and surveys.

An example worth mentioning here is the Experimental Population and Household Census of Costa Rica conducted in 1983 in a district of San Juan, San Ramón, as a preparatory activity for the 1984 national census. On that occasion, it was decided to study in more detail those activities performed by women considered inactive (according to definitions normally used) and who contribute to personal and household income and well-being. The purpose was to determine to what extent the typical census questionnaire does not ascertain economic activity performed by women who declare themselves to be inactive. A special questionnaire was prepared and applied to all women 12 years old and over within the District of San Juan and who had previously declared themselves occupied with domestic chores, or students, retired women or women not economically active. 22/ These women were asked if they had performed during that week and during the previous 12 months one or more of a list of 21 agricultural, artisan, commercial or service activities which were indicated on the questionnaire, the number of hours devoted to them and whether the job had been performed within or outside the household. 23/ The main characteristics of the women studied are summarized in annex tables A.5 (a) to A.5 (d). Relevant portions of the questionnaire used in the survey are shown in A.5 (e).

The main conclusions of the study are:

(a) The consideration of economic activities carried out by women classified as not economically active, according to the usual measurement methods, significantly increases participation rates; the comparison of rates according to the usual and modified computations shows an increment from 38.2 per cent to 48.3 per cent in urban areas and from 22.5 per cent to 45.3 per cent in the rural areas of the District of San Juan;

(b) Most of the activities declared are performed within the household or farm when the previous week is considered as the reference period, while these are carried out in very similar proportions within and outside the household when the reference period is the previous year. This can be explained in terms of the participation of women in coffee harvesting, an activity which is limited to a specific period of the year;

(c) On average, women in urban areas worked 18 hours a week and those in rural areas worked 12 hours, which indicates the importance of the contribution that women make to household income. If not included in national accounts this might represent a significant under-estimation of the national product;

(d) The activities declared by "inactive" women can all be classified in the urban informal sector (artisanry and family industry, commerce and services) or in the traditional agricultural sector, except for participation in harvesting coffee and other agricultural products, which they perform as paid workers, in which case they could be classified within the modern agricultural sector.

In general, it is suggested that special questionnaires in censuses be used for in-depth research of topics such as women's participation in the urban informal sector and in the so-called, traditional agricultural sector. Researching these topics, through the application of special questionnaires to the residents of pre-selected urban and rural areas, permits comparisons between responses to questions applied to the entire population and those coming from special questionnaires. If the selection of geographical areas for these studies takes account of such criteria as representativity and coverage, results could serve to permit generalizations to be made at the country level.

B. **Household surveys and the construction of household variables and tabulations for analysis of women's participation in the informal sector**

Some of the potential of household surveys to measure women's participation and income in the informal sector is described in this section. Four examples are given, each illustrating the construction of new variables using survey information and the elaboration of some tabulations for their analysis.

In all cases, access to survey microdata is assumed, as these examples consist of variables and tabulations which are not available in publications normally provided by statistical offices.

1. **Construction of a household classification and analysis of family income levels**

The first example illustrates a way of approaching the topic of women as household heads and the participation of women in occupations typical of the formal and informal sectors in different income strata. It has been stated that the lack of detailed data on the characteristics of women and of female-headed households reduces the efficiency of censuses and of most surveys to answer questions concerning the level of income of households under female heads and of women who assume such household headship. 24/ Although household surveys do not study household headship in this way, and women's role is only registered in the "relation to the head of household" variable, it is possible to identify households where no male spouse exists and consequently where effective headship is exercised by a woman.

One way of identifying these households is by means of a household classification which groups households according to the presence (absence) of various household members (spouse of head, children, other relatives and non-related members of head) as follows:

Spouse	Children	Other members	Type of household
No	No	No	Heads alone
No	No	Yes	Heads with other members
No	Yes	No	Heads with children
No	Yes	Yes	Heads with children and other members
Yes	No	No	Couples/no children
Yes	No	Yes	Couples with other members
Yes	Yes	No	Nuclear households
Yes	Yes	Yes	Extended and compound households

Clearly, the women-headed households are concentrated in the first four household types where there is no spouse. Data resulting from the Gran Buenos Aires Survey (October 1980) showed the following household distribution according to this classification:

Type of household	Percentage of households	Percentage of women heads of households
Heads alone	10.4	66.2
Heads with other members	8.1	80.8
Heads with children	4.9	47.0
Heads with children and other members	1.4	81.0
Couples/no children	16.8	0.9
Couples with other members	2.5	3.5
Nuclear households	47.2	0.8
Extended and compound households	8.7	1.8
TOTAL	100.0	17.7

Number of households: 2,647,400

A classification such as this permits identification of female-headed households and analysis of their internal composition according to their members, their activity, condition and participation in the formal and informal sector.

It has frequently been stated that female-headed households are an important target group since differences between households under the headship of men and women are being increasingly recognized. This is a relevant issue for social policy design, especially those differences referring to levels of family income and well-being, and which can be analysed using total family income to classify households. This variable can be constructed adding primary income, property income and current transfers received by all household members. Family income can then be dealt with as an additional individual variable referring to all persons, whether or not they are recipients of income. In the present example, households were classified into five groups according to the level of family income, to compare the types of occupations of women non-heads of households pertaining to the poorest 20 per cent and the richest 20 per cent of the households.

Occupations were classified as formal or informal, corresponding to typical activities in each sector. Table 9 shows the differences in the percentage of women non-heads of household employed in the informal sector (owners of retail businesses, peddlers, artisans in manufacturing industries, tailors and seamstresses, own-account workers in personal services, cooks, laundresses) according to the income strata of the household where they reside. In the three cities considered (Bogotá, Lima, Caracas) no less than 75 per cent of the women non-heads of household pertaining to the poorest 20 per cent declared having occupations typical of the informal sector, while the proportion which performed these occupations 25/ in the richest 20 per cent varies between 13.3 per cent and 19.1 per cent.

On the other hand, this example shows that family income, an indicator of the socio-economic status of the household, strongly conditions the access of women to occupations in the formal sector, occupations which are better paid and which make it necessary to rely on certain household services which facilitate working outside the household.

Table 9. Occupations of women non-heads of household, by family income group

(Percentage)

| Occupation | COLOMBIA | | PERU | | VENEZUELA | |
| | (Bogota, 1982) | | (Lima-Callao, 1982) | | (Caracas, 1982) | |
	Poorest 20 per cent	Richest 20 per cent	Poorest 20 per cent	Richest 20 per cent	Poorest 20 per cent	Richest 20 per cent
Formal sector occupation a/	21.8	77.2	15.1	79.8	15.4	86.4
Informal sector occupation b/	74.9	19.1	83.0	17.5	80.9	13.3
Other occupation c/	3.3	3.7	1.9	2.7	3.7	0.3
	100.0	100.0	100.0	100.0	100.0	100.0
Number of women (thousands)	(102.8)	(73.3)	(104.7)	(77.9)	(53.9)	(63.1)

Source: United Nations, ECLAC, "La mujer en el sector popular urbano: América Latina y el Caribe" (LC/G.1326), October 1984, pp. 275, 323, 341.

a/ Includes major groups 1, 2, 3 and 4 (except 4-1, 4-5, 4-9) of the International Standard Classification of Occupations (ISCO), Revised Edition, 1968.

b/ Includes groups 4-1, 4-5 and 4-9; major group 5 and groups 7-7, 7-9 and 8-0 of ISCO.

c/ Includes rest of major group 7, 8 and 9 and major group X of ISCO.

2. Relationships between women's employment characteristics and family circumstances

The following example shows the possibility of linking individual variables (the type of women's participation in the labour market) with household variables which describe different family situations. The example refers to the construction of variables which indicate that women's status in employment is very frequently conditioned by family situations which make it difficult to perform full-time jobs outside the households as salaried workers.

Information on marital status and the construction of a household classification make it possible to identify married women with or without children 26/ and to distinguish family situations which pose different degrees of difficulty for the performance of both domestic chores and work outside the household as salaried workers.

Table 10 shows data on a household survey carried out in Argentina (Gran Buenos Aires, 1980). Three extreme family situations are considered: single women without children residing in any of the household types defined in the first example; married women who live in households without children; and married women who live in households with children. In the last two groups, only those women living in "nuclear households" were considered. These are households with no other adult women who can help with domestic chores facilitating the participation of other women in economic activities outside the household.

As can be seen in table 10, the type of labour participation of women varies in the three family situations. As family situations changed to those which require a greater amount of domestic work - from single to married women and from married women with no children to married women with children - the proportion of those who participate in economic activity decreases sharply (from 84.5 per cent among single women to 27.9 per cent among married with children), and among those who declare themselves economically active, the percentage of self-employed increases, while the proportion among single women is 1 out of 10, and that for married women with children in the household amounts to 4 out of 10. Self-employment is largely carried out by women who have to cope with family situations which make remunerated work outside the household difficult.

Table 10 also shows that problems in measuring the participation of women in the labour force are concentrated among married women with children, a group in which only one out of every four women was counted as being economically active by the survey. It is on this group that attention should be focused to improve the assessment of woman's participation in the labour force by studying the economic activities of those who declare themselves as being "inactive".

Table 10. Employment status of working women 25-44 years, by family situation, Greater Buenos Aires, 1982

(Percentage)

			FAMILY SITUATION	
			Married women	
Employment status	Total	Single women	Without children	With children b/
Non-wage-earners	27.8	11.0	21.5	42.9
Own-account workers a/	25.7	10.5	16.2	40.0
Unpaid family workers	2.1	0.5	5.3	2.9
Wage-earners	72.2	89.0	78.5	57.1
In public sector	21.5	21.5	27.9	20.0
In private sector	50.7	67.5	50.6	37.1
TOTAL	100.0	100.0	100.0	100.0
Participation rate c/	41.9	84.5	60.5	27.9
Number of women (thousands)	(357.3)	(140.9)	(41.0)	(175.4)

Source: United Nations, ECLAC, Análisis estadístico de la situación de la mujer en países de América Latina a través de las encuestas de hogares, LC/R/418 (Sem. 24/2), p. 59.

a/   Includes employers.

b/   Refers to one or more children living in the household.

c/   Working women aged 25-44 years as percentage of all women of same age group.

The tabulation which has been used as an example can be supplemented for a more adequate analysis of the informal sector by including information about such aspects as average family income, number and age of the children and access to domestic services.

3. Relating characteristics of household members

Highlighted below are the possibilities which household surveys offer for analysis of women's participation in the informal sector based on the construction of variables which relate characteristics of different members within the same household.

The design of economic and social policies geared towards supporting the activities of those who participate in the informal sector means identifying the type of family members who participate in it. In the case of women, relevant information must refer to their position in the household and permit analysis of their relationship to the head of the household.

Table 11 shows that most of the women who work in the informal sector (own-account workers and unpaid family members, except professionals and technicians) are heads of household (22.2 per cent) or spouses of the head (55.4 per cent), while the highest proportion of those who work in the formal sector are daughters of the household heads (41.2 per cent). This raises the question: to what extent does the work of women in the informal sector take place in the same activities as performed by the heads of household. In order to make this type of analysis, it is necessary to relate, within each household, the activity of the head to that corresponding to other members. Table 12 also takes into account the status in employment of the heads of household, 80 per cent of which are men, and the branch of industry where women work, except women heads of household. The data, which refer to urban areas in Chile, show that two out of every three women in the informal sector live in households in which the head works on his own account, while in the formal sector only one out of every six women are found in that situation. Women tend to participate in informal economic activities in households where the head works in that sector.

This type of tabulation may be supplemented with information on income by sex and through a more exhaustive examination of the occupations of women in households in which the head or other economically active members participate in the informal sector.

Table 11.   Working women aged 15 years and over, by sector and
relation to head of household, Chile, urban areas,
1984

| Relation to head of household | Employment sector | |
	Informal a/	Formal
	(Percentage)	
Head of household	22.2	12.0
Spouse	55.4	22.8
Daughter	13.4	41.2
Other relatives	7.8	9.1
Non-relatives	1.2	14.9
TOTAL	100.0	100.0

Source: Instituto Nacional de Estadistica, Chile, Special
tabulation of National Employment Survey (October-December 1984).

a/   Includes own-account and unpaid family workers, except
own-account professionals and technicians.

Table 12.   Working women 15 years and over, by sector and
employment status of head of household, Chile,
urban areas, 1984

| Employment status of head of household | Employment sector | |
	Informal a/	Formal
	(Percentage)	
Employers	3.9	4.2
Employees	24.8	60.4
Own-account workers	61.5	17.2
Unemployed	9.8	18.2
TOTAL b/	100.0	100.0

Source: Instituto Nacional de Estadística, Chile, Special
tabulation of National Employment Survey (October-December 1984).

a/   Includes own-account and unpaid family workers, except
own-account professionals and technicians.

b/   Women heads of household (22.2 per cent) not included.

4. Estimation of undeclared income of women

This section describes a procedure to measure the underestimation of income of women in typical informal activities generally not declared in household surveys. It attempts to demonstrate that measurement of the "currently active population" (labour force approach) used in household surveys underenumerates a very high proportion of women performing economic activities, which is translated into a considerable underestimation of income and of their contribution to the gross product.

The data come from the ILO methodological survey in Costa Rica (June-October 1983). 27/ This survey provides information on status in employment and number of hours worked per week by currently economically active women. The survey also recorded the number of women who indicated their participation in "marginal" economic activities and the average number of weekly hours in those jobs.

Table 13 shows that, in the four periods during which information was collected, a very high proportion of these activities were in agricultural work and practically all of them were carried out on an own-account basis. Using the relationship between the average number of hours put in by own-account workers and those occupied in marginal activities, the number of "equivalent occupied own-account workers" can be calculated. This number represents between 52 per cent (information for the September-October 1983 period) and 88 per cent (June-July 1983) of the total number of occupied women in this category of employment.

The methodological survey does not provide data on population income. The computation of income underestimation attributable to marginal activities must therefore be made by resorting to some type of assumption on the relationship between the income averages for both groups of women. The three final items in table 13 indicate the percentages of underestimation, using three different hypotheses. These percentages range from 33.7 per cent (simple average of the four survey periods), assuming that income from marginal activities is equal to half the income of own-account women workers, and 67.4 per cent, assuming that there are no income differences between the two groups. The average percentage of underestimation of all measurements totals 50 per cent of the income of own-account women. These estimates indicate the need for surveys to research more thoroughly the activity of "inactive" women, incorporating into the questionnaire items especially directed to ascertaining the type of tasks performed and the number of hours put into such activity.

The same method can be used to make a monetary appraisal of the work performed by unpaid family workers when information is available to assign values by means of the input method (using the salary of an equivalent worker) or according to outputs (using the market price for equivalent goods and services obtained).

In this case, the income generated by unpaid family workers could be estimated by making reference to income declared by own-account workers, but linking such activities to the income generated by family enterprises within the same household. To this end, research must be conducted on the number of weekly hours which unpaid family members work, and this information registered in the survey, even when the number of hours worked is fewer than the minimum time working limit employed to meet the definition of economically active.

Table 13.   Income earned by own-account females engaged in
            marginal activities as a proportion of income
            earned by own-account working women, Costa Rica,
            June-October 1983

	June-July	July-Aug.	Aug.-Sept.	Sept-Oct.	Average all periods
			(Reference period:	one week)	
Number of employed own-account females a/	58	27	49	48	–
Average hours worked per week b/	28.2	35.1	24.6	28.5	–
Number of females engaged in:					
"marginal activities"	198	138	143	131	–
(in agriculture)	(118)	(105)	(104)	(85)	–
Average hours worked by women engaged in "marginal activities"	7.3	4.9	5.0	5.0	–
Percentage wholly own-account	92.9	99.3	100.0	96.9	–
Number of equivalent own-account occupied females c/	51	19	29	25	–
Ratio between average income of women in "marginal activities" and average income of own-account women (under-estimation of income earned by women in "marginal activities" as a percentage of total income earned by own-account women), on basis of three assumptions:					
Assumed ratio 1:1 informal/formal	87.9	70.4	59.2	52.1	67.4
Assumed ratio 3:4 informal/formal	65.9	52.8	44.4	39.1	50.6
Assumed ratio 1:2 informal/formal	44.0	35.2	29.6	26.1	33.7

Simple average of all percentages: 50.5

(Source and footnotes on following page)

(Source and footnotes to table 13)

_____

    <u>Source</u>: Calculations based on figures reported in ILO/DGEC (Costa Rica) Methodological Survey on the Measurement of Employment, Unemployment, Underemployment and Income 1983-1984, Costa Rica, June-October 1983, Basic Tables, Questionnaire C, Tables C18 and C31.

    <u>a</u>/   Includes unpaid family workers.

    <u>b</u>/   Weighted average of own-account and unpaid family workers.

    <u>c</u>/   Calculated as: $\dfrac{3 \times \text{line } 5}{\text{line } 2}$

IV. SUGGESTIONS FOR MEASURING WOMEN'S ROLE IN THE INFORMAL SECTOR BY USING HOUSEHOLD SURVEYS

The following suggestions on how to improve measurement of the informal sector using information from household surveys are based on the characteristics of the informal sector described in chapter III. They take account of what it seems feasible to achieve through the survey programmes of the countries of the region. The main objectives of these survey programmes are to examine the situation of the population over time in terms of levels of employment, unemployment and income.

Within these survey programmes, the following approaches can be considered:

(a) Include additional questions directed to some sub-group of the population which is potentially economically active or in the labour force, without introducing major changes in the design of the survey or the questionnaires used. For example, questions can be added concerning the size of establishments or economic units or to determine whether the activity declared is performed within or outside the household;

(b) Modify the formulation and sequence of the questions which determine the activity status of the population. For instance, it can be determined whether women who declare themselves as "housewives" have also performed economic activities, in order to include them in the economically active population. Their activities over a longer period of time, such as a month or a year instead of a week, can also be considered;

(c) Include in some rounds of a continuous household survey a special module to study the informal sector in depth, as has been done for other topics such as health and labour force qualifications in some surveys similar to the National Family Budget Survey (Pesquisa Nacional por Muestra de Domicilio) in Brazil.

A. Characteristics of women's role in the informal sector and ways of measuring it

1. Visible informal sector

Measurement of the visible informal sector can be undertaken without modifying the process used to determine the currently economically active population in most household surveys. It is assumed that people who form part of this sector are properly enumerated in the sequence of questions on the activity status during the reference week, so that identification of the visible informal sector can be achieved with questions on the characteristics of the establishments where women work. These questions can be used to study this sector according to varying definitions. They will be asked of people who state they were economically active in the reference period. Consequently, both paid and unpaid workers are included.

With national household surveys, it is convenient to separate the urban informal sector from the economic activities of the traditional agricultural sector which should be treated with specific questions within a specially designed module. In such cases, questions on the characteristics of establishments require an additional "filter" to select those employed outside agriculture (ISIC's divisions 1 and 2) to continue with the identification of the non-agricultural urban and rural labour force in each sector.

This process was used by the Methodological Survey on the Measurement of Employment, Unemployment and Underemployment sponsored by ILO and conducted by the National Statistics and Census Office of Costa Rica in 1983. 28/ This survey distinguishes between the formal and informal sectors on the basis of the following criteria:

(a) Whether or not the establishment has complied with legal registration requirements needed to operate, these registers differ from the permits issued by local authorities;

(b) The levels of organization of the economic units such as registration of workers in the Social Security and billing of goods and services provided by them;

(c) The size of the economic unit in terms of the number of persons occupied;

(d) The levels of technology considering the type of energy used. 29/

These criteria were translated into five questions in a special block 30/ used to classify workers into formal and informal sectors and, within the informal sector, in the registered, the non-registered, and a combined sub-sector. 31/ The advantage of the procedure is that it does not require a radical change in the design of the questionaires, except for questions pertaining to the additional module which are made for those found to be occupied during the reference week.

Some countries of the region already have experience in researching some characteristics which should be included in this special module. Surveys conducted by Argentina and Brazil, for example, have studied the size of the establishment and whether registered in social security institutions.

2. Invisible informal sector

As already indicated, activities within the invisible informal sector are chiefly performed by women whose "statistical invisibility" stems from the difficulties posed by their identification within the economically active population. The appropriate way to treat this sector in household surveys consists, therefore, in introducing modifications in that part of the questionnaire which researches the condition of activity of the potentially active population.

The procedure consists in posing a set of questions to people who declare not having worked in the week of reference and those who, not having worked, declare, furthermore, nor having had a paid job, enterprise or business. Within the module, questions are posed in terms of whether or not the person performed one or more activities from an extensive, previously established list. 32/ The greater or lesser probability of detecting these activities essentially depends on this list which the interviewer reads to the people being surveyed. It is very important therefore that such a list be based on knowledge of which activities are most frequently performed by the people surveyed, especially the economic activities that women perform in their household. This may require previous small surveys to develop listings of activities or the use of past research studies on specific sectors of the population where these types of situations are frequently found, such as studies on women in low-income sectors.

It should be noted that the location of a module of this type within the questionnaire determines the population segment which can be researched. In the methodological survey of Costa Rica, these activities were investigated among the not currently economically active as well as among the unemployed.

Furthermore, studying the time devoted to the various activities is important. The above-mentioned survey inquired as to the total number of hours per week dedicated to each activity as well as the destination of goods produced, and whether all or a portion was for sale or entirely for household consumption.

The module which is geared towards studying the informal sector makes possible the investigation of a broader spectrum of jobs performed by women within the household which are difficult to distinguish from typical domestic tasks, such as the care by minors of other people who are not household members, preparation of food for others, laundering and ironing outside the household. In these cases, however, additional information is required in order to establish whether the activities in question may or may not be classified as economic according to SNA and their appraisal in terms of contribution to gross domestic product may pose additional problems requiring another type of information. 33/

3. Petty trade

The results of Costa Rica's experimental survey indicated that four out of every five people who declared themselves to be performing "marginal" economic activities were women and that most of the tasks performed were centred in agricultural activity, the clothing industry and the construction sector. The average number of weekly hours worked by these women was 7.3 hours. 34/

The possibility of identifying small traders without fixed premises through household surveys depends on the particular conditions of this activity in each country. This sector deserves special attention because of its growing importance within urban employment, especially in the metropolises of some countries (for example, Mexico City, Lima, Santiago de Chile, Sao Paulo) and because it represents labour participation relatively distinguishable from other forms of invisible informality. The statistical invisibility of small traders results mainly from the variability of their occupations, the instability of the work over time, the fact that the activity is not generally declared when illegal activities are concerned and, in many cases, from difficulties in classifying the activities. In this sense, petty trade represents an intermediate situation between the visible and invisible informal sectors.

Recent household surveys such as the one conducted in 1984 in urban areas in Mexico City have included in the questionnaire a set of questions designed to identify own-account workers without fixed premises on the streets. This is done in a manner similar to that suggested to research marginal or "invisible" activities, that is, on the basis of an extensive list of specific occupations. The design of the questionnaire depends on whether it is to investigate only activities of the economically occupied populations or is also to investigate the population which was not occupied during the reference week, in the same manner as with "marginal" activities in the methodological survey of Costa Rica. In the first case, pertinent questions may be limited to occupied persons, whether paid or unpaid and declaring that their activity has no fixed location.

4. Domestic service

The unique characteristics of domestic service in the region make it advisable that it be treated as a separate sub-sector from the informal sector. The domestic service sector is unique because (a) it is the main occupation among economically active women, (b) the labour relationship is highly dependent as the worker lives in the same household where the work is peformed and (c) as opposed to other occupations, "modernization" of the activity is accompanied by a reduction of the number of regular employees engaged in it - that is, the workers' status changes from live-in (salaried) to daily work on own account.

Thus, in assessing domestic service, it is important to separate the two statuses, "live-in" employees and own-account workers. In addition, in studying family composition, it is important to separate domestic workers in households which have paid, live-in domestic employees from other household members.

B. Specific suggestions based on experience with household surveys in the region

The ECLAC Statistical Division has a Household Census data bank which has permitted the development of a considerable number of research studies on different topics in various countries throughout the region. The data bank now has 69 surveys available, which are part of continuous programmes carried out in 10 Latin American countries. Surveys cover a period of 10-15 years and include a large number of variables. 35/

A comparative analysis of nine surveys available reveals a series of problems and deficiencies in the identification and measurement of women's participation in the informal sector. Detailed evaluation of the information and the listing of variables studied 36/ in these surveys have been used to identify the main problems and prepare suggestions to overcome them. These are discussed below.

1.   In five of the nine countries considered, survey programmes provide information only on urban areas. In these countries, it is advisable for the programme to cover rural areas at least once a year, in order to take into account the specific conditions of agricultural activity. The means of studying women's activity in these cases would be through questionnaires that:

(a) Include activities carried out in reference periods exceeding that of a week, for instance, the preceding 12 months;

(b) Inquire about the activities carried out by women declared not economically active, according to the usual definition used by surveys based on international recommendations;

(c) Study activities performed by women within the household, especially in agricultural sectors where own-consumption activities constitute an important part of the production for support of family members.

2.   Although all of the surveys study the relationship of members of the household with the household head, none adequately studies the situation of household headship. In some cases, the family relationships are not studied either, nor is the position occupied by all the members within the household. In

such cases, it is not possible to identify the presence of domestic employees who live in the household or the existence of secondary family groups which live as relatives in the same home. In low-income sectors, this is a frequent situation and the presence of these relatives is accompanied by provision of services which correspond to an economic activity. The following suggestions can be made in this regard:

(a) Inquire about the condition of effective headship in the homes, beginning with the identification of the largest income contributor to the household or by means of some other criterion, especially when there are members who work in the informal sector, as women in those households tend to participate in the same activities carried out by the head (see chap. III, sect. B.3);

(b) Study the members' relationship with the household head in the most detailed manner possible and do not put those who habitually reside in the household in a single category such as "other relatives" or "non-related members of the household head". This information allows application of a household classification and study of its characteristics in relation to women who work in the informal sector. Given that these surveys do not study fertility, the information relative to family relationships with the household head is the only way to approximate the stage of the family life cycle. Therefore, a good record of this characteristic is central.

3. Two of the nine surveys analysed did not study the marital status of the population. It is desirable to include this question in the questionnaire and inquire about the marital situation of all the women who reside in the household. In addition, it is useful to identify those situations in which the male spouse has abandoned the household or is absent for relatively long periods of time because, for example, of carrying out agricultural activities outside the residence zone. In such cases, it is the women who support the household, typically participating in informal activities.

With regard to the variables which investigate the economic characteristics of the population, various deficiencies can be mentioned which pose difficulties in analysis of the informal sector.

4. None of the surveys provides information with regard to the physical location of the job relative to the household. In both urban and rural areas, the work of women is frequently carried out within (or near) the household.

The methodological survey of Costa Rica studied this variable through the following question: 37/

Indicate whether the place of work is located in your own home ...
Is located outside your own home ...
Has no fixed location ...

Analysis of data from this survey revealed that 38.5 per cent of the non-agricultural labour force in the informal sector worked in the household and that 48 per cent of those occupied in this sector were women. It is therefore desirable that surveys include this question and that, in those cases where the household head states he performs his activity within the household, it be investigated whether other members work with him. In this way, women who perform economic activities as unpaid family workers and who declare themselves not economically active could be identified.

5. Three of the nine surveys analysed do not study the size of the establishment or the economic unit. Employment characteristics are closely related with the size of the economic units (existence of social security for employees, formality of contractual relationships, occupational stability, technology used, etc.). This variable can thus serve as a proxy for other variables. Although it is known that the reliability of the data on the size of the establishment decreases as the number of persons occupied increases, it is desirable to include it in questionnaires in order to establish a criterion to identifiy those occupied in small enterprises when other criteria are not available to define the informal sector more precisely. 38/ This would allow identification of households which have access to domestic service in which it is more probable that women carry out activity outside their households.

Some surveys pose difficulties for the analysis of women's occupations owing to the high degree of aggregation in the classifications used. This makes comparability with other national and international classifications difficult. Frequently, this is due to the fact that, when recording the information on magnetic tapes, use is made of a classification at the level of major groups; specific occupations, such as domestic employment, peddlers and tailors and seamstresses, are not distinguished. It is therefore suggested that information on occupations be recorded at a high level of disaggregation and that comparability with international classifications be maintained.

When the classification of branches of industry (ISIC) is presented in an aggregate manner, it is not sufficient to have an idea of the characteristics of the establishments where the workers in the informal sector are employed. The National Urban Employment Survey of Mexico (1984) incorporated a question in the questionnaire on an experimental basis which adds to information on the type of establishment or economic unit and is very useful to identify the informal sector. The question, which followed upon the one used to study the branch of industry, presented a list of 21 types of establishments or places where the activity could be carried out, classified in accordance with the broad divisions of ISIC, as follows:

AGRICULTURAL, LIVESTOCK AND FISHING

1. Plots, boats, boards, puddles, ponds
2. Agricultural and livestock establishments, ships, fish farms

INDUSTRY AND CONSTRUCTION

3. Worker's, employer's or client's domicile
4. Workshops and other small-scale establishments or artisan shops
5. Engineers', architects' and other professionals' offices related to the industry
6. Factories: constructing and freezing, mines and other medium and large-scale establishments

SERVICES AND GOVERNMENT

7. Installation improvised on the street from door to door

8. Worker's, employer's and client's domicile
9. Services rendered on vehicles
10. Transportation line or route
11. Independent professionals' establishments
12. Guest houses, eating houses and other establishments of the same size and nature
13. Automobile or household appliance repair shops, laundromats and beauty shops which are not part of a chain
14. Vulcanizers, footwear repair shops, locksmiths and similar
15. Office of municipal, State or federal government and dependencies
16. Other medium and large-scale service establishments

COMMERCIAL

17. Floor stands or street peddlers
18. Worker's, employer's or client's domicile
19. Trading on vehicles
20. Grocery stores, permanent stands on the street, market places and other sales in similar barrios
21. Other medium and large-sized supermarkets and other commercial centres.

It is desirable that the surveys include a classification such as this to complement information on the branch of activity, as the latter does not explicitly consider the most frequent types of establishments in the informal sector.

C. Difficulties in the measurement of income
in household surveys

With regards to measurement of income, the household surveys analysed in this chapter offer a great variety. The type of information covered in selected household surveys is summarized in table A.3 of the annex. The importance assigned to the topic can be appreciated in the number of questions relative to income contained in the questionnaires. The extreme cases are represented by the surveys in which only primary cash income is investigated for the main occupation (Bolivia, Costa Rica 39/ and Venezuela) and those household surveys such as Brazil's PNAD which study all income flows in cash and kind of all recipients (active and passive) and in all occupations. This is not a general assessment of the quality of the measurement of income in the continuous household surveys, 40/ but simply underlines some limitations of the data available to analyse women's income levels and their contribution to the family income, especially in households supported by the informal sector.

In the publication entitled Improving Concepts and Methods for Statistics and Indicators on Women, four special income-measuring areas of interest are pointed out: (a) estimation of individual income of women in absolute terms; (b) importance of women's contribution to economy (income) and household welfare; (c) measurement of income levels of women heads of households; and (d) measurement of production income in own-consumption. Income flows normally studied in continuous household surveys pose different problems in all these areas.

If the levels of income in different occupations are to be measured, it is necessary to study, separately, income from work and remaining income, and to distinguish income obtained in the main occupation from incomes accruing from other occupations.

The first requisite is met in the nine household surveys analysed. These cover questions on primary income obtained in the activity (as salaried, own account, employees and employers) and on flows of remaining income (from property, transfers and other income). As for the second requisite, three of the nine surveys (Argentina, Colombia and Venezuela) pose difficulties as they inquire only about monetary income obtained in all occupations. In these cases, the problem may be alleviated by resorting to information on the number of occupations and limiting the analysis to the entire employed population which stated having worked in only one occupation during the period of reference. 41/ In this case, there is a loss of information equivalent to the percentage of the total employed persons who stated having more than one paid occupation. 42/ It is, therefore, desirable that questions on income be formulated in such a manner that income obtained from work in the main occupation can be separated from incomes obtained in the secondary occupation(s).

The second aspect refers to measurement of primary income from profits and benefits of employers and workers on their own account. Estimates of the understatement of this source of income, obtained from analysis of national accounts, indicate these fluctuate between 40 per cent and 60 per cent. 43/ This fact reduces the reliability of estimates of income accruing from activities carried out on an own-account basis and in the informal sector in general.

One of the reasons given to explain these high margins of understatement is the more sporadic and fluctuating nature of income obtained by own-account workers, which, in the case of women, is higher due to the higher turnover rate of women in the labour force. In this regard, it might be noted that the quality of the data may improve if questions are asked to obtain information on the income which unpaid workers "normally" obtain, taking into consideration a reference period longer than the previous week.

With regard to transfer income (social security, pensions, widows' pensions and other types of transfers), it is notable that, when dealing with cash income obtained on a regular basis (social security, for instance), understatement margins are quite low and similar to those for salaries and wages. Household surveys permit relatively reliable estimation of the levels of monetary income 44/ of the not economically active population.

In summary, it can be pointed out that continuous employment surveys permit analysis in a relatively reliable manner of cash income from salaries and wages obtained in the main occupation. Since this is not the main source of primary income in the informal sector, there are serious difficulties in measuring the contribution of this sector to national product, especially as regards own-consumption.

The high levels of understatement in other sources of primary income, namely profits and benefits earned by the self-employed, seriously limit the analysis of the contribution women make to family income and the measurement of income generated by women heads of household.

Some general suggestions to improve household information collected with household surveys are: (a) to separate primary income (salary and wages) from the main occupation from incomes earned in secondary occupations; (b) investigate the primary income of the self-employed and reduce understatement by using a longer period of reference; (c) separately, study income transfers in the entire active and not economically active population above a specific age.

Notes

1/   See C. D. Deere, "La división por sexo del trabajo agrícola: un estudio de la Sierra Norte del Perú", <u>Estudios de Población</u>, vol. II, No. 9 (Asociación Colombiana para el Estudio de la Población, September 1977).

2/   Felicia Reicher Madeira, "El trabajo de la mujer en fortaleza", <u>Demografía y Economía</u>, vol. XII, No. 1 (1978), p. 57.

3/   Zulma Recchini de Lattes and Catalina H. Wainerman, "El trabajo femenino en el banquillo de los acusados: la medición censal en América Latina" (Editorial Terra Nova and Population Council, 1981).

4/   International Labour Organisation, "Mujeres en sus casas; taller informal de consulta sobre el valor económico de las actividades del hogar" (Lima, 1984).

5/   Farhad Mehran, "The concept and boundary of economic activity for the measurement of the economically active population" (International Labour Organisation, Bureau of Statistics, Working Paper, May 1986).

6/   See, for example, Elizabeth Jelin, "Migration and labour force participation of Latin American women: the domestic servants in the cities", in <u>Women and National Development: The Complexities of Change</u> (Chicago, University of Chicago Press, 1977).

7/   International Labour Organisation and Dirección General de Estadísticas y Censos de Costa Rica, <u>Encuesta Metodológica sobre el Empleo, Desempleo y Subempleo en Costa Rica</u> (1983).

8/   International Labour Organisation, Regional Employment Programme for Latin America and the Caribbean, "Sectór informal: funcionamiento y políticas" (Santiago, 1978); and Dagmar Raczynsky, "Características del empleo informal úrbano en Chile", Estudios CIEPLAN No. 23 (April 1978).

9/   This is analysed in more detail in the following chapters.

10/   See United Nations Children's Fund, "Aspectos metodológicos de las políticas de desarrollo social", Estudios ILPES/UNICEF Sobre Políticas Sociales (Santiago, 1984).

11/   That is, domestic employees residing in the household where they work.

12/   See Thelma Gálvez and Rosalba Todaro, "La especificidad del trabajo doméstico asalariado y la organización de las trabajadoras (Chile)", in "<u>La Mujer in el sectór popular úrbano</u>" (United Nations publication, Sales No. S.84.II.G.14).

13/   Patricio Villagrán Streeter, <u>Sector Informal Urbano</u> (Santiago, Editorial Universitaria, 1985).

14/ Ibid., p.53.

15/ Ibid., p.55.

16/ This discussion refers to household surveys which are part of continuous programmes and not to other special surveys which have researched this subject in depth with other methodologies and ad hoc questionnaires.

17/ A detailed description of census information available in micro-data form and on the procedures to obtain new tabulations and other services provided by CELADE are found in CELADE, Boletín del Banco de Datos, No. 11 (Santiago).

18/ See ECLAC, "Análisis estadístico de la situación de la mujer en países de América Latina a través de las encuestas de hogares" (LC/R.418, Sem.24/2 and Add.1), 1985.

19/ See Arthur Conning, "Información censal geográficamente desagregada para la planificación en los países en desarrollo", Notas de Población, vol. XIII, No. 3 (San José, Costa Rica, CELADE, December 1985), pp. 9-24.

20/ Ibid., p. 9.

21/ Ibid., p. 16.

22/ A detailed description of the results of this experimental study is found in Pisoni L. Rodolfo, "El trabajo de las mujeres usualmente consideradas como económicamente inactivas" (paper presented at the Eighth National Demographic Seminar, San José, Costa Rica, September 1983); see sect. A.5 of the annex.

23/ Ibid., p. 1.

24/ Improving Concepts and Methods for Statistics and Indicators on the Situation of Women, (United Nations publication, Sales No. E.84.XVII.3).

25/ Includes groups 4-1, 4-5 and 4-9, major group 5 and groups 7-7, 7-9 and 8-0 of ISCO.

26/ Since continuous household surveys do not usually investigate fertility (number and age of the children of each woman), this variable can be constructed after identifying household members and the family relationship with the head of the household.

27/ See the extract from the survey questionnaire in sect. A.6 (a) of the annex.

28/ The methodology used and the results obtained in this survey are found in Trigueros M. Rafael, "La encuesta metodológica de la OIT para la medición del empleo, del desempleo y del subempleo en Costa Rica", Bulletin on Job Statistics (International Labour Organisation, 1986).

29/ Ibid., p. 14.

30/ See the questionnaire in sect. A.6 (a) of the annex.

31/ See the diagram with the definition of these sub-sectors in sect. A.6 (b) of the annex.

32/ See box 40 in the questionnaire in sect. A.6 (a) of the annex.

33/ See sect. B.4 above.

34/ Data refer to the period June-July 1983.

35/ See sect. A.1 of the annex.

36/ See sect. A.2 of the annex.

37/ See sect. A.6 (a) of the annex, questionnaire, box 70, question 78.

38/ The methodological survey of Costa Rica observed that employment in the non-agricultural informal sector is predominantly in very small economic units: 55 per cent of those employed in the informal sector work on their own, with no others involved in the activity; 35 per cent work in establishments employing between two and five employees; only 10 per cent work in establishments with six or more employees.

39/ The Costa Rican Survey (July 1982) questionnaire includes a question on payment in kind (housing, meals, other), but does not establish its equivalent in cash.

40/ A general evaluation of this type is found in Oscar Altimir, "Income distribution statistics in Latin America and their reliability" (Paper prepared for the eighteenth Conference of the International Association for Research on Income and Wealth, Luxembourg, August 1983).

41/ Of the three surveys mentioned, only that of Colombia lacks information on the number of occupations.

42/ Percentages of employed persons who state having more than one job are relatively small.

43/ The order of the magnitude of understatement of income from salaries is 10 per cent to 20 per cent of the value calculated on national accounts. In the case of property income, these figures are much higher and vary between 70 per cent and 90 per cent. See O. Altimir, op. cit., table 4.

44/ Surveys do not measure other types of transfers in kind, such as goods and services provided free or subsidized by the Government. Consequently, there is no possibility of obtaining information to evaluate the benefits of Government social programmes such as food distribution and primary health care programmes, which are becoming increasingly important and may represent an important fraction of household income.

Annex

ILLUSTRATIVE MATERIAL ON THE HOUSEHOLD AND INFORMAL SECTORS
FROM SELECTED HOUSEHOLD SURVEYS CONDUCTED IN LATIN AMERICA
AND THE CARIBBEAN

Annex

A.1. Household surveys in the ECLAC data bank

| Countries | Total | Number of surveys and geographical coverage | | | Year of survey | |
		National	Urban	Metropolitan area	Earliest available	Latest available
Argentina	9	–	1	8	1970	1986
Bolivia	12	–	9	3	1978	1988
Brazil	7	7	–	–	1977	1987
Colombia	22	4	17	1	1971	1987
Costa Rica	8	8	–	–	1967	1988
Chile	8	8	–	–	1971	1986
Guatemala	1	1	–	–	..	1987
Honduras	2	–	2	–	1986	1987
Panama	7	5	–	2	1970	1986
Peru	9	5	3	1	1974	1984
Uruguay	7	–	7	–	1980	1987
Venezuela	18	18	–	–	1971	1987

Source: ECLAC, Division of Statistics and Quantitative Analysis.

A.2. Variables included in selected household survey questionnaires

Variables a/	Argentina 1980	Bolivia 1982	Brazil 1982	Colombia 1982	Costa Rica 1982	Chile 1982	Panama 1982	Peru 1982	Venezuela 1982
Geographical coverage (Urban/rural)	U	U	U & R	U	U & R	U & R	U	U	U & R
Relation to head of household	x	x	x	x	x	x	x	x	x
Sex, age	x	x	x	x	x	x	x	x	x
Marital status	x	x	x	x	x	x	x	x	x
Education									
School attendance	x	x	x	x	x	x	x	x	x
Literacy	x		x	x		x			
Level of education (No. years)	x	x	x	x	x	x	x	x	x
Special training courses	x						x		
Migration									
Place of birth	x	x		x	x			x	x
Time living in present place of residence	x	x		x	x			x	x
Fertility									
Number of births		x	x						
Number of survivors		x	x						x
Economic characteristics b/									
Condition of activity c/	no limit	10	10	12	12	15	15	14	10
Employment status	x	x	x	x	x	x	x	x	x
Occupation	x	x	x	x	x	x	x	x	x
Sector of activity (industry)	x	x	x	x	x	x	x	x	x
Number of occupations	x	x	x	x	x	x	x	x	x
Hours worked in main occupations	x	x	x	x	x	x	x	x	x
Hours worked in all occupations	x	x	x		x	x		x	x
Size of economic unit	x	x			x		x	x	x
Social security			x			x			
Income	x	x	x	x	x	x	x	x	x

Source: ECLAC data bank.

a/ Some surveys investigate housing conditions; these variables were not considered.

b/ Economic characteristics of unemployed labour force have been excluded.

c/ Refers to current employment situation (one week reference period). Numbers indicate minimum age used for working age population.

A.3. Income variables in selected household surveys

Surveys	Wages & salaries (money in kind)	Gains & profits a/ (money in kind)	Property income b/ (money)	Property income b/ (imputed)	Transference c/	Other incomes d/
Argentina (Buenos Aires, 1980)	x	x	x		x	x
Bolivia (La Paz, 1982)	x	x				
Brazil (1982)	x	x	x		x	x
Colombia (Seven cities, 1982)	x	x	x			
Costa Rica (1982)	x	x				
Panama (Metrop. area, 1982)	x	x	x		x	x
Peru (Lima, 1982)	x	x	x		x	x
Uruguay (Urban areas, 1984)	x	x	x	x	x	x
Venezuela, 1982)	x	x				

Source: ECLAC data bank.

a/ Includes income declared by employers and own-account workers.

b/ Includes interest, dividends and rents. Imputed property income refers to rents imputed to homeowners.

c/ Includes pensions, net transferences from abroad and government payments.

d/ Includes scholarships, prizes and alimony.

A.4. Economically active population in the formal and informal sectors in Argentina, Brazil, Chile, Ecuador, Panama and Paraguay

(a) Definition of labour force sectors used in the study according to employment status, occupation and industry

Employment status: Occupation:	Employers and employees				Own-account and family workers				Employment- status not declared			
	Profes. & tech.	All other occup.	Occup.not declared	Domestic servants	All other occup.	Occup.not declared	Profes. & tech.	Domestic servants	Profes. & tech.	Domestic servants	All other occup.	Occup.not declared
Industry												
Agriculture	MA	MA	MA	DE	TA	TA	MA	DE	MA	DE	TA	TA
Mining					Labour force in mining							
Manufacture)												
Construction)												
Trade)	FS	FS	FS	DE	IS	IS	FS	DE	FS	FS	DE	DNK
Transport)												
Personal service)												
Other												
Seeking first job					Seeking first job							
Industry not declared	DNK	DNK	DNK	DE	DNK	DNK	DE	DE	DNK	DNK	DE	DNK

Note: MA = Modern agriculture.
TA = Traditional agriculture.
FS = Formal sector.
IS = Informal sector.
DE = Domestic employment.
DNK = Don't know.

-144-

(b) Percentage distribution of labour force, by sector and sex

ARGENTINA

Labour force sector	1970		1980		1970	1980
	Male	Female	Male	Female	Female (percentage of total)	Female
A. Formal	59.1	53.6	60.6	59.3	28.6	27.0
A.1 Manufacturing	8.2	18.6	19.1	12.1	20.3	19.4
A.2 Construction	8.2	0.5	8.5	0.8	2.0	8.2
A.3 Trade	8.5	8.6	9.9	10.8	25.8	29.8
A.4 Transport	5.8	0.5	8.9	0.6	3.3	5.5
A.5 Personal service	2.7	2.6	2.6	1.2	24.2	14.9
A.6 Other	16.2	27.7	16.6	33.8	36.8	48.5
B. Informal	11.6	10.0	16.0	9.7	22.7	18.6
B.1 Manufacturing	1.6	4.1	2.0	3.3	47.0	38.2
B.2 Construction	2.0	.0	4.9	.0	0.3	0.4
B.3 Trade	4.9	4.1	5.2	4.8	22.1	26.0
B.4 Transport	1.2	.0	1.1	0.1	1.2	2.0
B.5 Personal service	1.5	1.4	2.1	0.9	24.6	13.9
B.6 Other	0.5	0.4	0.7	0.5	20.4	23.4
C. Domestic service	0.2	23.0	0.1	20.5	97.9	98.3
D. Modern agriculture	11.7	1.7	9.5	1.5	4.8	5.6
E. Traditional agriculture	6.8	1.9	6.0	1.3	8.8	7.6
F. Mining	0.6	0.1	0.6	0.1	3.6	7.1
G. Seeking first job	0.6	1.2	0.4	0.6	40.8	36.3
H. Not stated	9.4	8.5	6.8	7.1	28.5	28.4
TOTAL	100.0	100.0	100.0	100.0	25.4	27.5

A.4 (continued)

(b) Percentage distribution of labour force, by sector and sex

BRAZIL

Labour force sector	1970 Male	1970 Female	1980 Male	1980 Female	1970 Female (percentage of total)	1980 Female (percentage of total)
A. Formal	36.9	39.5	49.6	53.4	22.0	29.0
A.1 Manufacturing	11.7	10.1	15.2	13.0	18.6	24.4
A.2 Construction	5.8	0.2	7.1	0.5	1.1	1.1
A.3 Trade	5.0	5.5	6.2	7.4	22.4	31.4
A.4 Transport	3.2	0.2	3.2	0.6	1.6	6.6
A.5 Personal service	0.2	0.8	3.1	2.5	52.0	23.4
A.6 Other	10.9	22.6	14.7	29.3	35.3	43.0
B. Informal	9.2	11.6	10.9	10.3	24.8	26.4
B.1 Manufacturing	1.8	8.2	1.0	0.9	54.4	25.1
B.2 Construction	1.4	.0	2.6	.0	0.2	0.1
B.3 Trade	4.2	1.9	3.1	2.2	10.6	21.5
B.4 Transport	1.1	.0	1.5	.0	0.1	0.2
B.5 Personal service	0.2	0.6	1.6	6.0	39.3	59.1
B.6 Other	0.5	0.9	1.1	1.1	32.2	27.8
C. Domestic service	0.2	26.6	0.4	18.9	97.7	95.2
D. Modern agriculture	14.2	3.6	15.2	4.8	6.3	10.7
E. Traditional agriculture	36.5	16.8	20.6	9.6	10.8	15.0
F. Mining	0.6	0.1	0.6	0.1	3.6	7.1
G. Seeking first job	0.6	1.2	0.4	0.6	40.8	36.3
H. Not stated	9.4	8.5	6.8	7.1	28.5	28.4
TOTAL	100.0	100.0	100.0	100.0	25.4	27.5

A.4 (continued)

(b) Percentage distribution of labour force, by sector and sex

CHILE

Labour force sector	1970 Male	1970 Female	1982 Male	1982 Female	1970 Female (percentage of total)	1982 Female (percentage of total)
A. Formal	47.5	44.4	52.0	52.1	21.9	26.7
A.1 Manufacturing	13.4	11.0	13.1	7.9	19.7	18.0
A.2 Construction	6.6	0.3	7.6	0.4	1.5	2.1
A.3 Trade	4.8	5.6	7.3	8.9	25.8	30.7
A.4 Transportation	5.2	0.5	4.9	0.8	2.5	5.4
A.5 Personal service	3.1	2.3	3.2	1.9	18.1	17.7
A.6 Other	14.3	24.7	16.0	32.2	34.1	42.3
B. Informal	11.0	15.9	11.6	10.2	30.4	24.2
B.1 Manufacturing	1.4	6.2	1.3	2.9	57.0	45.1
B.2 Construction	0.5	.0	0.7	.0	0.2	0.5
B.3 Trade	4.4	5.8	4.4	5.1	28.5	29.7
B.4 Transport	1.3	0.1	1.8	0.1	1.8	1.9
B.5 Personal service	2.9	2.9	2.8	1.3	23.0	14.5
B.6 Other	0.4	0.9	0.5	0.7	40.5	31.9
C. Domestic service	0.6	26.9	0.2	24.5	93.4	97.4
D. Modern agriculture	17.4	1.6	15.0	1.5	2.7	3.6
E. Traditional agriculture	9.2	1.2	8.4	0.7	3.9	3.0
F. Mining	2.5	0.2	2.6	0.2	1.9	3.0
G. Seeking first job	0.7	0.8	2.6	4.1	24.9	36.8
H. Not stated	11.0	9.0	7.6	6.6	19.6	24.0
TOTAL	100.0	100.0	100.0	100.0	23.1	26.6

A.4 (continued)

(b) Percentage distribution of labour force, by sector and sex

ECUADOR

Labour force sector	1974 Male	1974 Female	1982 Male	1982 Female	1974 Female (percentage of total)	1982 Female (percentage of total)
A. Formal	27.1	34.1	33.9	41.7	20.7	24.4
A.1 Manufacturing	6.3	7.8	7.0	7.6	20.4	22.4
A.2 Construction	4.2	0.5	5.5	0.5	2.3	2.6
A.3 Trade	2.8	4.9	3.1	5.7	26.4	32.8
A.4 Transportation	2.1	0.4	2.5	0.4	3.8	4.4
A.5 Personal service	2.7	2.4	2.6	1.8	15.3	15.0
A.6 Other	8.9	18.1	13.3	25.6	29.6	33.6
B. Informal	12.2	23.7	16.8	17.8	28.7	21.9
B.1 Manufacturing	3.3	12.5	4.0	6.4	43.9	29.6
B.2 Construction	0.9	0.1	2.5	0.1	1.4	1.5
B.3 Trade	4.6	8.5	5.6	8.9	27.5	29.5
B.4 Transport	1.1	.0	2.4	.0	0.3	0.4
B.5 Personal service	1.9	2.0	1.8	1.2	17.9	15.6
B.6 Other	0.4	0.7	0.4	1.1	27.4	39.2
C. Domestic service	0.4	20.1	0.3	14.5	91.9	93.7
D. Modern agriculture	20.0	4.0	16.4	0.4	4.0	0.7
E. Traditional agriculture	33.1	9.1	22.1	11.3	5.4	11.8
F. Mining	0.4	0.1	0.3	0.1	4.3	7.3
G. Seeking first job	1.6	1.4	2.2	3.6	15.6	30.5
H. Not stated	5.4	7.4	8.0	10.5	22.3	25.7
TOTAL	100.0	100.0	100.0	100.0	17.1	20.8

-148-

A.4 (continued)

(b) Percentage distribution of labour force, by sector and sex

PANAMA

Labour force sector	1970 Male	1970 Female	1980 Male	1980 Female	1970 Female (percentage of total)	1980 Female (percentage of total)
A. Formal	34.7	46.1	44.0	61.1	31.3	34.6
A.1 Manufacturing	6.4	5.1	9.3	6.2	21.4	20.4
A.2 Construction	5.9	0.6	5.6	0.8	3.3	5.4
A.3 Trade	6.4	8.9	6.9	9.8	32.2	35.1
A.4 Transport	1.9	1.2	1.2	0.3	17.7	7.8
A.5 Personal service	1.3	1.9	1.6	2.1	32.8	33.3
A.6 Other	12.8	28.5	19.4	41.9	43.4	45.1
B. Informal	7.7	11.8	7.8	5.9	34.4	22.3
B.1 Manufacturing	0.9	4.4	1.0	2.0	63.0	44.0
B.2 Construction	1.6	.0	1.8	.0	0.6	0.2
B.3 Trade	2.2	2.5	2.0	2.0	28.1	28.0
B.4 Transport	1.9	.0	2.0	0.1	0.1	1.0
B.5 Personal service	0.8	3.9	0.8	1.4	61.8	38.2
B.6 Other	0.5	0.9	1.1	1.1	32.2	27.8
C. Domestic service	0.6	24.2	0.8	16.1	93.3	88.7
D. Modern agriculture	10.8	1.2	10.7	1.9	3.5	6.3
E. Traditional agriculture	38.4	6.0	27.5	3.3	5.1	4.4
F. Mining	0.1	.0	0.2	.0	7.8	5.9
G. Seeking first job	2.2	7.4	2.9	5.8	53.2	43.6
H. Not stated	5.4	3.2	6.2	5.8	17.0	26.2
TOTAL	100.0	100.0	100.0	100.0	25.6	27.6

A.4 (continued)

(b) Percentage distribution of labour force, by sector and sex

PARAGUAY

Labour force sector	1972 Male	1972 Female	1982 Male	1982 Female	1972 Female (percentage of total)	1982 Female (percentage of total)
A. Formal	26.8	28.2	28.2	32.9	22.6	23.1
A.1 Manufacturing	7.8	7.3	7.1	5.6	20.4	16.9
A.2 Construction	3.2	.0	5.6	0.2	0.3	0.8
A.3 Trade	2.5	4.2	2.5	5.2	31.3	34.6
A.4 Transportation	2.5	0.3	1.3	0.2	3.1	2.8
A.5 Personal service	1.4	1.2	1.9	1.7	20.2	19.0
A.6 Other	9.3	15.2	9.6	20.0	31.1	34.9
B. Informal	9.5	32.9	11.0	25.7	48.9	37.7
B.1 Manufacturing	2.6	20.7	2.7	14.7	68.4	58.8
B.2 Construction	1.6	.0	2.6	0.1	0.1	0.6
B.3 Trade	3.2	9.5	3.4	8.5	45.0	39.3
B.4 Transport	0.7	0.0	0.7	.0	0.0	0.5
B.5 Personal service	1.1	2.4	1.2	1.9	37.8	28.7
B.6 Other	0.2	0.3	0.4	0.6	29.9	28.8
C. Domestic service	0.2	23.0	0.1	21.1	97.4	99.0
D. Modern agriculture	12.0	1.6	8.2	1.6	3.6	4.8
E. Traditional agriculture	47.3	11.4	44.5	10.0	6.2	5.5
F. Mining	0.2	.0	0.1	.0	.0	0.9
G. Seeking first job	1.2	1.1	0.6	0.4	20.2	15.5
H. Not stated	2.8	1.9	7.4	8.3	15.4	22.4
TOTAL	100.0	100.0	100.0	100.0	21.7	20.5

Source: Special tabulations of census samples in CELADE data bank. Reproduced by permission of PREALC.

A.5. 1983 experimental census conducted in Costa Rica to identify
economic activities of women classified as not economically
active according to usual census measurement of the labour
force: illustrative results and excerpt from the
questionnaire

(a) Number of women from San Juan District who are classified as
not economically active and performed economic activities
inside or outside their homes/farms, and average hours
worked, by urban and rural residence and week or year
reference period, May 1983

Women not economically active	San Juan District, total		San Juan, urban		San Juan, rural	
	Ref. week	Ref. year	Ref. week	Ref. year	Ref. week	Ref. year
Total	1 476	..	714	..	762	..
Not economically active who did not work	1 033	..	534	..	499	..
Not economically active who worked						
Total	370	659	146	269	224	390
Inside their home/farm	314	220	112	93	202	126
Outside their home	44	308	26	139	18	169
In and outside their home	12	132	8	37	4	95
Unknown	73	73	34	34	39	39
Average hours worked	16	..	18	..	14	..

Source: Pisoni L. Rodolfo, "El trabajo de las mujeres usualmente consideradas
como económicamente inactivas" (Paper presented at the Eighth National Demographic
Seminar, Dirección General de Estadísticas y Censos, San José, Costa Rica,
September 1983).

-151-

A.5 (continued)

(b) Economic activities performed by women from San Juan District
who are classified as not economically active, by urban and
rural residence and week or year reference period, May 1983

(Number of women)

Activity	San Juan District, total		San Juan, urban		San Juan, rural	
	Ref. week	Ref. year	Ref. week	Ref. year	Ref. week	Ref. year
All activities	445	929	169	359	276	570
Activities in or outside the house or farm	388	431	135	149	253	282
Agricultural tasks on the farm or family plot	26	29	8	9	18	20
Care and milking of cows	19	20	4	4	15	16
Livestock raising	131	134	23	25	108	109
Dressmaking and weaving	50	66	25	30	25	36
Cigars manufacturing	35	37	7	8	28	29
Craft manufacturing	4	8	1	3	3	5
Processing of food and drinks to sell	17	21	13	17	14	11
Care of family business	28	28	17	14	11	14
Sale of agricultural products and others from plots	17	21	5	7	12	14
Laundry for non-household members	25	24	13	9	12	15
Babysitting outside the home	24	28	12	15	12	13
Food selling or room-letting to boarders	5	6	4	5	1	1
Other activities	7	9	3	3	4	6
Activities outside the home	57	498	34	210	23	288
Coffee harvest	--	389	--	143	--	246
Cultivation of tobacco or others	3	8	1	2	2	6
Care of family business	12	18	7	12	5	6
Vendors	4	8	4	7	--	1
Domestic service	20	31	10	18	10	13
Child care	6	11	4	9	2	2
Community work	8	8	4	4	4	4
Other activities	4	25	4	15	--	10

Source: Pisoni L. Rodolfo, "El trabajo de las mujeres usualmente consideradas como económicamente inactivas" (Paper presented at the Eighth National Demographic Seminar, Dirección General de Estadísticas y Censos, San José, Costa Rica, September 1983).

A.5 (continued)

(c) Percentage distribution of economic activities performed by
women from San Juan District who are classified as not
economically active, by urban and rural residence and week
or year reference period, May 1983

Type of activity	San Juan District, total		San Juan, urban		San Juan, rural	
	Ref. week	Ref. year	Ref. week	Ref. year	Ref. week	Ref. year
Activities inside the house or farm	87.1	46.4	79.9	41.5	91.7	49.5
Agriculture and livestock	39.5	19.7	20.8	10.6	51.1	25.4
Crafts and family industry	23.9	14.2	27.2	16.1	21.7	13.0
Trade	10.1	5.3	13.0	5.9	8.3	4.9
Services	12.1	6.2	17.1	8.1	9.1	5.1
Other activities	1.5	1.0	1.8	0.8	1.4	1.1
Activities outside the house	12.8	53.6	20.1	58.5	8.3	50.5
Agriculture and livestock	0.7	42.7	0.5	40.4	0.7	44.2
Trade	3.6	2.8	6.5	5.3	1.8	1.2
Services	7.6	5.4	10.7	8.6	5.8	3.3
Other activities	0.3	2.7	2.3	4.2		1.8
Total	100.0	100.0	100.0	100.0	100.0	100.0

Source: Pisoni L. Rodolfo, "El trabajo de las mujeres usualmente consideradas como económicamente inactivas" (Paper presented at the Eighth National Demographic Seminar, Dirección General de Estadísticas y Censos, San José, Costa Rica, September 1983).

A.5 (continued)

(d) Economic activity of women in San Juan District, based on
self-declaration and on activity analysis, May 1983

	Economic activity based on self-declaration			Economic activity based on activity analysis		
	Total	Urban	Rural	Total	Urban	Rural
(Number of women)						
Total of female population	2 883	1 532	1 351	2 883	1 532	1 351
Women in non-active ages	745	377	368	745	377	368
Women in active ages	2 138	1 155	983	2 138	1 155	983
Not economically active women	1 476	714	762	1 106	568	538
Worked	370	146	224	–	–	–
Did not work	1 106	568	538	1 106	568	538
Economically active women	662	441	221	1 032	587	445
Worked	630	419	211	1 000	565	435
Did not work	32	22	10	32	22	10
(Percentage)						
Specific gross rate of participation	23.0	28.8	16.4	35.8	38.3	32.9
Global specific rate of participation	31.0	38.2	22.5	48.3	50.8	45.3
Occupation rate	29.5	36.3	21.5	46.8	48.9	44.2
Open unemployment rate	4.8	5.0	4.5	3.1	3.7	2.2

Source: Pisoni L. Rodolfo, "El trabajo de las mujeres usualmente consideradas como económicamente inactivas" (Paper presented at the Eighth National Demographic Seminar, Dirección General de Estadísticas y Censos, San José, Costa Rica, September 1983).

[Original: Spanish]

(e) Excerpt from questionnaire used in the experimental census
of San Ramón, May 1983

Questionnaire on the economic activity of women

For all women aged 12 and over who replied to the question on economic
activity status that they were housewives, students, pensioners, rentiers or others

Segment   Housing unit No.

Neighbourhood
or village   Home

Person No.

Name in full

Questions	Yes No	Hours worked last week	Months worked last year M J J A S O N D J F M A	Hours usually worked per week	Code
Apart from housework or studies, do you perform one or more of the following tasks inside your home or farm?					

1. Do you wash, iron or mend clothes for non-household members?

Yes
No

01

2. Do you do dressmaking, sewing or weaving for other people?

Yes
No

02

3. Do you do babysitting for pay?

Yes
No

03

4. Do you make crafts to sell?

Yes
No

04

5. Do you make food or beverages to sell?

Yes
No

05

6. Do you sell food or rent a room to someone (boarders)?

Yes
No

06

7. Do you sell some other type of product or service?
Please specify:

Yes
No

8. Do you look after or help look after a family business located inside or next door to your home?
Please specify kind of business:

Yes
No

9. Do you care for or help to care for farm animals such as poultry, pigs or rabbits?

Yes
No

20

10. Do you engage in, or help with, such tasks as milking, taking to pasture or rounding up animals such as cows, goats or horses?

Yes
No

21

11. Do you work on your farm or family plot on tasks such as preparing the land, planting, fertilizing, watering or irrigation, or harvesting of agricultural products?

Yes
No

22

12. Do you sell garden produce, milk, eggs or some other product from the farm or family plot?

Yes
No

23

13. Other tasks?
Please specify:

Yes
No

A.5 (continued)

Code

At some time of the year, do you go to work
<u>outside your home</u> to perform one or more of
the following activities?   M J J A S O N D J F M A

14. Do you do laundry or cleaning in other   Yes   51
    homes or establishments?   No

15. Do you do babysitting outside the home   Yes   .52
    for pay?   No

16. Do you engage in street vending of some   Yes
    type of product such as fruit, prepared   No
    food, lottery tickets, clothing, crafts
    or others?
    Please specify what products:

17. Do you look after or help look after a   Yes
    family business located outside your   No
    home?
    Please specify the type of business:

18. Did you work picking coffee during the   Yes   70
    last harvest?   No

19. Have you worked in tobacco farming   Yes   71
    during the past year?   No

20. Have you worked with some other crop   Yes
    during the past year?   No
    Please specify:

21. Have you worked at some other task   Yes
    outside your home during the past year?   No
    Please specify:

_____

REMARKS: Name of census taker   Signature of census taker

                            Date of census   Signature of reviser

POPULATION

PERSON NO.   NAME IN FULL

1.   RELATIONSHIP TO HEAD OF HOUSEHOLD

     Head of household   ( ) 1

     Spouse or companion   ( ) 2

     Son or daughter   ( ) 3

     Son-in-law or daughter-in-law ( ) 4

     Grandson or granddaughter   ( ) 5

     Parents or parents-in-law   ( ) 6

     Other family members   ( ) 7

     Domestic servant   ( ) 8

     Other non-family members   ( ) 9

2.   SEX

     Male ( ) 1   Female ( ) 2

3.   AGE

     Under 1 year   ( ) 00

     98 and over   ( ) 98

     Age at last birthday _____

4.   PLACE OF BIRTH

     Here   ( ) 8

     District

     County

     Province
     _____

     Country (if born abroad)

5. YEAR OF ARRIVAL IN COUNTRY

    Year (only for those born abroad)

    _____

6. DATE OF BIRTH

    Day

    Month

    Year

    _____

7. NATIONALITY

    Costa Rican by:

    Birth   ( ) 7

    Naturalization   ( ) 8

    Other nationality (Specify)

    _____

8. ORPHAN STATUS

    Mother: Dead ( ) 1   Living ( ) 2

    Year of death

    Father: Dead ( ) 1   Living ( ) 2

    _____

9. SOCIAL SECURITY

    Only direct insurance (Illness and Death) ( ) 1   Family   ( ) 4

    Only direct insurance (Disability,
    Old Age and Death)   ( ) 2   Other   ( ) 5

    Both   ( ) 3   Not insured   ( ) 6

    _____

ONLY FOR PERSONS AGED 5 AND OVER

---

10. PLACE OF RESIDENCE 5 YEARS AGO

Where was your customary place of residence 5 years ago?

    Here   ( ) 8

    District

    County

    Province

    _____

    Country (if you were living abroad)

---

11. SCHOOL ENROLMENT

    Are you enrolled in an ordinary education centre?

           Yes ( ) 1   No ( ) 2

---

12. LEVEL OF EDUCATION

What was the last year or grade you completed
successfully in ordinary education?

    None   ( ) 00

    Primary   ( ) 1

    Secondary   ( ) 2

    University   ( ) 3

    Major:

---

13. OUT-OF-SCHOOL EDUCATION

    Have you studied or are you studying out of school?

           Yes ( ) 1   No ( ) 00

    Please specify:

ONLY FOR PERSONS AGED 10 AND OVER

14. LITERACY

Do you know how to read and write?

Yes ( ) 1   No ( ) 2

15. MARITAL STATUS

Living together ( ) 1   Separated ( ) 2

Married   ( ) 3   Widowed   ( ) 4

Divorced   ( ) 5   Single   ( ) 6

ONLY FOR PERSONS AGED 12 AND OVER

16. ACTIVITY STATUS

What did you do during the week of 9-15 May?

Worked   ( ) 1

Looked for work for the first time ( ) 2

Was unemployed   ( ) 3

Housework   ( ) 4

Student   ( ) 5

Pensioner or rentier   ( ) 6

Other (Specify)   ( ) 7

ONLY FOR PERSONS AGED 12 AND OVER WHO REPLIED "WORKED" OR "WAS UNEMPLOYED"

17. MAIN OCCUPATION

What occupation or kind of work were you engaged in during the week of 9-15 May, or at your last job?

18. OCCUPATIONAL CATEGORY

Wage-earner   Non-wage-earner

Government   ( ) 1   Self-employed   ( ) 4

Public body   ( ) 2   Employer   ( ) 5

Private sector ( ) 3   Non-wage family ( ) 6

---

19. BRANCH OF ACTIVITY

What is the main type of work performed at
your place of work or where you last worked?

---

20. SIZE OF THE PLACE OF WORK

How many people work at the place where you
are working now or where you last worked?

Less than 5 ( ) 1   5 or more ( ) 2

---

21. LOCATION OF THE PLACE OF WORK

Where is your current or last place of work
located?

Here   ( ) 8

District

County

Province
_____

Country (if you worked abroad)

---

22. MAIN MEANS OF TRANSPORT USED

Bus   ( ) 1   Walk   ( ) 4

Train ( ) 2   Other means ( ) 5

Car   ( ) 3   None   ( ) 6

ONLY FOR PERSONS AGED 12 AND OVER WHO REPLIED
"WORKED"

23. HOURS WORKED

How many hours did you work during the week
of 9-15 May?

24. INCOME

What income did you receive for your work?

¢ _____ per _____
          (Week or month)

ONLY FOR WOMEN AGED 15 AND OVER

25. CHILDREN BORN ALIVE

None   ( ) 00

          Children

26. DATE OF BIRTH OF LAST CHILD BORN ALIVE
    (Either still living or dead)

Has not had any ( )   Day   Month   Year

27. CHILDREN CURRENTLY ALIVE

None   ( ) 00

          Children

REP. DE COSTA RICA — MINISTERIO DE ECONOMIA Y COMERCIO / DIRECCION GENERAL DE ESTADISTICA Y CENSOS

CENSO EXPERIMENTAL DE SAN RAMON
Mayo de 1983
Cuestionario sobre actividad económica de la mujer
1883 - Centenario de la DGEC - 1983

Para todas las mujeres de 12 años y más que en la pregunta sobre condición de actividad respondieron: oficios domésticos, estudiantes, pensionados, rentistas u otros

Segmento ☐☐☐☐☐☐☐ Vivienda Nº ☐☐
Barrio o Caserío: _____ Hogar ☐☐
Persona No. ☐☐ ☐☐☐☐☐☐☐
Nombre-Apellidos: _____

Preguntas	SI NO	Horas trabajadas última semana	M J J A S O N D E F M A	Horas semanales habituales	Código
Aparte de los cuidados de la casa o de estudiar realiza alguno o varios de los siguientes trabajos *dentro de su casa o finca?*					
1. ¿Lava, plancha o arregla usted ropa ajena?	Sí / No				01
2. ¿Hace usted ropa, costuras o tejidos para otras personas?	Sí / No				02
3. ¿Cuida o atiende niños ajenos percibiendo por ello algún ingreso?	Sí / No				03
4. ¿Hace usted artesanías para vender?	Sí / No				04
5. ¿Hace usted comidas o bebidas para vender?	Sí / No				05
6. ¿Vende usted comida o alquila habitación a personas (pensionistas)?	Sí / No				06
7. ¿Vende usted algún otro tipo de producto o servicio? *Especifique:*	Sí / No				
8. ¿Atiende usted o ayuda en la atención de algún negocio familiar ubicado dentro o a la par de su casa de habitación? *Especifique clase de negocio:*	Sí / No				
9. ¿Se dedica usted o ayuda en la cría o cuidado de animales de granja tales como aves, cerdos o conejos?	Sí / No				20
10. ¿Se dedica usted o ayuda en el ordeño, pastoreo o arreo de animales tales como vacas, cabras o caballos?	Sí / No				21
11. ¿Trabaja usted en su finca o huerta familiar en tareas de preparación de tierra, siembra, abono, riego o cosecha de productos agrícolas?	Sí / No				22
12. ¿Vende hortalizas, leche, huevos o algún otro producto de la finca o huerta familiar?	Sí / No				23
13. ¿Otras tareas? *Especifique:*	Sí / No				
En alguna época del año sale usted a trabajar *fuera de su casa* para hacer una o varias de las siguientes actividades?			M J J A S O N D E F M A		
14. ¿Lavar, planchar, cocinar o hacer la limpieza en otras casas o establecimientos?	Sí / No				51
15. ¿Cuida o atiende niños ajenos percibiendo por ello algún ingreso?	Sí / No				52
16. ¿Realiza venta ambulante de algún tipo de productos tales como frutas, comidas, lotería, ropa, artesanía u otro? *Especifique producto:*	Sí / No				
17. ¿Atiende usted o ayuda en la atención de algún negocio familiar ubicado fuera de su casa? *Especifique clase de negocio:*	Sí / No				
18. ¿Ha trabajado cogiendo café en la última cosecha?	Sí / No				70
19. ¿Ha trabajado en el cultivo del tabaco durante el último año?	Sí / No				71
20. ¿Ha trabajado en algún otro cultivo durante el último año? *Especifique:*	Sí / No				
21. ¿Ha trabajado en alguna otra tarea fuera de su casa durante el último año? *Especifique:*	Sí / No				

OBSERVACIONES: _____

Nombre del Enumerador _____ Firma del Enumerador _____
Fecha de Enumeración _____ Firma del Revisor _____

POBLACION

2 PERSONA No.	NOMBRE Y APELLIDO:

1 RELACION CON EL JEFE

- Jefe..................................... ○1
- Esposa (o) o compañera (o)....... ○2
- Hijo (a)................................ ○3
- Yerno o nuera........................ ○4
- Nieto (a)............................... ○5
- Padres o suegros..................... ○6
- Otros familiares...................... ○7
- Servicio doméstico................... ○8
- Otros no familiares.................. ○9

2 SEXO

Hombre ○1   Mujer ○2

3 EDAD

- Menos 1 año............ ○ 00
- 98 años y más.......... ○ 98
- Años cumplidos ____

4 LUGAR DE NACIMIENTO

Aquí........ ○8

Distrito ____

Cantón ____

Provincia ____

País ____ (Si nació en el extranjero)

5 AÑO DE LA LLEGADA AL PAIS

Año ____ (Solo para nacidos en el extranjero)

6 FECHA DE NACIMIENTO

- Día ____
- Mes ____
- Año ____

7 NACIONALIDAD

Costarricense por:

- Nacimiento.................. ○7
- Naturalización .... ○8
- Otra nacionalidad ____ (E specifique)

8 CONDICION DE ORFANDAD

Madre: Muerta ○1   Viva ○2

Año de fallecimiento ____

Padre: Muerto ○1   Vivo ○2

9 SEGURO SOCIAL

- Solo directo (E y M) ○1   Familiar .... ○4
- Solo directo (IVM) ○2   Otros......... ○5
- Ambos casos.... ○3   No asegurado.. ○6

SOLO PARA PERSONAS DE 5 AÑOS Y MAS

10 LUGAR DE RESIDENCIA HACE 5 AÑOS

¿Dónde residía habitualmente hace 5 años?

Aquí................. ○8

Distrito ____

Cantón ____

Provincia ____

País ____ (Si residía en el extranjero)

11 MATRICULA ESCOLAR

¿Está matriculado en algún centro de enseñanza regular?

Sí ○1   No ○2

12 NIVEL DE INSTRUCCION

¿Cuál es el último año o grado que aprobó en la enseñanza regular?

- Ningún grado...... ○ 00
- Primaria............. ○1 ____
- Secundaria.......... ○2 ____
- Universitaria....... ○3 ____

Carrera : ____

13 ESTUDIO EXTRA ESCOLAR

¿Realiza o ha realizado estudios de enseñanza extra regular (extra escolar)

Sí....... ○   No... ○ 00

Especifique ____

SOLO PARA PERSONAS DE 10 AÑOS Y MAS

14 ALFABETISMO

¿Sabe leer y escribir?

Sí ○1   No ○2

15 ESTADO CONYUGAL

- Unido............ ○1   Separado...... ○2
- Casado........... ○3   Viudo........ ○4
- Divorciado...... ○5   Soltero .... ○6

SOLO PARA PERSONAS DE 12 AÑOS Y MAS

16 CONDICION DE ACTIVIDAD

¿Qué hizo la semana del 9 al 15 de mayo?

- Trabajó................................. ○1
- Buscó trabajo por primera vez.......... ○2
- Estuvo desempleado .... ○3
- Oficios domésticos.................. ○4
- Estudiante......................... ○5
- Pensionado o rentista.............. ○6
- Otro ____ (E specifique) ○7

SOLO PARA PERSONAS DE 12 AÑOS Y MAS EN CONDICION DE "TRABAJO" O ESTUVO "DESEMPLEADO"

17 OCUPACION PRINCIPAL

¿Qué ocupación o clase de trabajo desempeñó la semana del 9 al 15 de mayo, o en su último empleo? .

____

____

18 CATEGORIA OCUPACIONAL

Asalariado   No asalariado

- Gobierno........ ○1   Cuenta propia.... ○4
- Autónomas..... ○2   Patrono .... ○5
- Sector privado.. ○3   Fam sin sueldo.. ○6

19 RAMA DE ACTIVIDAD

¿Qué se hace principalmente en el lugar de trabajo o donde trabajó la última vez?

____

____

20 TAMAÑO DEL LUGAR DE TRABAJO

¿Cuántas personas trabajan en el lugar actual o donde trabajó la última vez?

Menos de 5. ○1   5 ó más .... ○2

21 LOCALIZACION DEL LUGAR DE TRABAJO

¿Dónde está ubicado el lugar de trabajo actual o donde trabajó la última vez?

Aquí......... ○8

Distrito ____

Cantón ____

Provincia ____

País ____ (Si trabajó en el extranjero)

22 PRINCIPAL MEDIO DE TRANSPORTE QUE UTILIZA

- Bus............ ○1   A pie.......... ○4
- Tren......... ○2   Otro medio... ○5
- Carro.......... ○3   Ninguno...... ○6

SOLO PARA PERSONAS DE 12 AÑOS Y MAS EN CONDICION DE "TRABAJO"

23 HORAS TRABAJADAS

¿Cuántas horas trabajó en la semana del 9 al 15 de mayo?

Horas: ____

24 INGRESOS

¿Cuál fue el ingreso por su trabajo?

¢ ____ por ____ (Semana, mes)

SOLO PARA MUJERES DE 15 AÑOS Y MAS

25 HIJOS TENIDOS NACIDOS VIVOS

Ninguno . ○ 00

Hijos ____

26 FECHA DE NACIMIENTO DEL ULTIMO HIJO NACIDO VIVO
(Ya sea que esté vivo o haya muerto)

No ha tenido ○   ____ Día Mes Año

27 HIJOS VIVOS ACTUALMENTE

Ninguno . ○

Hijos ____

A.6. Methodological survey on the measurement of employment, unemployment and underemployment, Costa Rica, 1983

(a) Excerpt from questionnaire used in the survey

BOX 10

Information concerning the preceding 365 days

---

10. Activity during the major part of the preceding 365 days

    Habitually active   ( ) 1   Habitually inactive ( ) 2
    (working, seeking work
    or available for work)

---

11. (a) Most of this time was   11. (b) Was mainly

    Working   ( ) 1 ——> 12   Student   ( ) 1

    Seeking work or   Housewife   ( ) 2
    available for work ( ) 2 ——> 15
                                                Pensioner   ( ) 3   ——> 15

                                                Person of inde-
                                                pendent means ( ) 4

                                                Other   ( ) 5

---

12. Describe the activity of the firm or main business for which the person works

---

13. Describe the type of work (occupation) done by the person

---

14. Indicate the category of occupation:

    Self-employed

                                Employ others   ( ) 1
                                Work alone   ( ) 2
                                Work without pay   ( ) 3

    Paid employee

                                Permanent employee ( ) 4
                                Temporary employee ( ) 5
                                Other   ( ) 6

---

15. Were you engaged in any (secondary) paid activity during the preceding 365 days?

Yes ( ) 1   No ( ) 2 ———> 20

16. Describe the (secondary) activity of the firm or business for which the person was working

17. Describe the type of work (occupation) done by the person in that firm or business

18. Indicate the category of occupation

(Use codes from 14)   / / ———> 20

BOX 20

20. Indicate if you worked this last week

      Yes ( ) 1   No ( ) 2 ———> 30

---

21. Did you work last week at more than one job, firm or own business?

      Yes ( ) 1   No ( ) 2

---

22. How many hours did you actually work last week (in one or more jobs or own businesses)?

             Monday   hours
             Tuesday   hours
             Wednesday   hours
             Thursday   hours
             Friday   hours
             Saturday   hours
             Sunday   hours

             Total ....   hours

If the total is 30 hours or more   ( ) 1 ———> 70

If the total is less than 30 hours ( ) 2

---

23. How many hours do you usually work per week?

Less than 30 hours ( ) 1   30 hours or more ( ) 2

---

24. (a) Why do you usually work less than 30 hours per week?   24. (b) Why did you work less than 30 hours last week?

Illness or accident	( ) 1
Public holiday or vacation	( ) 2
Strike, stoppage or lockout	( ) 3
Reduction of economic activity	( ) 4
Bad weather	( ) 5
Personal or family commitments	( ) 6
Only found part-time work	( ) 7
Did not want to work full-time	( ) 8
Worked full-time less than 30 hours	( ) 9
Other	( ) 0

70. Describe the activity of the firm or main business for which the person was working

71. Describe the type of work (occupation) done by the person

72. Indicate the category of occupation:

Self-employed

Employ others	( ) 1
Work alone	( ) 2
Work without pay in family business	( ) 3

Paid employee

Permanent employee	( ) 4
Temporary employee	( ) 5
Other	( ) 6

BOX 30

30. Even though you did not work last week did you have a job or your own firm/business?

Yes, I had paid employment ( ) 1 __

Yes, I had a firm or business ( ) 2 __

No ( ) 3 ———> 40

---

31. Why did you not work last week?

Illness or accident ( ) 1

Public holiday or vacation ( ) 2

Strike, stoppage or lockout ( ) 3

Reduction of economic activity ( ) 4

Temporary disruption of work ( ) 5

Bad weather ( ) 6

Personal or family commitments ( ) 7

Study leave ( ) 8

Maternity leave ( ) 9

Other ( ) 0

---

32. How many weeks have you been absent from work?

_____ weeks

---

33. How many hours do you usually work each week?

Less than 30 hours ( ) 1

30 hours or more ( ) 2 ———> 35

---

34. Why do you usually work less than 30 hours a week?

(Use the code from question 24) /__/

---

35. Note to the enumerator

If in answer to question 30 you checked code 2, move on to ———> 70

If in answer to question 30 you checked code 1, go to the next question

---

A.6 (continued)

36. Are you being paid for the time you did not work last week?

     Yes ( ) 1   No ( ) 2

37. Are you assured of returning to work or do you have any agreement regarding the date of return?

     Yes ( ) 1 ———> 70   No ( ) 2 ———> 70

BOX 40

40. Did you engage in any of the following activities last week?

Preparation of soil, sowing/planting, cultivation (weeding, watering, etc.) or harvesting, in relation to sugar cane, coffee, beans, yucca, other, fruits, vegetables .... ( ) 11

Raising and care of livestock, fowl, etc. and production of milk, eggs, etc. .... ( ) 12

Other activities relating to agriculture, mining, hunting, fishing, forestry .... ( ) 13

Industrial processing or treatment of foodstuffs .... ( ) 35

Production of baskets, carpets/straw mats, other crafts .... ( ) 37

Making yarn, fabric, women's/men's clothing .... ( ) 38

Other manufacturing activities .... ( ) 39

Construction, repair, maintenance of:

    Farm house .... ( ) 51

    Own house/dwelling .... ( ) 52

    Other construction-related activities .... ( ) 53

Helping in places of sale/distribution of food/drink .... ( ) 61

Helping in the sale of agricultural produce and other retail sale establishments .... ( ) 62

A.6 (continued)

Transport of freight for marketing/storage .... ( ) 71

Other transport-related activities .... ( ) 72

Repairing tools, shoes, etc. .... ( ) 92

Collecting wood, fetching water, other services .... ( ) 93

---

41. Note to the enumerator

If more than one activity   If no activity is
is checked   checked ———> 50
              ↓

---

42. Insert codes (up to 4 activities), check the appropriate circle and put down
    the total number of hours then go to 50

Code	All or part for sale	All for household consumption	No. of hours
/ / /	( ) 1	( ) 2	_____
/ / /	( ) 1	( ) 2	_____
/ / /	( ) 1	( ) 2	_____
/ / /	( ) 1	( ) 2	_____

A.6 (continued)

BOXES 50 and 60

50. During the past month, have you looked for paid employment or tried to establish your own business?

Yes ( ) 1   No ( ) 2 ———> 60

51. What did you do during the last month to find work or to establish your own business or firm?

	Yes	No
Contacted an employment agency	( ) 1	( ) 2
Approached potential employers directly	( ) 1	( ) 2
Asked in various places of work, farms, etc.	( ) 1	( ) 2
Asked friends and relatives	( ) 1	( ) 2
Placed or answered ads in the newspapers	( ) 1	( ) 2
Looked for sites, buildings and so forth to establish your own business or firm	( ) 1	( ) 2
Took steps to obtain financial resources and to establish your own business or firm	( ) 1	( ) 2
Requested permission or authorization to establish your own business or firm	( ) 1	( ) 2
Other _____	( ) 1	( ) 2
Nothing _____ ( ) 3 ———> 60		

52. Could you have started to work last week?

Yes   ( ) 1

No, because

      Attending the training centre   ( ) 2

      Personal or family commitments   ( ) 3

      Other reasons   ( ) 4

53. Have you ever worked before?

Yes, during the past year ( ) 1

Yes, between one and five years ago ( ) 2 ——> 70

Yes, more than five years ago ( ) 3

No, I have never worked ( ) 4 ——> 80

---

60. Do you wish to work right now for wages/salary or bonus/commission at home or outside the home?

Yes, at home ( ) 1 ___   No ( ) 3 ——> 64b

Yes, outside the home ( ) 2 ___   Don't know ( ) 4 ——> 64a

---

61. What type of work do you want?

Permanent full-time paid employment ( ) 1

Permanent part-time paid employment ( ) 2

To be self-employed ( ) 3

Other ( ) 4   Want to work _____ hours per week

---

62. Describe the type of work (occupation) you want.

---

63. Give reasons why you have not sought work nor done anything to establish your own business/firm during the past week.

	Yes	No
Personal illness or accident	( ) 1	( ) 2
Attending school, college, etc.	( ) 1	( ) 2
Personal or family commitments	( ) 1	( ) 2
Waiting to go back to your job	( ) 1	( ) 2
Waiting for answers from potential employers	( ) 1	( ) 2
Waiting for the busy season in agriculture	( ) 1	( ) 2
Found another job	( ) 1	( ) 2
Thought there was no work available in the region	( ) 1	( ) 2
Did not know how to go about looking for work	( ) 1	( ) 2
Other	( ) 1	( ) 2

64. (a) Why were you unable to accept
         a job last week?

64. (b) (Ask only if circle 3 in
         question 60 is checked)
         Why don't you want to work now?

Because attending training centre   ( ) 1

Because of personal or family commitments ( ) 2

Other   ( ) 3

65. Have you ever worked before?

    (Use codes from box 53)   / /

    If 1, 2 or 3 checked ———> 70

    If no ———————————> 80

BOX 70

70. Describe the activity of the firm or main business for which the person was
    working.

71. Describe the type of work (occupation) the person does.

72. Indicate category of occupation:

    Self-employed

                    Employ others   ( ) 1
                    Work alone   ( ) 2
                    Work without pay
                    in family business   ( ) 3

    Paid employee

                    Permanent   ( ) 4
                    Temporary   ( ) 5
                    Other   ( ) 6

A.6 (continued)

73. Note to the enumerator:

If in 70 you checked 1 and
in 20 you checked 1 _____   If no ———> 80

In in 70 you checked 1 and
in 30 you checked 1 or 2 ____

74. Type of institution in which you were employed

Government (central, autonomous, semi-autonomous,
municipality)   ( ) 1

Private and registered, clinic, hospital, school, college,
firm of lawyers, engineers, similar form of independent   ( ) 2   ——> 80
professionals

Bank, insurance, corporation, co-operative   ( ) 3

                                                                      Don't
                                                                      know

Registered establishment (company, firm, factory, private
or public)   ( ) 4   ( ) 7

Other - registered   ( ) 5   ( ) 8

Unregistered   ( ) 6   ( ) 9

75. (a) Were you covered by some pension   75. (b) Does your firm bill the sale
        or other social security system   of goods and services?
        paid for by the firm?

    Yes ( ) 1 No ( ) 2 Don't know ( ) 3   Yes ( ) 1 No ( ) 2 Don't know ( ) 3

76. How many people worked in the establishment or firm?

    10 or more ( ) 1   Less than 10 ( ) 2

77. The principal work equipment of the establishment, firm or business is operated:

    Manually   ( ) 1

    On fuel   ( ) 2

    On electricity ( ) 3

    Other   ( ) 4

---

78. Indicate whether the place of work is

    Located in your own home   ( ) 1

    Located outside your own home   ( ) 2

    No fixed location   ( ) 3

---

79. Indicate the average monthly income derived from the work:

    _____   colones per month ———> 80

BOX 80

80. Status of daily activity of this person during the past month

    Note:
        2 for a complete day of activity
        1 for half a day's activity

	M	Tu	W	Th	F	Sat	Sun	Total
At work								
Has job or own business/firm but not at work								
Without work and available for work (whether seeking or not searching for work)								
Without work and not available for work								
Total	2	2	2	2	2	2	2	14

Bloque 10
Información sobre los 365 días precedentes

10. Actividad durante la mayor parte de los 365 días precedentes.

Habitualmente activa (trabajando, buscando trabajo o disponible para trabajar) ◯ 1   Habitualmente inactiva ◯ 2

11. a) La mayor parte de este tiempo estaba

Trabajando ◯ 1 → 12

Buscando trabajo o disponible para trabajar ◯ 2 → 15

11. b) Era principalmente

Estudiante ◯ 1
Ama de casa ◯ 2
Pensionado ◯ 3   → 15
Rentista ◯ 4
Otro ◯ 5

12. Describa la actividad de la empresa o negocio principal en donde trabaja la persona

13. Describa la clase de trabajo (ocupación) que hace la persona

14. Indicar categoría de ocupación:

Trabajador independiente:
Patrono ◯ 1
Por cuenta propia ◯ 2
Familiar no remunerado ◯ 3

Empleado asalariado:
Asalariado permanente ◯ 4
Asalariado temporal ◯ 5
Otro ◯ 6

15. ¿Estuvo ocupado en alguna actividad (secundaria) remunerada en los 365 días precedentes?

Sí ◯ 1   No ◯ 2 → 20

16. Describa la actividad (secundaria) de la empresa o negocio en donde trabajaba la persona.

17. Describa la clase de trabajo (ocupación) que hace la persona en esta empresa o negocio.

18. Indicar categoría de ocupación (Usar los códigos de 14) □ → 20

Bloque 20

20. Indicar si la semana pasada trabajó

Sí ◯ 1   No ◯ 2 → 30

21. ¿Trabajó la semana pasada en más de un empleo, empresa o negocio propio?

Sí ◯ 1   No ◯ 2

22. ¿Cuántas horas trabajó efectivamente la semana pasada (en uno o más empleos o negocios propios)?

Lunes _____ horas
Martes _____ horas
Miércoles _____ horas
Jueves _____ horas
Viernes _____ horas
Sábado _____ horas
Domingo _____ horas

Total _____ horas

Si el total es de 30 horas o más ◯ 1 → 70
Si el total es de menos de 30 hs. ◯ 2

23. ¿Cuántas horas trabaja habitualmente por semana?

Menos de 30 hs. ◯ 1   30 hs. o más ◯ 2

24. a) ¿Por qué razón trabaja habitualmente menos de 30 horas por semana?   **24. b)** ¿Por qué razón trabajó menos de 30 horas la semana pasada?

Enfermedad o accidente ◯ 1
Días festivos o vacaciones ◯ 2
Huelga o paro ◯ 3
Reducción de la actividad económica ◯ 4
Mal tiempo ◯ 5
Obligaciones personales o familiares ◯ 6
Solo encontró trabajo a tiempo parcial ◯ 7
No quería trabajo a tiempo completo ◯ 8
Trabajó a tiempo completo menos de 30 horas ◯ 9
Otros ◯ 0

70. Describa la actividad de la empresa o negocio principal en donde trabajaba la persona.

71. Describa la clase de trabajo (ocupación) que hace la persona.

72. Indicar categoría de ocupación:

Trabajador independiente:
Patrono ◯ 1
Por cuenta propia ◯ 2
Familiar no remunerado ◯ 3
Empleado asalariado:
Asalariado permanente ◯ 4
Asalariado temporal ◯ 5
Otro ◯ 6

Bloque 30

30. Aunque no haya trabajado la semana pasada ¿Tenía algún empleo o empresa/negocio propio?

Sí, tenía un empleo asalariado .... ○¹
Sí, tenía una empresa o negocio .... ○²
No ○³ → 40

31. ¿Por qué no trabajó la semana pasada?

Enfermedad o accidente .... ○ 1
Días festivos o vacaciones .... ○ 2
Huelga o paro .... ○ 3
Reducción de la actividad económica ..... ○ 4
Desorganización temporal del trabajo ..... ○ 5
Mal tiempo .... ○ 6
Obligaciones personales o familiares ...... ○ 7
Licencia de estudios .... ○ 8
Licencia por maternidad .... ○ 9
Otros .... ○ 0

32. ¿Cuántas semanas ha estado ausente del trabajo?

_____ semanas

33. ¿Cuántas horas por semana trabaja habitualmente?

Menos de 30 hs. ○¹   30 hs. o más ○² → 35

34. ¿Por qué trabaja habitualmente menos de 30 hs. por semana?

(Use los códigos de la pregunta 24) ☐

35. Control para el enumerador

Si en pregunta 30 marcó código 2 pase a ———→ 70

Si en pregunta 30 marcó código 1 pase a la siguiente

36. ¿Percibe salario por el tiempo no trabajado la semana pasada?

Sí ○¹   No ○²

37. ¿Tiene seguridad de regresar al trabajo o algún acuerdo sobre la fecha de regreso?

Sí ○¹ → 70   No ○² → 70

Bloque 40

40. ¿Realizó alguna(s) de las siguientes actividades la semana pasada?

Preparar la tierra, sembrar/plantar, cultivar (desyerbar, regar, etc.), o cosechar, en relación con caña de azúcar, café, frijoles, yuca, otros, frutas, hortalizas..................... ○ 11
Criar y cuidar ganado, aves, etc., y producir leche, huevos, etc. ...... ○ 12
Otras actividades de agricultura, minería, también caza, pesca, silvicultura..................... ○ 13

Trabajar en procesos o tratamientos industriales de productos alimenticios........................ ○ 35
Fabricar canastos, alfombras/esteras, otras artesanías ... ○ 37
Hacer hilados, tejidos, vestidos de mujer/hombre........... ○ 38
Otras actividades manufactureras........................ ○ 39

Trabajar en la construcción, reparación, mantenimiento de:
Casa de granja........................ ○ 51
Casa/vivienda propia........................ ○ 52
Otras actividades relativas a la construcción.......... ○ 53

Ayudar en lugares de venta/distribución de comidas/ bebidas .... ○ 61
Ayudar en ventas de productos agrícolas y otros establecimientos de ventas por menor .... ○ 62

Transportar cargas para mercadeo/almacenamiento .... ○ 71
Otras actividades relativas a transporte .... ○ 72

Reparar herramientas, zapatos, etc. .... ○ 92
Recoger leña, ir por agua, otros servicios .... ○ 93

41. Control para el enumerador

Si se anotó por lo menos una actividad ↓   Si no se anotó actividad ———→ 50

42. Anotar códigos(hasta 4 actividades), marcar el círculo apropiado y anotar número total de horas-luego pase a la 50.

Código	Todo o parte para vender	Todo para consumo del hogar	Número de horas
☐☐☐	○ 1	○ 2	_____
☐☐☐	○ 1	○ 2	_____
☐☐☐	○ 1	○ 2	_____
☐☐☐	○ 1	○ 2	_____

Bloques 50 y 60

50. ¿El mes pasado estuvo buscando empleo asalariado o tratando de establecer su propia empresa o negocio?

60

Sí ◯¹   No ◯²

51. ¿Qué hizo el mes pasado para buscar trabajo o establecer su propio negocio o empresa?

	Sí	No
Estableció contacto con oficina de empleo.....	◯1	◯2
Gestionó directamente ante empleadores........	◯1	◯2
Gestionó en lugares de trabajo, granjas, etc....	◯1	◯2
Gestionó valiéndose de amigos y familiares.....	◯1	◯2
Puso avisos o respondió a ofertas aparecidas en los periódicos....	◯1	◯2
Buscó terrenos, edificios, etc., para establecer su propio negocio o empresa........	◯1	◯2
Gestionó para obtener recursos financieros y establecer su propio negocio o empresa.......	◯1	◯2
Solicitó permiso o licencia para establecer su propio negocio o empresa........	◯1	◯2
Otros: _____	◯1	◯2
Nada _____	◯3	60

52. ¿Podía haber empezado a trabajar la semana pasada?

Sí .... ◯1

No, porque

Asistía al centro de enseñanza .... ◯2

Tenía obligaciones personales o familiares........ ◯3

Tenía otras razones.. ◯4

53. ¿Ha trabajado antes?

Sí, en el transcurso del año precedente......... ◯1 ⎤
Sí, hace de uno a cinco años........................ ◯2 ⎬ 70
Sí, hace más de cinco años........................... ◯3 ⎦

No, nunca ha trabajado................................. ◯4 → 80

60. ¿Desea trabajar ahora mismo por sueldo/salario o ganancia/beneficio en la casa o fuera de ella?

Sí, en la casa............ ◯1 ⎤ No............ ◯3 → 64b.
Sí, fuera de la casa..... ◯2 ⎦ No sabe...... ◯4 → 64 a.

61. ¿Qué tipo de trabajo desea?

Empleo asalariado permanente a tiempo completo........ ◯1

Empleo asalariado permanente a tiempo parcial............ ◯2

Trabajo independiente... ◯3

Otro..... ◯4   Desea trabajar _____ hs. por semana

62. Describa la clase de trabajo (ocupación) que desea.

63. Indicar razones por no haber buscado trabajo ni hecho nada para establecer negocio/empresa propia la semana pasada.

	Sí	No
Enfermedad o accidente personal	◯1	◯2
Asistió a la escuela, colegio, etc.	◯1	◯2
Tuvo obligaciones personales o familiares...........	◯1	◯2
Espera ser reintegrado a su trabajo...................	◯1	◯2
Espera respuesta de empleadores.......................	◯1	◯2
Espera el período de gran actividad agrícola........	◯1	◯2
Había encontrado nuevo trabajo.......................	◯1	◯2
Creía que no había trabajado disp. en la region	◯1	◯2
No sabía cómo proceder a buscar trabajo............	◯1	◯2
Otras...	◯1	◯2

64.a) ¿Por qué no pudo tomar un trabajo la semana pasada? | **64.b) (Preguntar solo si marcó 3 en 60) ¿Por qué no desea trab. ahora?**

Porque asiste al centro de enseñanza .... ◯1

Porque tiene obligaciones personales o familiares............... ◯2

Otros... ◯3

65. ¿Ha trabajado antes?

(Utilizar los códigos de 53)

Si marcó 1,2 o 3 → 70

Si no → 80

Bloque 70

70. Describa la actividad de la empresa o negocio principal **en donde** trabajaba la persona.

71. Describa la clase de trabajo (ocupación) que hace la persona.

72. Indicar categoría de ocupación:

Trabajador independiente:
- Patrono .... ○1
- Por cuenta propia .... ○2
- Familiar no remunerado .... ○3

Empleado asalariado:
- Asalariado permanente .... ○4
- Asalariado temporal .... ○5
- Otro .... ○6

73. Control para el enumerador.
Si en 70 marcó 1 y en 20 marcó 1 — Si no → 80
Si en 70 marcó 1 y en 30 marcó 1 ó 2

74. Clase de institución en que estaba empleado
- Gobierno (Central, autónomas, semi-autónomas y Municipalidades) .... ○1
- Privada y registrada: dispensario, hospital, escuela, colegio firma de abogados, de ingenieros, empresa similar de profesionales independientes .... ○2 →80
- Bancos, seguros, sociedades, cooperativas .... ○3

No sabe
- Establecimientos registrados (compañía, firma, fábrica, privada o pública) .... ○4 ○7
- Otras - registradas .... ○5 ○8
- No registradas .... ○6 ○9

75. a) Estaba cubierto por algún sistema de pensiones u otro de Seguridad Social pagado por su empresa.
Sí ○1 No ○2 No sabe ○3

75. b) ¿Su empresa factura la venta de bienes o servicios?
Sí ○1 No ○2 No sabe ○3

76. ¿Cuántas personas estaban ocupadas en el establecimiento o empresa?
Diez o más ○1   Menos de diez ○2 ____

77. El principal equipo de trabajo del establecimiento, empresa o negocio es operado:
- Manualmente .... ○1
- Con combustible .... ○2
- Con electricidad .... ○3
- Otros .... ○4

78. Indicar si el lugar de trabajo está
- Situado en el propio hogar .... ____ ○1
- Situado fuera del propio hogar ... ____ ○2
- Sin asiento fijo .... ____ ○3

79. Indicar el promedio de ingreso mensual proveniente del empleo:
____ Colones por mes ____ 80

Bloque 80

80. Condición de actividad diaria de esta persona durante la semana pasada. Anotar: 2 por un día completo de actividad; 1 por medio día de actividad	LUNES	MARTES	MIERCOLES	JUEVES	VIERNES	SABADO	DOMINGO	TOTAL
En el trabajo								
Con empleo o negocio/empresa propia pero no en el trabajo.								
Sin trabajo y disponible (buscando o no) para trabajar.								
Sin trabajo y no disponible para trabajar								
Total	2	2	2	2	2	2	2	14

A.6 (continued)

(b) Operational definition of urban informal sector in the survey

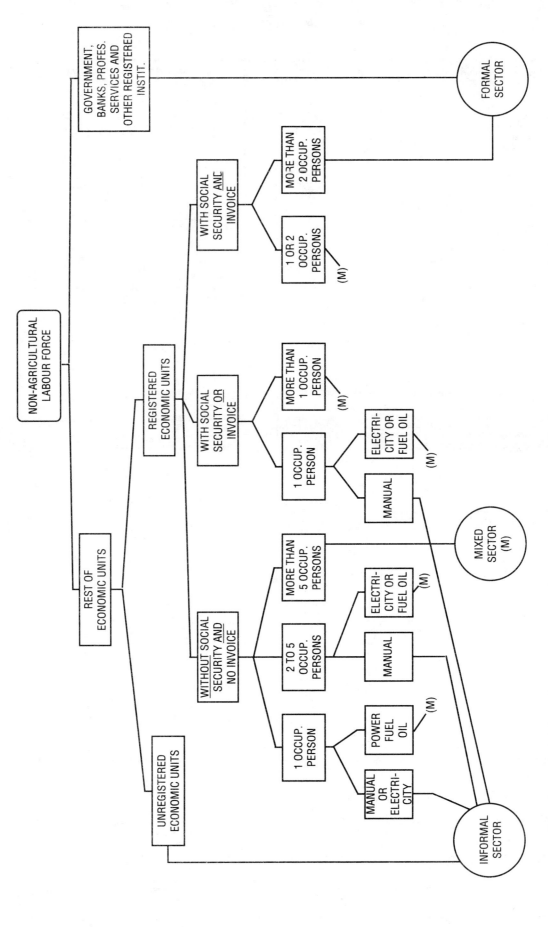

Source: Rafael Trigueros M., "Algunos aspectos relacionados con la definición actual del empleo, del desempleo y del subempleo a través de encuestas de hogares" (Some aspects related to the current definition of employment, unemployment and underemployment in household surveys) (Santiago, Chile, ECLAC, November 1985).

Part Four

MEASURING THE ECONOMIC SITUATION OF WOMEN:
AN ALTERNATIVE APPROACH*

_____

    *   Prepared by Stein Ringen, a consultant to the International Research and
Training Institute for the Advancement of Women and the Statistical Office,
Department of International Economic and Social Affairs, United Nations Secretariat.

INTRODUCTION

This part of the report describes statistical indicators for measuring the economic situation of women, which differ considerably from labour force indicators derived from concepts of economic activity recommended by the International Labour Organisation and the United Nations. These indicators are designed to make the economic activities of women more visible and this can be a step towards taking the situation of women into consideration in development planning. By using statistical indicators, as opposed to more qualitative methods, the situation of women is described in such terms as development planners are accustomed to using as a basis for their work.

This study rests on some simple assumptions:

(a) As is often suggested, some established statistical procedures may have a sex bias or assume certain sex-based stereotypes. The statistical description of the situation of women should therefore not necessarily take as given, accept, or be bound by established statistical procedures;

(b) Description of the economic situation of an individual or group calls for a kind of double-entry bookkeeping or input-output analysis. There is, on the one hand, the person's economic activity (contribution to production), and on the other hand, his/her economic welfare (reward from production). The input and output sides are obviously related to each other, as it is usually through work that we gain claims to income or consumption but, since such claims are not determined by work alone, the input and output sides need to be described separately. For example, the female member(s) of a household may carry a large part of the household's total work burden and yet enjoy only a small part of its total consumption;

(c) The concept of "welfare" is used, as in welfare economics, as a short-hand form for "people's well-being" (as distinguished, for example, from the use of the term to mean social assistance from government). Chapter I contains a discussion of the concept and measurement of welfare. It is usually (perhaps only) because income is held to be a relevant indicator of welfare that we are interested in the analysis of income and income distribution. Chapter II deals with income as an indicator of welfare seen from the perspective of the specific conditions of women. Methods for more direct measurement of welfare are illustrated in chapter III below.

The description of the economic situation of women presents some special challenges which arise from the structure of female activity. Economic activity can take place in a formal market or can be informal, for example, within the household. Economic rewards can be in monetary form or can be received in kind. From the point of view of measuring welfare, distinctions between formal and informal economic activity, between economic activity conducted within and outside of the household, and between monetary and in-kind rewards are not important. Non-market economic activity, including the production of goods and services within the household for consumption by household members, is just as much economic activity as work that happens to be paid. In-kind compensation is compensation just as much as compensation that happens to come in the form of money. The consumption of goods produced by oneself is consumption just as much as the consumption of goods that are bought in a store. If we are interested in describing what people have and do economically, we should be interested in and ideally treat equally all economic activities and rewards. Thus, unless we are able to incorporate informal economic activity and in-kind economic rewards in statistical measurements, we will not be describing the economic welfare of individuals but only their attachment to the formal sector of the economy. The treatment of informal activities and in-kind rewards is a difficulty in any description of economic conditions, but more so in the description of the situation of women since so much of their activity is usually in the informal sector. The failure to incorporate informal activities and in-kind rewards is an important cause of sex bias in economic statistics because less of the economic activity of women than that of men is thereby considered and accounted for. This failure also introduces bias into comparative economic statistics between developing and developed countries.

In order to interpret a description of the economic situation of women, some standard of reference is needed against which their observed situation can be compared. Since a basic underlying concern in socio-economic analyses which focus on women is discrimination, the obvious choice is to compare women's situation with the situation of men. This is the approach used in the present paper. It should be noted, however, that this is not necessarily the most appropriate comparison. These comparisons are based on the assumption, stated or implicit, that the situation of men represents an ideal towards which women should strive. This is, of course, not necessarily the case. The demonstration of an underprivileged situation of women in comparison to men and the use in this connection of concepts such as integration and emancipation, as will be done below, can therefore in some cases be controversial. Another approach could be to compare the observed situation of women with a normative understanding of what their situation ought to be. In practical terms, however, this is difficult and is not likely to be less controversial.

One aim of the following chapters is to go beyond a discussion of concepts and principles and to include examples from available statistics. They explore how far it is possible to go towards compiling a simple set of indicators on the economic situation of women by drawing on statistical material which is presently widely available. Such a set of indicators could be used on a more or less regular basis to monitor main trends in the economic situation of women. The exploration is, however, done in a tentative manner. The examples are taken mainly from Norwegian public statistics and from a small number of statistical publications from a few developing countries. Norway has a well-developed system of statistics and the examples indicate the extent to which relevant data are available in such a system. Within the scope and time available for preparing the present study, it was not possible to undertake a systematic search of available statistics or literature for developing countries, but it is assumed that the material fairly reflects the situation with regard to available statistics in at least some of them.

I. MEASURING ECONOMIC ACTIVITY

It is now widely argued that there is an economic aspect to almost all activity, namely, choice in the use of limited means, and that therefore the distinction between economic and non-economic activity is not very meaningful. It is common in welfare economics to hold "utility" to be the ultimate product of any activity. Since no activity is conceivable if it does not produce "utility" for someone, the distinction between productive and non-productive activities is, in this view, equally dubious. Although such distinctions are for many practical purposes necessary, such as the present one of comparing the level of economic activity of women and men, it should be recognized that the quest for objective criteria is futile and that all such distinctions are largely arbitrary.

Thus, all activity that can intuitively be regarded as "work" is in the present study considered to be economic activity. This includes work both in the formal and in the informal sectors, inside as well as outside of the household, and unpaid as well as paid work. Economic activity should, ideally, according to this understanding, include the following:

(a) Work as employee and in self-employment, including travel to/from work, time spent for meals at work, and the like;

(b) Work in family businesses, whether paid or unpaid;

(c) Production of goods and services within households, whether for consumption within the household or for trade, barter, gifts and the like (household work). This is not to say that all household activity is work. Only the production of goods and services is included. But no distinction is made between production for outside use and production for consumption within the household;

(d) Education (investment in/preparation for more "productive" work later);

(e) The activity of looking for work (which is an investment in future work, much like education);

(f) National service, military or civilian (the production of defence and other collective goods).

Non-economic activity is a residual category.

The most commonly available source of statistics on economic activity is labour force statistics. Time-use data are also an important source, although less widely available. Each of these sources is considered below.

A. Labour force statistics

In labour force statistics, individuals are classified by their main activity (current or usual activity). The basic distinction is between the economically active and the not economically active, with more or less detailed disaggregation applied to these main categories.

Table 14 presents statistics on economic activity in Norway and Indonesia. These statistics are from labour force surveys which were conducted in accordance with ILO recommendations. However, the distinction in the table between economically active and not economically active does not follow ILO or United Nations recommendations. Only a relatively simple battery of five to six survey questions is necessary to produce these statistics.

The main features indicated by the table are:

(a) The level of economic activity is high in both populations. When classified by main activity, about 90 per cent of all persons are economically active;

(b) The level of economic activity of women is about the same as that of men, slightly higher in Norway and slightly lower in Indonesia;

(c) The difference in economic activity between women and men is found more in the structure of activity than the level of activity. Women, more than men, have household work as their main activity. Hence, women do not differ from men primarily in their level of economic activity but in the degree to which they are integrated into the labour market. This is reflected also, particularly in Indonesia, among those who work in the primary sector. Between 1979 and 1984 in Norway, there was for both women and men little change in the level of economic activity. However, the structure of economic activity is stable for men but has changed considerably for women, the trend being that more women have their main activity in the labour market and fewer in household work;

(d) The level of economic activity appears to be slightly higher in Indonesia than in Norway, but this may be due to a lack of comparability in the data. To the extent that these statistics can be generalized, they suggest that the difference between developing and developed countries as to economic activity is found not in the level but in the structure of activity, notably in the importance of the primary sector.

These statistics for Norway and Indonesia are roughly comparable. The survey designs are about the same. In both cases, current activity is recorded (activity last week). The categories of activity are, as far as can be determined from the respective publications, defined in more or less the same way. There is some difference in sample coverage. The Norwegian survey covers the population 16 to 74 years of age. The Indonesian survey covers the entire population but the figures reproduced here are for the population aged 10 and older. The effect of the difference in coverage is that the Indonesian statistics, compared to the Norwegian ones, probably overestimate somewhat the level of educational participation and thereby the level of economic activity. This problem could be eliminated by estimating statistics from the Indonesian survey covering only the population 16 to 74 years of age, in which case near-perfect comparability would be achieved. This shows that it is possible, on the basis of existing ILO recommendations on labour force statistics and with simple means, to produce comparative statistics on economic activity in developed and developing economies on the basis of the broad concept of economic activity which is applied here.

Table 14. Activity status of the population, Norway and Indonesia

(Percentage)

| | NORWAY a/ | | | | INDONESIA b/ | |
| | 1979 | | 1984 | | 1976 | |
	Women	Men	Women	Men	Women	Men
Economically active	90.5	88.2	89.9	87.4	92.9	94.2
Gainful employment c/	52.8	76.9	56.5	75.1	45.4	75.5
Household work	30.2	0.9	24.6	1.2	33.7	1.1
Other d/	7.6	10.4	8.7	11.1	13.8	17.6
Not economically active	9.5	11.7	10.0	12.6	7.1	5.9
Retired	4.9	6.7	5.2	7.5)	5.8)	4.6
Disabled	4.4	4.6	4.6	4.5)	)	
Other e/	0.1	0.4	0.3	0.6	1.3	1.3
Total	100.0	100.0	100.0	100.0	100.0	100.0
Memoranda						
Unemployed f/	1.3	1.2	1.9	2.2	0.9	1.5
Education g/	7.1	7.6	8.0	7.5	12.8	16.1
Primary sector, h/						
employees	..	..	0.5	2.0	6.0	7.7
Self-employed	..	..	0.5	4.3	8.1	28.6
Family workers	..	..	1.5	0.5	18.6	12.8

Source: Norway – Labour Market Statistics 1984 (Central Bureau of Statistics).

Indonesia – 1976 Intercensal Population Survey, Series 2 (Central Bureau of Statistics.

a/   Population aged 16-74.

b/   Population aged 10 years and older.

c/   Includes persons temporarily absent from work.

d/   Education, unemployed seeking work, and (in Norway) military service.

e/   Persons not employed and not seeking work.

f/   Persons seeking work, including persons presently active in household work or education.

g/   Includes persons presently active in education who are seeking work.

h/   Agriculture, husbandry, hunting, forestry, fishing.

These simple estimates provide a great deal of information on economic activity, including the following:

(a) They correspond well to a reasonable understanding of the concept of economic activity, which equates economic activity with "work", and hence give a meaningful description of the level of economic activity;

(b) They are sensitive to differences in the structure of economic activity between women and men;

(c) They are sensitive to differences in the structure of economic activity between developing and developed economies;

(d) They are sensitive to change over time in the structure of economic activity of women.

An important feature of this way of organizing and presenting the statistics is that the level of economic activity is shown to be high and to be about the same for women and men. This is an important and, many would argue, entirely appropriate result. In this view, production of goods and services within the household (and for the benefit of household members) is an economic activity just as much as is work against monetary payment in the market. Preparation for more "productive" work, such as education or job seeking, is economic activity (an investment of time and effort for present enjoyment or in the anticipation of a benefit later on), and certainly not a form of passivity. The production of collective goods in some form of national service (compulsory or voluntary) may be less rewarding for the individual than some other activities, but it is certainly production and work. Under-employment can occur just as easily in labour market jobs as in household work.

Labour market statistics can, however, be organized so as to give a different picture, in particular in the comparison of the level of economic activity between women and men. For example, in the ILO Year Book of Labour Statistics 1985, 23 per cent of Indonesian women are classified as economically active as compared to 48 per cent of men; and 41 per cent of Norwegian women as compared to 59 per cent of men. These figures are estimated, in principle, according to national accounts standards. The ILO data, in comparison to the data in table 14, suggest that the overall level of economic activity in Indonesia is quite low and that fewer women than men are involved in economic activity.

Table 15 shows some main results from the Botswana Labour Force Survey of 1984/85. In this table, "work" and "employment" are defined in relation to market activity. (The terminology in the table is the one used in the source.) These figures are not comparable to those in table 14. It here appears, as in the ILO statistics, that women are less active than men. The Botswana survey is conducted "broadly" (as stated in the publication) according to ILO recommendations on labour force statistics. It is therefore likely that statistics comparable to those in table 14 on labour force statistics can be estimated from these survey data.

It can fairly be argued that, in table 14, labour force statistics are organized so as to describe economic activity, whereas in table 15 (and the ILO Year Book) they are organized more so as to show the degree of integration into the market economy. There is no question that one way of organizing the statistics is more "correct" than the other - that depends on what one wants to demonstrate with

Table 15. Distribution of population by activity status, usual activity basis and current activity basis, Botswana, 12 months ending 30 April 1985 a/

(Percentage)

	Urban			Rural			Total		
	Male	Female	Total	Male	Female	Total	Male	Female	Total
Usual activity basis b/									
Working	62.0	37.0	48.4	46.0	27.4	35.1	49.6	29.3	37.9
Not working but available	13.4	28.4	21.6	22.0	35.4	29.8	20.1	33.9	28.0
Not working and not available:									
Students, etc.	18.8	19.4	19.1	21.0	17.1	18.7	20.5	17.6	18.8
Home duties	4.0	13.4	9.1	7.5	16.3	12.7	6.7	15.7	11.9
Permanently unable to work	0.8	1.2	1.0	2.9	3.3	3.2	2.4	2.9	2.7
Other	0.8	0.8	0.8	0.5	0.6	0.5	0.6	0.6	0.6
Sub-total not available	24.4	34.6	29.9	31.9	37.3	35.1	30.2	36.8	34.0
Not stated	0.2	0.1	0.1	0.0	..	0.0	0.1	0.0	0.0
Current activity basis c/									
Employed	61.7	37.8	48.7	55.0	40.8	46.7	56.5	40.2	47.1
Unemployed	16.1	27.1	22.1	12.8	15.4	14.3	13.5	17.8	16.0
Not in labour force	22.1	35.0	29.1	32.2	43.7	39.0	29.9	42.0	36.9
Not stated	0.1	0.1	0.1	0.0	..	0.0	0.1	0.0	0.0
Total	100.0	100.0	100.0	100.0	100.0	100.0	100.0	100.0	100.0

Source: Botswana Labour Force Survey 1984-85 (Gaborone, Central Statistical Office).

a/ Excludes children under 12 years. Relates only to occupants of private dwellings and excludes occupants of temporary and institutionalized dwellings, diplomats and their families and foreign staffs.

b/ Main activity in 12 months preceding the interview.

c/ Activity in the week preceding the interview.

the statistics - but a question can be raised about the adequacy of the label of "working/not working" and "active/inactive" in the case of table 15 and the ILO Year Book. These statistics do not include under the headings of "working" and "active" all persons who in fact work. If the basic assumption adopted for this study is accepted - namely, that the distinction between household work and other work is in principle irrelevant - the organization of the statistics shown in table 14 is to be preferred.

A substantive point can be added. The statistics contained in table 15 and in the ILO 1985 Year Book indicate that there is less economic activity among women than men and less in developing than in developed economies. This suggests that the remedy to the relative deprivation of women and of developing countries is more work. The statistics in table 14 show that, as between developed and developing countries and between the sexes, there is little difference in the level of economic activity. Rather, they suggest that the remedy is to be found in a reorganization of economic activity (more productive activities in developing countries) and in a redistribution of available consumption, notably between women and men.

B. Time-use statistics

In time-use statistics, persons are described according to how their available time is distributed among various forms of activity according to a more or less detailed classification of activities. This is a relatively new field of data collection and research. Time-use data are not generally available in official statistics in the majority of developing countries.

Table 16 shows the distribution of time for women and men by main categories of activity in Norway in 1971/72 and 1980/81. In this table, the main categorization is by activity, whereas in tables 14 and 15 it is by persons. These statistics are from time-use surveys conducted, 1971/72 and 1980/81, with nationally representative samples (sample size about 3,000 and 3,300 respondents, respectively) of the population 16-74 years of age. The respondents filled in a detailed time diary covering two days and answered a set of conventional survey questions. The surveys were distributed over a one-year period so that annual average figures could be estimated and biases due to possible seasonal variations in time-use patterns could be avoided.

Some main features of the table are the following:

(a) Women and men on average have about the same level of economic activity, according to the definition of the present study, although women work slightly more than men and have slightly less leisure;

(b) The structure of this economic activity is different for women and men in that women do more of their work as household work and men do more of their work in gainful employment;

(c) Between 1971/72 and 1980/81, there is for both women and men little change in the level of economic activity, although both have some more leisure. The structure of economic activity for women has, however, changed noticeably. Time spent on household work is reduced by an hour and the extra available time is shared between more time in gainful employment and more leisure.

Table 16.   Use of time by main categories, Norway, 1971/72
            and 1980/81 a/

(Hours per day)

	1971/72		1980/81	
	Women	Men	Women	Men
Economic activity	8.0	7.9	7.7	7.6
Gainful employment	1.9	5.4	2.4	4.7
Employment/self-employment b/	1.4	3.9	1.9	3.6
Family business, primary sector c/	0.2	0.7	0.1	0.4
Other	0.3	0.8	0.4	0.7
Household work d/	5.8	2.1	4.8	2.4
Education e/	0.3	0.4	0.5	0.5
Non-economic activity	16.0	16.1	16.3	16.5
Personal needs f/	10.8	10.5	10.3	10.3
Leisure	5.0	5.3	5.9	6.1
Other	0.2	0.3	0.1	0.1
Total	24.0	24.0	24.0	24.0

Source: Time Budget Surveys, 1971/72 and 1980/81 (Oslo, Central Bureau of Statistics).

a/   Based on representative samples of the population, 16-74 years of age.

b/   Main and secondary job, including overtime, travel to/from work, meals at work, etc.

c/   Agriculture, forestry, fishing; paid and unpaid work.

d/   Food preparation, private production of food, cleaning, maintenance, family care, purchases and the like.

e/   Time spent in education, including preparatory work at home, travel to/from, etc.

f/   Sleep, meals, personal care.

These time-use statistics give broadly the same picture as do the labour force statistics for Norway in table 14. In both cases, the indications are that the level of economic activity is about the same for women and men, that the structure of economic activity is different, and that the structure of activity has changed a great deal for women. Indeed, for this purpose of simple statistical description, the statistics based on time-use data do not add much information to what is already known from labour force statistics.

There are very few international comparisons of time-use statistics available. Time-use surveys are not conducted in many countries; such surveys are conducted in various ways which may make them non-comparable; and there are no international statistical guidelines in this area.

As an illustration, table 17 gives figures for Finland and Norway. Although approximately the same survey method has been used in both cases (time diaries), the statistics are not perfectly comparable, most importantly because the Finnish survey does not cover the entire year. The difference between women and men in the time spent in gainful employment is less in Finland than in Norway. This is what would be expected in the light of other knowledge about the economic situation of women in these two countries but, because of the lack of comparability in the data, the possibility can not be excluded that some of the observed differences are spurious.

Table 18 shows the use of time in rural Botswana. The data used to produce this table were collected as part of the Rural Income Distribution Survey 1974/75 by a different method from the one used in the Norwegian and Finnish surveys. Respondents were asked to list by duration their main activities during the previous day, from the time they got up in the morning until bed-time. These figures can therefore not be compared directly to those in tables 16 and 17. While the main features are the same - women work more than men and men have more leisure than women - the survey methods and definitions of categories are so different that more detailed comparisons are not meaningful. No re-analysis of the data in table 18 would make it possible to estimate statistics that are truly comparable to those in tables 16 and 17.

Table 17. Use of time by main categories, Finland, 1979, and Norway, 1980/81

(Hours per day)

	Finland a/ 1979 (Sept.-Nov.)		Norway b/ 1980/81 (all year)	
	Women	Men	Women	Men
Gainful employment	3.4	4.8	2.4	4.7
Household work	3.9	2.0	4.7	2.3
Meals	1.4	1.4	1.3	1.3
Sleep	8.4	8.4)	9.0)	8.9
Other personal needs	0.7	0.7)	)	
Leisure, education and the like	6.1	6.6	5.9	6.1
Other	0.1	0.1	0.7	0.7
Total	24.0	24.0	24.0	24.0

Source: L. Aatola, "Tidsanvandningsundersokningar i de nordiska landerna" (Nordic Council, mimeo.).

Note: The definition of categories is slightly different from that in table 16.

a/   Population aged 15-64 years.

b/   Population aged 16-74 years.

Table 18. Distribution of activity time of adults, by sex and
household composition, rural Botswana, 1974/75

(Percentage)

| Activities | Males | Females | | | |
		MH-MP a/	MH-NMP b/	FH-MP c/	FH-NMP d/
Crops	6.8	11.1	14.0	10.1	9.6
Animal husbandry	12.6	1.5	0.3	0.9	0.4
Wage	8.8	0.8	0.3	1.8	2.8
Trading, vending, manufacturing services	1.2	0.9	0.3	2.4	3.1
Hunting and gathering	2.4	2.6	3.5	2.1	2.7
All income-earning activities	31.8	16.9	18.5	17.3	18.6
Repairing, new building	3.1	3.9	5.1	6.2	4.4
Fetching water	1.4	7.1	8.0	6.8	6.8
Childcare	0.3	3.6	4.3	5.0	2.8
Housework	3.8	21.8	16.5	19.4	18.7
All housekeeping activities	8.6	36.4	34.0	37.5	32.6
Schooling	0.6	0.7	0.1	0.3	0.5
Illness and health care	3.3	5.0	5.6	6.4	6.8
Meetings	5.0	0.7	0.5	0.2	0.4
Leisure	54.2	40.1	41.3	38.3	41.0
All non-work activities	58.9	45.9	47.4	44.9	48.2
All activities	100.0	100.0	100.0	100.0	100.0

Source: S. Kossoudji and E. Mueller, "The economic and demographic status of
female-headed households in rural Botswana" (University of Michigan, Population
Studies Center, mimeo.).

Note: Activity time was measured for approximately 12 hours from morning to
bed-time, omitting meals. There is reason to believe that minor activities were
underreported and that leisure time is therefore overstated. Such errors should
affect all household composition groups in a similar manner so that comparisons
between groups are valid.

a/   MH-MP = recognized male head - male aged 20-64 present.

b/   MH-NMP = recognized male head - no male aged 20-64 present.

c/   FH-MP = recognized female head - male aged 20-64 present.

d/   FH-NMP = recognized female head - no male aged 20-64 present.

C. Comments

It has been shown in this chapter that comparative statistics on economic activity, using a broad definition of that term, can be estimated from labour force survey data to the extent that the surveys were conducted according to ILO recommendations. It has been suggested that the estimation of comparative statistics covering both developing and developed countries on the basis of time-use surveys is for the time being probably not a realistic ambition. For the purpose of simple statistical monitoring of trends in economic activity and of the difference in economic activity between women and men, information from time-use surveys at present probably does not add much to what can be learned from labour force surveys, if the broad concept of economic activity proposed here is used. This is not to say that time-use surveys are not important for other purposes or that they would not be important for the purpose discussed here if more time-use surveys with comparable designs were available.

II. MEASURING ECONOMIC WELFARE

Main indicators of economic rewards and welfare could include the following types:

(a) Wages: This is the economic compensation to labour which is sold in the labour market (the formal economy). It should include cash wages, payments in kind, and "fringe benefits" (which may include anything from pension rights and free services to leisure and consumption at work, e.g. enjoyable travel). Ideally, income from self-employment should be treated in the same way as wages, but in practical terms this is usually difficult;

(b) Personal income: This includes all individual income, such as wages and salaries, income from self-employment, income from capital, pensions, and public and private transfers;

(c) Household income: This is the aggregate income of all household or family members. Since many income components are not individual but owned and used collectively by the family or household, income beyond wages is usually recorded on a household or family basis. In principle, "free" public services such as education and health care should be included, but there are difficult theoretical problems in doing this, such as to determine the value of "free" services and to allocate their consumption to households;

(d) Consumption: This should be estimated as the sum of all purchases and in-kind receipts, and the value of consumption produced within the household. (The latter is also regarded as income and included in the measure of household income.) While income is an "indirect" measure of welfare (welfare in this case is measured by the available resources, irrespective of how the resources are used), consumption - and the two types of indicators mentioned below - are "direct" measures of welfare (welfare in this case is measured directly by how people live);

(e) Living conditions: This concept goes beyond an "economic" measurement of welfare in terms of income or consumption to a broader "social indicators" kind of measurement which includes indicators on, for example, health, nutrition, education, social and cultural activity;

(f) Utility: This concept, which is commonly used in theoretical welfare economics, goes beyond the recording of objective resources and conditions to the recording of subjective satisfactions. This concept is not considered further in the present study.

Each of the concepts (a)-(e) above is discussed below.

A. Wages

In table 19, estimates of the relative wage level of women compared to that of men are reproduced for full-time workers in selected developed economies. This table shows both how female and male wages can be compared and about how far it is possible to come in production of such statistics on a comparative basis. The main features are:

Table 19. Women's earnings as a percentage of men's earnings in selected sectors of 17 market-economy countries

| | | All sectors | | | Manufacturing | | Trade | | | | Public administration |
| | | Total (1) | Manual (2) | Non-manual (3) | Manual (4) | Non-manual (5) | Wholesale trade (6) | Retail trade (7) | Banking (8) | Insurance (9) | (10) |
	Year										
Austria	1983	77.6	72.1	75.7	..	..	(74.2)	..	(79.2)	..	82.2
Belgium	1982	..	..	..	72.6	59.3	65.0	71.1	71.2	68.4	..
Canada	1979	63.3	..	..	..	..	..	..	..	..	..
Denmark	1983	..	..	73.8	88.6	71.4	74.4	75.5	76.4	68.1	..
Finland	1981	..	..	..	76.8	76.1	69.4	87.3	78.6	68.5	74.0
France	1982	75.0	75.5	83.1	77.7	61.7	69.7	67.5	74.5	66.1	83.9
Germany, Federal Republic	1982	..	..	64.8	72.7	66.7	68.3	65.9	77.4	76.8	..
Greece	1980	..	..	..	67.4	57.0	..	70.0	..	..	..
Ireland	1982	..	..	..	68.5	..	56.4	58.5	67.1	58.9	..
Italy	1982	..	..	..	86.7	..	79.0	85.8	79.5	71.1	..
Netherlands	1981	76.8	75.5	..	74.7	..	61.1	61.2	56.6	60.4	..
Norway	1982	..	..	..	83.2	65.3	70.5	80.6	77.5	65.5	82.9
Portugal	1980	75.6	..	..	72.0	74.6	79.4	79.2	81.8	84.6	..
Sweden	1982	80.7	..	..	90.3	72.7	72.5	95.0	76.9	71.7	88.3
Switzerland	180	..	..	66.9	67.7	66.4	74.7	63.0	78.2	72.6	78.8
United Kingdom	1980	65.7	61.9	61.2	60.3	53.2	54.1	56.1	(49.9)	..	60.9
United States	1981	59.1	61.2	52.8	57.6	60.1	58.3	59.7	(47.8)	..	67.0

Source: "The pay differential for women: some comparison for selected ECE countries" (Economic Commission for Europe, 1984).

Note: All weekly, monthly and yearly earning data refer to full-time workers.

(a) Female earnings are, with no exception, lower than male earnings;

(b) There is a great deal of difference both between sectors and countries in the degree to which this is true;

(c) While wage statistics within sectors are available in many countries, data allowing the estimation of the wage level for all workers are available in only a few countries.

Table 19 does not include any developing economies but it must be assumed that such statistics are less available in developing economies than in developed economies.

When interpreting statistics such as these, it should be kept in mind that there may be many reasons why average female wages are lower than male wages. Women may work shorter hours than men. (Although these statistics are for full-time workers, average working hours are not necessarily the same.) Women may work in different industries or types of businesses or jobs than men, and they may have a different background in education and experience. Hence, wage discrimination (lower wages for women than men in comparable jobs) is only one of several factors which may contribute to the observed wage differentials in table 19.

Wage statistics can give only very limited information about the economic situation of women. They indicate something about the situation of women who are in paid employment in the formal sector of the economy, but they cannot be taken as indicators of the standard of living of these women and say nothing about the situation of women who have the main part of their activity in the household or in the informal sector of the economy. Such statistics should be interpreted as indicators of the degree of equal treatment of women who are active in the formal economy, rather than as indicators of economic welfare. While employment statistics show the degree of integration of women into the formal economy, wage statistics show the degree of emancipation of those who are integrated. The estimates reproduced in this study suggest, not surprisingly, both that women are generally less integrated into the formal economy than are men and that those women who are in the formal economy generally occupy inferior positions in comparison to men.

B. Individual income

To the degree that it is practically possible to allocate income beyond wages to individuals, as opposed to families or households, it is possible to compile statistics on individual income. This can be done, for example, in systems where tax return data are a reliable basis for income statistics and where the individual is the main tax unit.

Table 20 gives an overview of the distribution of individual income in Norway. These statistics are based on personal tax returns and they cover all income earners. An income earner is a person who has filed a personal tax return. The income concept in principle includes all forms of income, although only some minor forms of in-kind income are included (certain forms of in-kind compensations for wage earners, some consumption of own production, mainly in the primary sector, and imputed income from home ownership). Most in-kind income and consumption from informal economic activity, as well as the value of "free" public services, are not included.

Table 20. Distribution of individual income in Norway,
by sex, 1982

(Mean income in each decile as percentage of total mean)

		Gross income		Net income	
		Women	Men	Women	Men
Median (N. Kroner)		38 000	98 000	40 000	80 000
Deciles	1	1.1	8.3	0.0	6.3
	2	17.4	30.0	11.3	29.7
	3	42.9	49.5	37.9	50.8
	4	60.1	73.6	58.6	74.3
	5	72.0	91.7	71.5	93.4
	6	90.2	103.6	88.9	106.6
	7	115.4	114.6	115.2	119.0
	8	150.3	129.4	152.8	133.6
	9	189.0	151.6	195.0	156.7
	10	261.6	247.7	268.7	229.6

Source: Wages, Salaries and Income, 1982 (Oslo, Central Bureau of
Statistics).

Note: Gross/net income = income before/after taxes.

The main features of table 20 are:

(a) The level of individual income is lower for women than for men;

(b) The difference between women and men is less in net than in gross
income. This is because of progressive taxation whereby women, having lower
incomes than men, also have a lower rate of taxation;

(c) The distribution of individual income is more inegalitarian among women
than among men. This probably reflects, among other things, a difference between
the sexes in their pattern of economic activity whereby there is more variation
among women than men in the amount of formal sector economic activity.

The interpretation of the kinds of estimates reproduced here is somewhat
problematic. The unit of observation is the person who files a tax return. This
is, from a welfare point of view, an arbitrary unit. The result is statistical
information on the level and distribution of whatever income is recognized and
recorded in the process of taxation among individuals who according to current tax
laws are required to file a tax return (and who in fact do so).

Statistics on individual income are not always (perhaps not even usually)
estimated in income statistics publications, the household being the usual unit.

Often, surveys are not designed so as to allow individual income to be estimated. But even when individual income figures are available for several countries, the possibility for international comparison is very limited. The reason for this is that both the unit of observation and the concept of income invariably differ. For example, in the Sri Lanka Labour Force and Socio-economic Survey 1980/81 (Department of Census and Statistics), "income receivers" are defined as all persons who report monetary income in the survey questionnaire. In this group, 74 per cent are men and 26 per cent women. In the estimate of individual income, only monetary income is included. In the Norwegian statistics reported in table 20, which are based not on survey data but on tax return data, all persons who file a tax return are "income earners". This group divides about equally between men and women. With the exception of imputed income from home ownership and a few other small items, income is limited to monetary income. The income definitions are therefore close to each other in both these data sources, but since monetary income must be assumed to cover a larger part of total income in Norway than in Sri Lanka, the income coverage is still different. The ratio of female to male average individual income in the Sri Lanka survey is .61, as compared to .39 in Norway (see table 20, gross). This suggests that the differences in average individual income between men and women may be greater in Norway than in Sri Lanka, but intuitively this does not appear to be likely, and because of the lack of comparability in the data no such conclusion can reliably be drawn.

C. Household income and consumption

In statistics on income and consumption, the household and not the individual is most commonly the unit for which income and consumption are recorded. From the point of view of the present discussion, this poses three problems: the appropriate recording of income and consumption, international comparability, and the distribution of household income and consumption among household members so that something can be said about the welfare of individuals.

To illustrate different methods of recording income for statistical purposes, table 21 compares the methods used in Norwegian income statistics (Central Bureau of Statistics, Oslo, compiled at regular intervals, sample based on tax returns) and the Botswana Rural Income Distribution Survey 1974/75 (Central Statistical Office, Gaborone, sample survey data).

The income concepts in these two cases potentially differ from one another in two ways. First, although both record in-kind as well as monetary income, in-kind income is a larger share in total income in the Botswana case. Since this is because subsistence economic activity (production for own consumption) is relatively more important in Botswana than in Norway it does not necessarily make the income concepts non-comparable. Secondly, in the Botswana survey, some forms of products from household work are included as imputed income. No such income is estimated in the Norwegian statistics. This difference makes the income concepts to some degree non-comparable. In neither case is housework, such as cooking, cleaning, and child care incorporated.

Table 21. Income components in income statistics, Botswana and Norway

Type of income a/	Botswana	Norway
Employment income		
Monetary	Wages	Wages, sick-pay, unemployment compensation
In-kind	Housing benefits, non-contributory pensions, free food, medication, travel and the like	Some, e.g. imputed income from use of company car, surplus on travel per diem
Self-employment income		
Monetary	All sales of products (goods and services), net	Net income in self-employment
In-kind (business)	Value of all products not sold (consumed or saved)	Consumption of food from own production
In-kind (household)	Hunting, fishing, gathering (e.g. wild fruit, firewood) for own consumption; housebuilding, clearing of land and the like	Not included
Private transfers		
Monetary	Money gifts	Alimony
In-kind	In-kind gifts	Not included
Public transfers		
Monetary	Poor relief	Social security, family assistance, scholarships
In-kind	Food	Not included
Capital income		
Monetary	Interest, rent, dividends and the like	Interest, rent, dividends and the like
In-kind rent	Imputed income from own home	Imputed income from own home
In-kind value added	Weight gain of livestock, value of house improvements and the like	Not included

a/   The sum of all these income components is total income. Total income minus direct taxes (central and local) is disposable income.

Both studies, but in particular the Botswana study, show that it is possible to record household income so that non-monetary income is included. The reason housework is not included is not for want of technical means of doing so, but simply that it was decided not to regard the product of such work as income. Had housework been incorporated, an imputed income could have been estimated in much the same way that imputed income from other non-paid work is estimated. One possible way of doing this is to estimate the value of the time invested in housework. Another possibility is to estimate the market value of the goods and services produced (e.g. food cooked, clothing cleaned, children cared for, and so on). Hence, the problem of recording household income comprehensively can be solved, at least in principle.

Table 22 shows the distribution of available income per household in Botswana and Norway according to the income concepts explained in table 21. Table 22 does not show the absolute income level but only the distribution around the mean in each country. The distribution is more inegalitarian in Botswana than in Norway, mainly because the income level of the upper deciles is higher relative to the mean in Botswana.

Table 22. Distribution of disposable household
income, Botswana and Norway

(Mean income in each decile as percentage
of total mean)

Deciles	Botswana a/	Norway b/
1	28.9	25.5
2	44.3	46.9
3	57.8	63.8
4	72.2	77.8
5	90.3	92.9
6	103.0	108.0
7	139.0	125.0
8	169.5	144.1
9	272.2	169.0
10	497.8	244.3

Sources: The Rural Income Distribution Survey in
Botswana, 1974/75 (Gaborone, Central Statistical Office);
Income Statistics, 1982 (Oslo, Central Bureau of Statistics of
Norway).

a/   1974-75, rural households.

b/   1982, all households.

The distribution of income in Botswana and Norway can be compared directly from the statistical publications since both publications give figures for the relative distribution over decile groups. This is not always the case. For example, in the Sri Lanka Labour Force and Socio-economic Survey 1980/81, income is recorded in a way comparable to that used in the Botswana survey but the publication gives distribution figures only for income intervals rather than deciles. This prevents any comparison of the distributions in these two countries without first re-analysing the Sri Lanka data.

The recording of household consumption starts with a record of consumption expenditure. This can be recorded directly or indirectly. In the first case, in a typical procedure, a sample of households keeps detailed books on their spending over a period, say, of two weeks, and information on large purchases over the year is added. In the second case, consumption expenditure is estimated by subtracting from gross income direct taxes, other transfers out of the household and savings.

Statistics on consumption expenditure show how much households spend on goods and services in the market. This is obviously important information for many purposes but it does not necessarily reveal much about economic welfare. Not all consumption is purchased in the market and some of the things bought in the market are subsidized so that their consumption value must be assumed to be higher than their price. To consumption expenditure should therefore be added, first, the value of subsidies, secondly, the value of "free" consumption, the main forms being "free" public services (e.g. health care, education), and thirdly, consumption which is produced within the household.

Techniques are available for measuring statistically the value of the consumption of "free" and subsidized goods. The standard procedure is that the value is taken to be expressed in the costs to government of the subsidy or of producing "free" goods, and these values are allocated to households in proportion to their consumption of "free" or subsidized goods and services. This procedure is based on a number of controversial assumptions but is nevertheless an established and broadly accepted procedure.

As to the consumption which is produced within the household, this value can be recorded as explained above. The quantity in question (i.e. the value of cooking, cleaning, child care, and so on) can be called "a product" if it is seen from the point of view of how much work it takes to bring it forth and who does the work. If it is seen from the point of view of who benefits from or uses it, it can be called "consumption" (or "saving" as in the case of improvements to dwellings or other capital goods). As long as this quantity is measured for the household as a whole, the product will be identical to the consumption (or consumption plus saving). This quantity can be added to other household income. Thus, the problem of income recording will be solved. However, if attention is shifted from the household as a whole to the individual members of the household, new problems arise. Although this form of product and consumption is the same for the household as a whole, the same is not true for the individual members of the household, except in the unlikely case where work and consumption are shared absolutely equally. For example, if a wife does all the housework in a family, her own consumption of such goods and services will be lower than her production of these goods and services. This brings us to the issue of distribution within the household, which is discussed below.

In order to say something about the income or consumption of women as individuals on the basis of information on household income or consumption, three procedures can be suggested. First, one can compare the income (or consumption) of female-headed households with that of male-headed households. This is a highly indirect approach since it is still not individual incomes that are compared, but it does indicate something about the relative status of women and men. This kind of information is at least occasionally available in income statistics publications. For example in Norway in 1982, the ratio of disposable income for female-headed households to male-headed households was 0.60, and of available income per unit of consumption 0.86 (female-headed households are on average smaller). Hence, female-headed households, on average, have a lower standard of living than male-headed households, although the difference is reduced when income is adjusted for household size and composition.

The second possibility is to allocate to each individual member of the household a certain fraction of the household's total income and to analyse the material using the individual rather than the household as the unit of observation. The simplest way of doing this is to divide household income equally between all members, but this is not very appropriate since no allowance is made for economies of scale in large households. The alternative is to divide household income by an equivalence factor which is a function of the size and composition of the household. For example, in a family of two adults and one child, household income will be divided by a factor of 2.2 if the first adult is weighted by 1.0, the second adult by 0.7, and the child by 0.5. The underlying assumption is that household income divided by the equivalence factor can be taken to express the standard of living of each member of the household. This, again, assumes that income and consumption is distributed "fairly" and in the same way within all households.

Equivalence factors can be estimated in several ways, depending on what relative weight the various household members are given. The Luxembourg Income study shows that the choice of weights and hence of equivalence factors can strongly influence the subsequent estimates of the distribution of income. (This is illustrated in the annex.) Since there are no objective criteria for determining what weights are "correct", this choice can only be made by best judgement. This brings an element of arbitrariness into income distribution statistics based on equivalent incomes which has previously perhaps not been fully recognized.

A third possibility is to study the process of distribution within households directly. This would be desirable if the assumption that income and consumption are distributed "fairly" and in the same way within all households were rejected as unrealistic, as obviously it is. The problem, however, is that it has not appeared practical up to now to capture the result of within-household distributive processes in large-scale surveys and statistical descriptions.

Table 23.   Distribution of income in seven developed countries

	Market income gini a/	Total income gini a/	Available income gini a/	Pre-transfer poverty rates b/	Post-transfer poverty rates c/
Canada	0.398	0.327	0.299	25.600	12.100
Germany, Fed. Rep. of	0.505	0.363	0.355	28.300	7.200
Israel	0.459	0.382	0.333	29.000	14.500
Norway	0.400	0.289	0.243	24.100	4.800
Sweden	..	0.249	0.205	41.000	5.000
United Kingdom	0.414	0.297	0.273	27.900	8.800
United States	0.440	0.371	0.326	27.300	16.900

	Available income gini relative to market income gini	Available income gini relative to total income gini	Available income gini relative to market income gini	Level of transfers d/	Level of taxes e/
Canada	0.82	0.91	0.75	9.1	15.2
Germany, Fed. Rep. of	0.72	0.98	0.70	16.5	22.5
Israel	0.83	0.87	0.73	8.3	28.7
Norway	0.72	0.84	0.61	14.1	25.3
Sweden	..	0.82	..	29.2	29.7
United Kingdom	0.72	0.92	0.66	17.2	16.9
United States	0.84	0.88	0.74	8.0	21.0

Source: S. Ringen, "Difference and similarity: two studies of comparative income distribution" (Swedish Institute for Social Research, 1986).

Note: Gini = measure of inequality (1.000 = maximum inequality, 0.000 - total equality).

Poverty rate = percentage of persons belonging to families with equivalent income below half of the media for all families.

Equivalent income = family income adjusted for family size.

a/   Family equivalent income as distributed among persons.

b/   Family equivalent market income, less taxes.

c/   Family equivalent disposable income.

d/   Public transfers as percentage of gross income.

e/   Personal income tax, including payroll tax, as percentage of gross income.

f/   This figure is not available for Sweden but for other comparisons between Norway and Sweden, it is known to be lower than the Norwegian figure.

D. Comments

Four types of indicators of economic welfare have been considered: wages, individual income, household income and household consumption. The requirements that need to be met by an indicator for the purpose of measuring and comparing men's and women's economic welfare are:

(a) That it is based on a concept of income or consumption that is relevant from a welfare perspective;

(b) That income or consumption is recorded comprehensively, i.e. that some forms of income or consumption are not by definition disregarded;

(c) That the unit of observation is the individual;

(d) That comparative data are available.

The suitability of the indicators considered relative to these requirements is assessed in table 24.

Table 24. Suitability of various indicators for measuring
women's economic welfare

	Wages	Individual income	Household income	Household consumption
Relevant concept	no	no	yes	yes
Comprehensive recording	no	no	yes	yes
Individual unit	yes	yes	no	no
Comparative data	no	no	yes	no

Wages and individual income are not applicable for the present purpose of identifying welfare-relevant indicators because all forms of income which are collective within the household are by definition disregarded. When income or consumption is analysed on a household basis, the theoretical concepts and methods of recording are in principle the appropriate ones, with the exception that income/consumption generated in usual housework is disregarded (although this need not theoretically be the case). The difficulties in the use of these indicators are in part that relevant data are hardly available, but above all that the necessary unit for recording is the household and the necessary unit of observation the individual. This poses an inescapable dilemma. In order to record income comprehensively, it is necessary to use the household unit, but in order to analyse income so that women and men can be compared, it is necessary to use the individual unit. Since there is no way of uniting these two requirements in statistical description without assuming that there are no problems of distribution within the household, the conclusion must be that none of the indicators considered can fulfill the purpose of economic welfare comparisons between women and men in a fully satisfactory manner.

III. COMPARISON OF APPROACHES

The question asked in this study is the following: Is it possible to identify a set of simple statistical indicators on the economic situation of women, describing both their economic activity and their economic welfare, and to find comparative data for such indicators from available statistical sources? What has been found is not altogether encouraging.

A. Economic activity indicators

Indicators of economic activity should ideally describe the amount of "work" people do, irrespective of whether the work is performed in the formal or informal sectors of the economy. Statistical indicators which conform to this ideal can be identified. The two techniques considered are a classification of individuals by main activity and recording the time used for various activities. The statistics produced by both techniques show that economic activity is on about the same high level for women and men but that the structure of economic activity differs between women and men in that women perform more of their economic activity outside of the formal economy, although this difference appears to be narrowing, at least in developed economies.

Statistical techniques are available for providing the data needed to calculate these indicators. Activity is recorded in labour force surveys and the distribution of time between activities in time-use surveys.

Since labour force surveys are conducted more or less regularly in a large number of countries and since they are generally conducted more or less in accordance with ILO standards, there is reason to believe that the necessary data are available for producing indicators on the economic situation of women across a relatively wide range of countries. This is already done in the ILO Year Book of Labour Statistics, but not according to the broad concept of work used in this study. The same data sources can, however, be used to estimate economic activity more comprehensively, which is to say that there is a basis, both with regard to relevant indicators and available comparative data, for an alternative and more comprehensive statistical series on economic activity. This would, however, require reanalysis of a large number of national data sets. The necessary statistics are probably not generally estimated in available publications, and certainly not on a comparative basis. The degree to which such re-estimations could practically be carried out with successful results could be determined only after a careful review of national data sets.

Time-use surveys have been conducted only in a minority of countries and the ones that have been conducted are not easily comparable. This, therefore, is to be seen more as a potential than current technique. The advantage of time-use surveys over labour force surveys for describing economic activity is that they give much more information, including the information labour force surveys give. If the purpose is only to produce rough statistics on the level of economic activity, time-use surveys may not add much to what can be learned from labour force surveys, but if the purpose is a more detailed analysis of economic activity, time-use surveys can be invaluable, in particular for analysing the activity of women and men in a comparative way and for analysing economic activity in developing economies, where a relatively large share of all economic activity is performed in the informal sector of the economy.

The great advantage of the time-use technique is that the unit of measurement - time - is universal. Most economic statistics use, directly or indirectly, money as the unit of measurement. Money accrues only to economic activity in the market. The imputation of monetary values for non-market activities and transactions is fraught with theoretical and methodological difficulties. This creates some biases in economic statistics, such as in the comparison of developing and developed economies and of the economic activity of women and men. In cases where more of total economic activity is in the non-market sector, economic statistics will tend to underestimate economic activity and income. In time-use surveys, all economic activity is in principle recorded, irrespective of whether it occurs within or outside of the market. This technique therefore offers the possibility of comparing economic activity "fairly" and of overcoming some of the biases in "conventional" economic statistics. There is perhaps a tendency to regard time-use surveys as belonging to the category of "social" statistics and as being not very relevant for "economic" statistics. But this view underestimates the potential of the time-use technique. This technique can be seen not only as a possibility for catching some phenomena which slip through the net of "conventional" statistics, but as a basis for a fully alternative kind of national accounting based on the universal measure of time rather than the "arbitrary" measure of money, which is anyway used mainly for want of a better alternative.

The time-use technique is still not universal. Because of its many advantages, it should, and there is reason to believe that it will, be used more in the future. The main difficulties in the use of the technique are:

(a) Data collection is more complicated than in conventional surveys, resulting for example in higher non-response rates;

(b) The very richness of the data make the analysis and the full exploitation of their potential difficult; new techniques of analysis need to be developed;

(c) The many possible ways of conducting time-use surveys are a threat to their comparability.

There is here much need for methodological work and international standardization. Promoting and improving time-use techniques should be an important task for those who are concerned with improving the situation with regard to statistics on women.

B. Welfare indicators

While the economic activity of women can be described with available or potentially available statistical techniques and data, the same is not true for their economic welfare on the basis of income statistics. There are several difficulties in trying to do this, but the basic problem is that while income can be recorded comprehensively only for households or families, the analysis of individual economic welfare must use the individual as the unit of observation. On the basis of income statistics, and using the broad concept of income, little can be said therefore about the economic welfare of women, unless it is assumed that the economic welfare of each individual member of the household follows directly from the total income/consumption of the household and its size and composition. This would be to disregard the whole issue of within-family distribution, which again would be to assume away one of the most important processes which determine individual economic welfare, in particular that of women. This difficulty is basic in income statistics and has nothing to do with the availability of income surveys or the quality of data.

Because of this basic dilemma in income statistics, it is suggested that for the purpose of describing the economic welfare of women, the avenue of analysing or reanalysing conventional income statistics is not a very fruitful one. In addition, there are problems of comparability in income data which require an intensive process of co-ordination and adjustment in order to make meaningful comparisons. Instead, work of a more developmental kind should be considered. Some relevant areas of work can be suggested.

First, how can household income/consumption be recorded comprehensively?

(a) Recording, in addition to income, of expenditure, savings, and transfers out of the household. The recognized problem here in surveys of income and consumption, as confirmed, for example, in the Botswana Rural Income Distribution Survey referred to above, is that these quantities, once recorded, tend not to add up consistently;

(b) The incorporation of income/consumption which is produced and consumed within the household. This is essential for understanding the economic situation of women since so much of what women produce is consumption for household members, such as meals, cleaning, maintenance, care. This task is related to that of describing the economic activity of women;

(c) The incorporation of "free" consumption which is transferred to the household from the outside, such as gifts in kind, e.g. the contribution of grandparents to younger generation families through gifts and other help, and, in particular, public services, e.g. education, health care. Even if income could be recorded comprehensively, the problem of its distribution within the household would remain.

Second, the distribution of consumption within households is a question of studying the processes which determine who gets what within households. Important variables could be, for instance, food consumption, e.g. calorie intake, clothing, space, work, leisure, sleep and so on, and even "psychological" variables such as the amount of attention parents give their various children. Comparisons between women and men would be important, as would comparisons between girls and boys, considering that the welfare of children, given the total resources of the family, is determined almost totally within the family and by others than themselves. Within-family distributions are a much neglected issue in social research, having been considered mostly a "private" domain not to be penetrated by outsiders. Special purpose surveys and time-use surveys might be of some use for this purpose, but case studies, for example using anthropological methods, are probably more suitable and necessary. In any event, this is not a matter of producing standard statistics but of in-depth research.

Third, how can the living conditions of women and men best be compared? For the present purpose it is probably more fruitful to compare the welfare of women and men through direct measurement than through the indirect measure of income. There is now a great deal of experience in many countries with the use of broad levels of living surveys. The idea behind this approach is to measure welfare directly in terms of how people live rather than indirectly through the resources which theoretically determine how they live. The argument is, on the one hand, that it is difficult to measure resources accurately and fully, and on the other hand, that people have different abilities to transform resources into welfare. Through direct measurement, welfare is described in a set of social indicators which are applied simultaneously, such as education, housing, employment, health, leisure, social activity, and so on, in addition to conventional economic indicators such as income and consumption.

These three areas of study are obviously closely related to each other. A common denominator is the need for more knowledge about economic life within the family/household.

C.   Direct and indirect measurement

The issue of direct as opposed to indirect measurement merits some additional comments.

The concept of welfare is an abstract, theoretical concept. It is a shorthand term for people's well-being. The empirical measurement of this concept must be done with the help of operational indicators. Such indicators can be either "direct" or "indirect". Indirect indicators are assumed to reflect determinants of welfare. The most important indirect welfare measure is income. Direct indicators reflect how people live. The use of such indicators brings one closer to a direct measurement of the outcome of the various factors which determine how we live. It is generally recognized that direct measurement requires the simultaneous use of several indicators. The main argument in favour of the income approach is that the use of a single indicator is methodologically convenient. The problem, however, is that income is only one of several factors which determine welfare and that there can therefore be considerable differences between income and welfare. It can probably be said as a general rule that direct measurements of welfare correspond to broad concepts of welfare.

This study argues that, for the purpose of measuring the overall welfare of women, the income approach is not very useful. Income (or for that matter consumption) can be recorded comprehensively only for the household. No statistical technique is available for allocating this aggregate income (or consumption) to individual household members without disregarding the possibility of inequitable distribution within the household. Direct measurement therefore seems preferable to measure overall welfare.

Comparisons of direct and indirect measurement have shown that the two approaches can give different results. The choice of approach is hence not merely an academic issue but one which it must be assumed influences the conclusions which are eventually drawn from the research in question. Since income can only be an approximate, and probably inaccurate, measure of the welfare of women, it is likely that direct and indirect measurement will result in noticeably different conclusions from the analysis of the situation of women.

To illustrate, let us take poverty as an aspect of welfare. Poverty, as other aspects of welfare, can be measured directly or indirectly. The incidence of poverty is measured indirectly with the use of the income poverty line. By this measurement, all persons who have an income below a specified level are considered to be poor. The poverty line is, for example, set in many studies at half of the median income of the entire population. On the other hand, it can be argued that a direct measurement of poverty is made by the use of several indicators at the same time and by taking the accumulation of deprivation as the criterion of poverty. According to this approach, people are considered poor if they are deprived not simply in income terms but in several areas at the same time, so that the way they live adds to a situation of general deprivation.

Compare, for example, the result of measuring poverty as accumulated deprivation to the result of using the income poverty line measure in Sweden. The data are from two identical Swedish surveys conducted in 1968 and 1981 with representative panel samples of the population 15 to 74 years of age. Students and school pupils are excluded from the analysis because of their transitory situation.

The income poverty lines are defined in relation to median income in each year. The other resource and way of life indicators are defined in the same way for both 1968 and 1981 in relation to a judgement of the meaning of deprivation in a society such as the present Swedish one. Results are reported in table 25.

Three low-income groups are identified:

(a) Persons belonging to families with a disposable income per unit of consumption below 40 per cent of the median for all families;

(b) Persons belonging to families with a disposable income per unit of consumption between 40 and 50 per cent of the median for all families;

(c) Persons belonging to families with a disposable income per unit of consumption between 50 and 60 per cent of the median for all families. Disposable income per unit of consumption is estimated with the following equivalence scale: 0.95 for single persons, 1.65 for couples, and 0.40 for each child. Persons other than spouses/co-habitants and children belonging to larger households are counted as independent families.

The low-income groups are compared to all other persons (those belonging to families with a disposable income per unit of consumption above 60 per cent of the median) and to the entire sample. Since poverty is a question of falling behind the average standard in one's society, and not simply of falling behind the rich, no comparisons between low-income and high-income groups are included.

The three low-income groups together make up about 14 and 9 per cent of all persons in 1968 and 1981 respectively. Those below 50 per cent of the median - the most commonly used poverty line - make up 7 and 5 per cent respectively. The size of the lowest income group, those below 40 per cent of the median, has remained almost unchanged, going down only from 3.6 per cent in 1968 to 3.1 per cent in 1981. This is about the incidence of low income we should expect from previous studies.

Table 25. Low income and deprivation, 1968 and 1981

Income group	1968					1981				
	I	II	III	Other	All	I	II	III	Other	All
Sample										
1. Number of observations	182	175	388	4 379	5 124	172	102	231	4 987	5 492
2. Percentage	3.6	3.4	7.6	85.5	100.0	3.1	1.9	4.2	90.8	100.0
					(Percentage)					
Resources										
3. Small cash margin	38	31	31	15	17	26	14	26	11	12
4. Non-ownership	62	55	63	29	34	35	30	21	20	21
5. Low personal capability	29	25	25	17	18	13	13	14	9	9
Housing										
6. Crowded	28	28	28	23	24	15	10	10	5	6
7. Low standard	54	53	45	18	23	10	8	7	4	4
8. Inferior quality (6 and/or 7)	63	63	60	36	39	22	15	15	8	9
Consumption										
9. Does not have phone	19	15	16	8	9	6	1	3	2	2
10. Not away on holiday last year	75	75	72	44	48	53	39	49	33	35
11. Not occasionally/ often relatives in	16	12	11	10	10	16	12	8	9	9
12. Not occasionally/ often friends in	13	10	8	6	6	9	2	5	4	4
Accumulated deprivation										
13. (5 + 8)	21	15	19	9	10	5	3	4	1	1

Source: S. Ringen, The Possibility of Politic (Oxford, 1987).

The chosen indicators of deprivation in resources other than income include:

(a) Small cash margin - the respondent cannot raise a certain amount of money in one week, Swedish kronor 2,000 in 1968, adjusted for inflation to Sk5,000 in 1981;

(b) Non-ownership - the respondent/respondent's family does not own either house/flat, car, vacation house/cottage, pleasure boat, or camper;

(c) Low personal capability - the respondent does not judge himself/herself to have the ability to make a written complaint against a decision by an authority.

These are two indicators of economic resources and an indicator of personal resources which can be expected to influence one's ability to use economic resources efficiently and otherwise to cope in society.

Deprivation in resources other than income is generally higher in the low-income groups than in the rest of the population, but the difference is moderate compared to what one would expect if these groups, in fact, included the poor and excluded the non-poor. The low-income groups are far from homogenous with regard to resources. Nor is there a uniform correlation across low-income groups in the level of absolute deprivation in other resources.

The chosen indicators of deprivation in way of life include:

(a) Housing: crowded - more than two persons per room, kitchen and one additional room not counted; low standard - lacking one or more of the following facilities: running water, bath/WC, central heating, modern stove, refrigerator; inferior quality - crowded and/or low standard;

(b) Other forms and patterns of consumption.

Again, deprivation is more frequent in the low-income groups than in the rest of the population but the difference is not very large. As judged by these indicators, the low-income groups are no more homogenous in way of life than in resources.

Three indicators are taken into consideration in an attempt to approach a measure of accumulated deprivation: low income, low personal capability, and inferior quality of housing. This is to move only cautiously away from the income poverty line method. Low income is retained as the basic indicator, one non-economic resource indicator is added, and only one way of life indicator with self-evident relevance in relation to poverty is included. The housing indicator stretches the idea of deprivation in housing as far as possible by being defined as crowded and/or low standard; it is enough not to have a modern stove to be classified as deprived.

In 1968, 3.6 per cent of the population belonged to the lowest income group and 21 per cent of these had both low personal capability and inferior housing, bringing the percentage in accumulated deprivation according to these three indicators to 0.75 per cent of the population. In 1981, the lowest income group comprised 3.1 per cent of the population, but only 5 per cent of these were deprived according to the two other indicators, so that the number of persons in accumulated deprivation had fallen to 0.15 per cent of the population.

D. Summary of conclusions

The most important conclusions from this study in terms of suggestions for further work are the following:

(a) Concerning the measurement of economic activity:

(i) It appears to be a worthwhile and relatively simple task to estimate time-series indicators of economic activity based on a comprehensive concept of work, and on a comparative basis, from available labour force surveys;

(ii) There is a need for further methodological work on the application of time-use data, and above all for guidelines for international standardization of time-use surveys;

(b) Concerning the measurement of welfare:

(i) Studies of the processes of production and distribution within households may be more important for understanding the situation of women than is statistical information on income which is recorded for the household as a whole;

(ii) The direct method of measurement of welfare using sound indicators appears to be a more fruitful approach to the empirical analysis of the overall welfare of women than does the indirect income approach.

EQUIVALENCE FACTORS AND POVERTY RATES

This annex shows the proportion of elderly persons and children estimated to be in poverty in six developed nations when different equivalence factors are applied. The percentage of persons in each category with disposable income below the official United States poverty line, converted to other currencies using purchasing power parities published by the Organisation for Economic Co-operation and Development, is shown. Hence, the income poverty line is the same in all estimates; only the equivalence factor is different.

Equivalence factors

Family size	Reference person's age	No adjustment	Rainwater	United States poverty line	Luxembourg Income Study	Per capita
1	65 or older	1.00	.70	.60	.50	.33
1	Less than 65	1.00	.70	.66	.50	.33
2	65 or older	1.00	.88	.76	.75	.67
2	Less than 65	1.00	.88	.84	.75	.67
3	All ages	1.00	1.00	1.00	1.00	1.00
4	All ages	1.00	1.18	1.28	1.25	1.33
5	All ages	1.00	1.27	1.52	1.50	1.67
6	All ages	1.00	1.35	1.71	1.75	2.00
7	All ages	1.00	1.43	1.86	2.00	2.33
Each additional person		0	+.08	+.15	+.25	+.33

Estimates of percentage of population who are in poor households

Country	Luxembourg Income Study		Rainwater		United States poverty line	
	Elderly	Children	Elderly	Children	Elderly	Children
Canada	3.0	9.5	10.6	6.4	4.8	9.6
Germany, Federal Republic of	2.3	7.7	24.0	4.0	15.4	8.2
Norway	5.5	7.7	32.5	4.5	18.7	7.6
Sweden	0.0	4.9	6.4	3.3	2.0	5.1
United Kingdom	23.5	11.0	55.2	6.0	37.0	10.7
United States	11.7	17.4	22.3	11.7	16.1	17.1

Source: Smeeding, Torrey and Rein, "The economic status of the young and the old in six countries", Luxembourg Income Study, Working Paper No. 8, mimeo.